SAGA OF THE SUPERFORTRESS

SAGA OF THE SUPERFORTRESS

The Dramatic Story of the B-29 and the Twentieth Air Force

STEVE BIRDSALL

1980

DOUBLEDAY & COMPANY, INC., *Garden City, New York*

Also by Steve Birdsall

THE B-17 FLYING FORTRESS

THE B-24 LIBERATOR

HELLS ANGELS

THE A-1 SKYRAIDER

LOG OF THE LIBERATORS

FLYING BUCCANEERS

Unless credited otherwise, all photographs appearing in this book are from the files of the United States Air Force in Washington. Life photographs are © 1944 Time, Inc.

CONTENTS

I

A Global Bomber

The Boeing B-29 Superfortress was the greatest airplane of World War II. It was the gleaming realization of a concept of strategic airpower, a concept that could be traced back to the earliest days of military aviation. The B-29 fought against heavy odds from the beginning, with the true believers often outnumbered and outranked by those who doubted or opposed the doctrine. The battle for an American strategic air force cost lives and it cost careers. Throughout the early years the B-29 would need friends in high places.

Boeing's Superfortress may be traced back as far as March 1938, when the company produced a design study, Model 334, for the Air Corps. This was essentially "a pressurized version of the B-17 with tricycle undercarriage," a logical next step. With the Air Corps struggling to obtain appropriations for aircraft, it was up to the Boeing Company to take some of the risks. By July 1939 they had conceived Model 334A, the first direct link with the B-29, and, still with Boeing money, they built a mock-up in December. In the first nine months of that year the company was showing a loss of over $2,500,000. In the big-bomber field, Boeing's fortunes hinged naturally on the fortunes of the military, and major changes were occurring.

The man who would assure the B-29's future was General Henry H. "Hap" Arnold, who had become chief of the Air Corps in September 1938. Arnold had carefully built his career without resorting to the "do or die" tactics of other, more colorful advocates of strategic air power. Working from within the entrenched system, Hap Arnold was succeeding where others had failed, and among some of his hotter-blooded contemporaries his caution had gained him a reputation as a man whose loyalty was directed where it would gain him the most. The rebels of the Air Corps, under General Frank Andrews at Langley Field, home of America's tiny heavy-bomber force, were fighting their own battle for airpower, epitomized at that time by Boeing's Flying Fortress. A situation existed where the apparent foresight of some was balanced by the sad lack of it in others. Against this background, Boeing continued their studies.

In May 1939 General Arnold had formed a board to examine all kinds of aircraft and suggest exactly what the Air Corps should develop and procure. Headed by General Walter Kilner, the board included aviator Charles Lindbergh, who had come back from Europe with a lot of knowledge and an unpopular respect for Germany's Luftwaffe, Colonel Carl Spaatz, and two other officers. The Kilner board's comprehensive report was completed by the end of June, and among the recommendations was the development of several long-range heavy bombers.

In November Hap Arnold set about getting official approval to let contracts for a very long-range, very heavy bomber, and received the green light at the beginning of December. A "statement" of the requirements was prepared by Captain Donald Putt, an Air Corps test pilot and engineer who had survived the crash of the first Flying Fortress back in 1935. The Air Corps was looking for a speed of 400 miles per hour, 5,333 miles range, and the capacity to carry a 1-ton bomb load half that distance. The "super bomber" was supposedly conceived as a defensive airplane, for long-range reconnaissance and strikes against the enemy at sea, but with the thinking prevalent in the Air Corps at the time this was never more than a ruse. As far back as September 1939 Colonel Spaatz had suggested that the future bomber might be used against Japan from bases in Luzon, in Siberia, or the Aleutians.

Putt's document was sent to various aircraft companies late in January 1940. These specifications for the super bomber reached Boeing's president, Philip Johnson, on February 5, 1940, and within three weeks the company's Model 341 had been submitted.

Boeing had been well prepared because during the spring and summer of the previous year company people like Claire Egtvedt, Wellwood Beall, and Edward Wells had discussed super bombers with Wright Field and Air Corps officers—General Frank Andrews, Colonel Oliver Echols, Major Bill Irvine, and others, sometimes even Arnold himself. From these meetings Boeing had "acquired the conviction" that the bomber would be built, despite the fact that official approval was still half a year away.

As the war in Europe burgeoned, lessons were being learned, and the Air Corps specification was soon amended to include armor, fuel-tank sealing, and defensive armament. With these amendments in mind, preliminary design teams in Seattle worked on Model 345. There were early problems: Leakproofing the gas tanks would mean adding 3,000 pounds weight, in turn meaning that 2,000 pounds more fuel had to be carried if range was not to shrink. The total changes added around 13 tons to the design.

When the revised bids were received at Wright Field in May, a board of officers headed by Colonel Oliver Echols looked hard at them. Boeing and Lockheed were the winners, but Boeing's Model 345 was considered superior; the Air Corps gave it the designation XB-29 and named Captain Putt as project officer. In June Arnold approved contracts for both Boeing and Lockheed to proceed with wooden mock-ups.

Boeing was appropriated some $85,000 for further study and wind-tunnel tests, and more money was forthcoming later in June. Finally, on August 24, the company received $3,615,095 to build two prototypes and a model for static testing. The contract was dated September 6, 1940, and was amended in December to include a third prototype. To offhandedly call this a "gamble" is to denigrate Boeing and Air Corps experts who worked on the Superfortress. Boeing had a wealth of experience, and if any company was ready to build a "super bomber" it was Boeing.

However, it was a tremendous undertaking, and there was a great deal of theory yet to be proved in flight. The designers were facing fundamental challenges. How to propel more than twice the weight of the B-17 through the air at a greater speed? Engines giving almost twice the power were available, but there was a basic law to be considered: The horsepower goes up as the cube of the velocity, meaning around eight times the power was required to double the speed. When the weight was doubled the induced drag was increased, again demanding more power.

Minimizing drag was the primary consideration.

The staff engineers at Boeing controlled research and development in the many areas involved in producing such a bomber — aerodynamics, armament, power plant, vibration, weight control and so on, while group engineers did the detailed design, such as the fuselage, nacelles, wings, control surfaces, and landing gear. Marrying all the specialties together was the project engineer, who approved all designs before they were passed to manufacturing for fabrication and assembly of the airplane.

There had to be an extremely delicate balance of considerations, right along the line, and under normal circumstances, developing an aircraft like the Superfortress would be expected to take five years. The complex and numerous problems required patience, experiment, and lengthy testing, although the bold steps taken with the B-29 were not into totally unknown areas. Boeing had the experience of the XB-15, the B-17, and the Stratoliner with its pressurized cabin, and in June 1940 the project was accelerating. The key Boeing men were Wellwood Beall, chief engineer; his assistant, Edward Wells; Edmund Allen of Flight Test and Aerodynamics; and the chief aerodynamicist, George Schairer. They could and would remain within proven concepts, refining and adapting them to suit the B-29. Wright Field and the Air Corps' Materiel Division represented the military.

The B-29 had much in common with the B-17 — for example, the B-17's tail was one step in the development of the B-29 tail. Other features were copied directly, and a lot of experimentation to check ideas was done using a B-17. However, there were areas where the new bomber was revolutionary. The wing had to have low drag at cruising speed and good high-speed and stall characteristics. To find the bomber's wing, Schairer and Allen spent two months negotiating with David Davis, designer of the laminar flow wing, which was considered the best for a long-range airplane. In the end, when no agreement could be reached, Wellwood Beall decided that Boeing should develop its own wing, and the design of eight potential wings consumed thousands of hours. When the Air Corps increased the gross weight of the aircraft, an even greater-performance wing was required, and finally the Boeing "117" wing was developed. It featured the world's largest wing flap, equivalent to one fifth of the B-29's total wing area, which would allow pilots to get the B-29 into the air, where the low-drag, high-speed, long-range characteristics of the wing would pay their way.

The wing structure was fairly standard and proven, consisting of a center section, two inboard panels, two outboard panels, and wingtips. Self-sealing fuel tanks were installed in the inboard wing structure. The two wing spars were the longest and heaviest Duralumin extrusions ever used in a production aircraft.

The fuselage was made up of five joined sections. The three sections that would contain the crew were pressurized. To allow passage from the pressurized nose section to the pressurized waist, a tunnel, large enough for a man to crawl through, crossed the bomb-bay section. To hold the diameter of the airplane to a minimum, and reduce drag, a tandem bomb bay was used. One was forward of the wing and the center of gravity, the other behind, meaning that one could not be emptied before the other without the center of gravity going out of limits; accordingly, an intervalometer was used to alternate the release of bombs from each bay.

The structure of the fuselage was composed of circumferential frames, pressure bulkheads, and stringers, with butt-jointed, stressed aluminum-alloy skin. Flush riveting was used, again to reduce drag, except around turret mounts, where added strength was needed, and in areas out of the slipstream. The skin was riveted to the longitudinal members only, which would save thousands of man-hours in mass production.

The circular cross section of the fuselage was continuous, varying only at the wing and stabilizer. Besides allowing standardization of parts and ease of fabrication, the use of this circular body section provided the most efficient means of compartment pressurization, since the skin was then in uniform tensile stress. The pressurized areas were kept leakproof by riveting the skin seams and sealing them with a compound, and control cables passed through synthetic rubber bushing, which grasped the cables without interfering with their function and without excessive leaking of air. Boeing developed an automatic pressure regulator and vacuum relief valve, and compressed air was drawn from a gear-driven compressor on the left inboard engine on early models and later from one supercharger on each inboard engine.

The engines were Wright R-3350's, the most powerful and complicated ever built. They were a conventional radial design, with two staggered banks of 9 cylinders each, and were a development of a design that harked back to the Cyclone 9 of the '20s, a 525-horsepower engine. During 1937 and 1938 it had been designed and tested, and was developed to produce 2,200 horsepower with no increase in frontal area, bore, or cylinder displacement. The enormous power came from higher compression, greater revs, and supercharging. The engine came close to delivering one horsepower for every pound of engine weight.

The Wright R-3350 first flew in 1939 on the huge Douglas XB-19, but less than 100 engines had been built when it was adopted for the B-29. Boeing was aware that cooling problems had plagued earlier use of the engine, so care in this area was paramount; if the engines were not efficient, performance would fall short. Yet in the B-29 airflow to the engine had to be reduced to the minimum requirement; the cowlings had to admit enough air, but not increase drag at high speed, and maintain low drag during all cruising operation.

The B-29 induction system used only one air inlet for each engine, on

the leading edge of the cowl. Two General Electric exhaust-driven turbosuperchargers, automatically controlled by an electronic system, were
used on each engine because no single unit could provide the necessary
volume of air. A mock-up of the duct system was designed and built, and
blower sections of the turbosuperchargers were installed to simulate the
240,000 cubic feet of air that would be blasted through the 4 engines
every minute. A complete section of wing with a nacelle and power plant
was built and tested.

The propellers had to turn the raw power of the engines into useful
thrust with maximum efficiency for heavy takeoffs and long missions, and
an entirely new propeller gear ratio was used for the B-29. The propellers had to be of great size, and tip speed was critical—normal speeds
would be "too fast" and would cut high altitude performance. Wright
Aeronautical engineers were consulted, and they suggested a gear ratio
that would make the B-29s' propellers the slowest-turning on any airplane. After extensive testing the Hamilton Standard three-bladed propeller was adopted for the XB-29s and some of the YB-29s, and then a
four-blade version was used.

The B-29 had to have ample defensive fire power, but again adding as
little drag as possible. The periscope turrets produced by Sperry were
good from the point of view of keeping the airplane "clean," but their
field of vision was limited, and in battle the system was never really any
good. In November 1941 Wright Field representatives went to Seattle to
talk about arming the B-29, and their instructions were clear: Tell Boeing
to put power turrets on the B-29. The whole delicate balance of the
design was in jeopardy. It was an impasse: The periscope-sighted turrets
were unacceptable to Wright Field; power turrets were unacceptable to
Boeing. In the end Colonel Roger Williams of the Wright Field armament section came up with an alternative. The General Electric fire-
control system, which was still in an experimental stage, might be the answer. The design work began in earnest in January 1942, General Electric engineers working closely with Boeing and the Materiel Division at
Wright Field. The new central fire-control system was made up of a small
computer that made corrections for speed, range, altitude, bullet drop,
wind, deflection, and temperature. It also meant that any gunner except
the tail could use more than one turret at a time, by the use of a switch
box. All the guns except those in the tail were sighted and fired from stations remote from the actual turrets, so gunners were not hindered by
vibration or recoil. The system increased range far beyond the usual 600
yards by automatically establishing the correct lead.

All the advances in the Superfortress required greater amounts of electric power, and existing generator equipment was inadequate, so new electric motors had to be developed. Battle experience had revealed that electrical wiring was less susceptible to battle damage than hydraulic or pneumatic tubing, and easier to maintain. The B-29 had what was essentially a completely electrical system. The landing gear, flaps, turrets, bomb-release control, automatic pilot . . . in the end there were over 150 electric motors of all kinds in the airplane, all drawing their power from a 6-generator system driven from the engines. When the engines were not running, power was drawn from the Auxiliary Power Unit, a 7-horsepower gasoline engine located in the rear fuselage. The only hydraulic system on the B-29 was the brakes.

* * *

Throughout the formative months of the Superfortress there were constant changes. The Army Air Corps still had doubts about the extremely high wing loading: 69 pounds per square foot. Colonel George Kenney called Wellwood Beall to his office at Wright Field, and graphically put the question to him. After writing the gross weight, wing loading, and ceiling of the B-24 Liberator on a blackboard, Kenney then added the gross weight and wing loading of the XB-29. A large question mark followed the chalked word "ceiling." Beall parried this with the point that there was no true comparison, because the turbosupercharger installations differed radically. Beall argued that the B-24's limited ceiling was caused by this rather than by the high wing loading.

The Air Corps was also experiencing serious problems with the takeoff and landing characteristics of the Martin Marauder. It was felt that these were caused by high wing loading and a resultant lack of low-speed control. The Superfortress became guilty by association, and the debate between Boeing and Wright Field grew so heated that at one time "orders" from Washington demanded more wing area for the B-29. This would play havoc with performance. In a nerve-wracking meeting at an office in Boeing's Plant 2 in Seattle, Echols and Putt put the Air Corps' case for change. Beall, Wells, Schairer, Allen, and N. D. Showalter defended their own figures, based on wind-tunnel tests, and decided that an attack was the best defense. They studied the B-26 Marauder and reached the conclusion that its landing and stall characteristics were not due to the high wing loading, but to a combination of maladjusted forces—high wing loading and low aspect ratio of the wing, a poor airfoil section, poor wing-flap design, and improper loading of the airplane. Overall, poor design. It was Boeing's assertion that the B-26's faults were designed into it. Boeing won the argument.

As the war in Europe intensified, air-power advocates in the military were winning more than their usual share of victories. Germany had shown vividly what could be achieved with an overwhelming air force, and in May 1940 President Franklin D. Roosevelt asked the nation for 50,000 airplanes. Soon the Army and Navy were unleashing an unparalleled flow of contracts to the aircraft industry. Business boomed as the lean years suddenly ended with a huge demand for labor, raw materials, and thousands of other items. It was just one year later when Boeing began another mock-up and were told that they would be receiving an order for 250 B-29s to be built in a new government-owned factory at Wichita, Kansas. This contract was signed in September 1941 and subsequently doubled in quantity in January 1942, after the shattering events of December had left no lingering doubts about the United States and world war. Sixteen hundred Superfortresses would ultimately be ordered before the prototype had flown.

With these new orders, new problems rose to be solved. A factory complex had to be planned, built, equipped, manned. Production and engineering personnel from Wichita were brought to Seattle to watch and learn about the B-29. While steam shovels were rearranging the Kansas prairie, Boeing was gathering the equipment the factory would require, and people had to be found who could build the B-29s.

The system of precompleting major sections of the airplane on separate production lines before final assembly was chosen. The B-29 design was broken down into component parts, and an analysis was made of final assembly. Critical labor shortages were imminent, and the process had to be simplified so that quickly recruited, hastily trained workers could put the B-29 together as quickly and perfectly as possible.

Toward the end of 1941 the company was working under pressure to finish their aerodynamic research, detailed design and engineering, tool design, and the construction of the first XB-29. In Kansas there was a similar haste to build roads and housing, recruit workers, and construct and equip the plant.

The B-29 continued to make history long before it took to the air. Only the Martin Marauder had ever been ordered "off the drawing board" before, but the B-29 was a far, far greater program. It embraced a large section of the aviation industry and it was a revolutionary airplane — the first pressurized bomber, first with remote-controlled turrets, the heaviest production airplane ever built, with the most powerful engines and highest wing loading.

With the design finalized, the huge manufacturing program getting under way, and wind-tunnel tests still being carried out, the first XB-29 was destroyed in a massive structural test program. The fuselage was tested first; put on the rack at Seattle, it was pulled down at both ends until it finally broke at the rear turret in a jagged tear. After that the fin, rudder, elevators, and stabilizers were broken, then the ailerons and wing flaps. The wing was trussed up and a simulated load over four times that of the airplane was applied by means of hydraulic jacks. It stood all that was required before it finally gave way with a deafening roar. The final torture was by gunfire: Cannon shells were pumped through crucial places to find out just how much punishment the Superfortress could withstand.

The building of the first Superfortress to fly had begun in Seattle 6 months before all aerodynamic work was completed and a year before drawings of all parts were available. The XB-29 had to be ready to fly by early August 1942, and an initial team of 50 mechanics would grow to over 700 people before the airplane was finally rolled out. Cradling the airplane in wooden jigs, they built the fuselage in a single piece, working on areas for which they had drawings first, leaving holes where the drawings were unavailable.

In February 1942 Boeing was informed that other companies would build B-29s. The original scheme involved Bell Aircraft at Marietta in Georgia, North American in Kansas City, and the General Motors Fisher Body Division in Cleveland. To thrash out the details, General Oliver Echols assembled some of the key military and industrial people involved. Among them were General Kenney, Colonel K. B. Wolfe, Larry Bell, and more than a dozen others. Chairing the meeting in the General Motors Building in Detroit was General Motors Vice President O. E. Hunt.

Hunt gave General Motors' position bluntly: While the company had the most enormous production capacity in the world, it was already snowed under, and wanted no part of the B-29. Addressing the meeting, Echols equally bluntly stated that General Motors had to be in the program. The sessions led to a joint production plan whereby Wichita would produce and assemble B-29s, Bell would build them in Georgia in a specially built plant, North American would build them in Kansas City, and Fisher Body would build them in a new factory at Cleveland. Boeing was required to provide all engineering data to the primary contractors, passing on all design changes as they were made, and to supply master gauges to maintain true interchangeability of parts.

The plan would never become reality in this original form. When the Navy wanted land-based bombers in August 1942, North American's Kansas City facility was "traded" for the Navy's Boeing factory at Renton, twelve miles south of Seattle. Fisher Body at Cleveland was switched to fighter production, and its part in the B-29 program, except for subassemblies, was taken over by the Glenn L. Martin factory at Omaha, Nebraska.

To tackle the massive pile of paperwork and organization a Superfortress Liaison Committee was formed, headed by Colonel K. B. Wolfe. As the key man in the co-ordination process, he was more and more associated with the Superfortress in Arnold's mind, and became the logical choice to take the first B-29s into action two years later.

Hap Arnold believed in the B-29, seeing in it the future and a postwar independent Air Force. After Pearl Harbor the "rebels" of the Air Force had seen an opportunity to make their point, and there was a movement, in the press and in Congress, for a separate Air Force. They felt that Arnold had deserted them, but they were unaware of his special relationship with General George C. Marshall. Marshall believed in the concept of a separate Army, Navy, and Air Force, and when he became chief of staff in September 1939 he had insisted on having Arnold as one of his deputies. Arnold was promised anything he needed, within the current structure. Marshall's reasoning made sense: The Army had a massive supporting organization, which the Army Air Forces could lean on. Marshall encouraged Arnold to bring his own best people to the top, and convinced Roosevelt that Arnold should be included in conferences and attend meetings of the War Council. Arnold, always part politician, "short-circuited" the independence movement, and on March 9, 1942, the Army Air Forces achieved equality with the Army's ground and service forces. Marshall kept his part of this "bargain" and Arnold kept his: the war would be over before there was a truly independent Air Force, but the foundation was firmly laid, and the B-29 would play a key role. The Superfortress had a powerful friend in Washington. She would need him soon.

"She Flies"

Boeing's Flight Test and Aerodynamic Research Unit was faced with the greatest test program ever undertaken. As production was getting

The first flight-test XB-29. The airplane had a wingspan of 141 feet, 3 inches, and was 99 feet long, with a design gross weight of 50 tons, and a maximum alternate gross weight of 114,500 pounds. At 25,000 feet the speed was 382 miles per hour. The XB-29 was identical to Model 345 except that it weighed about a ton more, was 62 inches longer, and when armed its turrets were not retractable, as was originally planned. Also, pointed aerodynamic features were added to the trailing edge of the inboard wing to obtain improved flap characteristics. (Boeing)

under way, hundreds of items were waiting to be proved in the air. At the beginning of the tests the airplane would be flown in a stripped condition, and in the spring of 1942 Eddie Allen had estimated that the airplane would need two hundred hours of test flight. This had to be compressed into four or five months. The flight tests would take place at Boeing Field, Seattle, where there were the necessary testing laboratories and numerous engineers needed to get the work done as rapidly as possible.

There were delivery delays and other difficulties, but on September 9 it was possible to run up the XB-29's four engines and begin taxi tests. Trouble with carburetion and the engines forced engineers to work around the clock. On September 15 the huge airplane was "hopped" from the runway to about fifteen feet three times in preliminary exercises. There was already an indication of future trouble: During these comparatively minor tests on the ground, fifty-seven hours was the longest any engine had operated without indicating distress.

September 21 was bright and hot. The XB-29's engines coughed,

Eddie Allen was thin, balding, 43 years old; the high-voiced vegetarian had been the first to bridge the gap between test pilot and designer, engineer and manufacturer. He considered it pointless for a manufacturer to build an airplane and then ask a test pilot to make it work right. Allen was considered a foremost authority on stability and control in heavy aircraft. (Boeing)

caught, and eased to a steady, deep roar. The turbine wheels on the superchargers whined. At three-forty in the afternoon the Superfortress was roaring down the runway. Then she was flying, and seventy-five minutes later she landed and Allen smiled and said, "She flies." He elaborated in a written report that night, and the following day Colonel Putt took the airplane into the air for the Army Air Forces. He was more effusive than Allen, noting it was "unbelievable for such a large plane to be so easy on the controls . . . easier to fly than a B-17 . . . stall characteristics remarkable. . . ."

The engines threw the test schedule into turmoil. After just seven hours of flight, tests were suspended on September 30 for ten days. During October the carburetors were reworked, adjustments were made to the propeller governors, and many other changes were made. By late in the month the XB-29 was flying again, but an engine failed, so ground tests continued while it was replaced. The engine problems continued. In late November and early December tests were centered on power-plant operation, cooling, and supercharger performance. The XB-29 was successfully flown to an altitude of twenty-five thousand feet, and then Allen and his team began determining the minimum distance required for takeoffs and landings at various gross weights.

On December 26, after less than thirty minutes of flight, an engine failed and after the XB-29 was safely landed two engines were changed. Later that week another failed.

There were other problems—carburetors, leaking fuel cells, propeller feathering controls, electric motors—but overriding everything was the battle with the engines.

As the second flight-test XB-29 was making its first flight on December 30, fire broke out in the No. 4 engine at three thousand feet. The prop refused to feather, and the extinguisher did not control the fire. Allen told the engineer to give it another bottle, but still the fire raged. Smoke was filling the cockpit. Half a mile from the field, a third bottle of extinguisher was used, which seemed to smother the blaze, but the XB-29 was filling with smoke and carbon dioxide. Allen got her down safely; then the fire took hold again, but it was quickly put out by a ground crew.

The XB-29 was laid up for a month while still more adjustments were

The second flight-test XB-29, which crashed at Seattle on February 18, 1943. None of the XB-29s were fitted with armament while *Boeing was conducting the test program. (Boeing)*

made. On January 30 the airplane was flown for about two hours without serious problems and was then prepared for a high-altitude flight. The next day an engine went at twenty thousand feet and the test had to be abandoned.

Tragedy at Seattle

The first XB-29 was grounded for repairs and revisions for three weeks from January 28, 1943, but flight tests on the second aircraft were resumed. On February 18 Eddie Allen and his men took the second XB-29 up just after midday. Fire broke out in the No. 1 engine nacelle at five thousand feet, so they feathered the prop. The engineer closed the cowl flaps and operated the extinguisher, smothering the fire. The control tower at Seattle received the report; everything seemed to be under control.

Five minutes later the XB-29 was at twenty-four hundred feet and asking to be cleared for an immediate landing. One propeller was feathered and still the problem was "not serious," but the flight crew asked for crash equipment to be alerted. The next message came two minutes later, as the silvery giant passed over Lake Washington Bridge at fifteen hundred feet. Following a normal approach, the XB-29 flew over Seattle's commercial district at twelve hundred feet, but a trail of smoke marked her path, and pieces of hot metal were falling in her wake.

Seattle control was told to "have fire equipment ready . . . am coming in with wing on fire." That was the last call.

Steadily losing height, the XB-29 headed for the field, but she was being devoured by blazing gasoline. Fuel from the fillernecks of the tanks ran to the leading edge of the wing.

On the ground, people watched the flaming airplane as it lost altitude and skimmed the downtown business area. Two policemen saw it over the Yesler residential district, and to them it seemed only one of the four propellers was turning. A second or two later, people on the twenty-first floor of the Exchange Building saw the XB-29 apparently heading right for them. Chilled with horror, they saw it race by and head west.

The people in the control tower, numbed, overheard a few words from the blazing bomber: "Allen, better get this thing down in a hurry. The wing spar is burning badly."

Tongues of flame were racing from the wing into the cockpit. As the pilots held the XB-29 level, the forward hatch was opened and the radio

The Proving Ground Command at Eglin Field conducted a three-pronged armament test on the B-29. They fitted a B-29 with the General Electric fire-control system, a YB-29 with locally controlled turrets, and this, the first flight-test XB-29, with a Sperry fire-control system, controlled remotely with periscopic computers. While the Proving Ground found locally controlled turrets superior to both systems, both the Sperry and General Electric designs were placed in production, the former a $75,000,000 "insurance alternative" if for some reason the General Electric system could not be used. (Boeing)

operator jumped. The XB-29's propeller blades nicked some high-tension wires; the radio operator struck the wires too, his parachute billowing over him. There was a vivid flash.

In a last desperate attempt, Allen and his copilot hauled back on the controls, racking the B-29 into a left turn and apparently trying to land in a marshy open area. The fire in the cockpit was visible to the people on the ground. The XB-29's left wingtip smacked a cattle chute, but the airplane continued in its steep bank, ramming the fifth floor of the Frye Packing Plant in Airport Way. There was a huge explosion and a boiling fire. The crash killed nineteen people in the building, a fireman, and Allen and his remaining crew. Two more of the crew fell or jumped, much too low to hope to live.

Hap Arnold was stunned by the news and ordered an immediate investigation to isolate the fire problem with the engines. During March and

April Senator Harry S. Truman's investigating committee also looked into the B-29 program, and found that a lot of substandard, defective engines had been produced. The committee was blunt: With orders for the engine totaling over forty thousand, quality had run second to quantity. The committee also laid part of the blame on the Air Force for the pressure it had applied to the Wright company. While the investigations went on, the B-29 program lost momentum, but whenever there was any wavering Arnold simply said, "We are going to build it."

Special Project

Colonel Leonard "Jake" Harman, as bombardment project officer at Wright Field, had been closely connected with the B-29 and had flown with Eddie Allen and his crew. Harman was scathing in his criticism, particularly of Allen's habit of coming in long and flat over Seattle. He recalled that the crash "made me so damn mad . . . here was a perfectly good airplane lost, and it was just due to human error."

Harman then came up with the idea that would reshape the B-29 program. "I told K. B. Wolfe, my boss, we ought to package a whole deal . . . a special project on the B-29, to consist of flight test, production, training the crews," Harman said. "So K.B. said, 'Well, write it down and we'll go in to show the Old Man.' I made about a half a page letter saying, 'a special project is hereby formed to have complete control over the B-29 consisting of control over production, flight tests, training . . . to get this airplane in combat with the least possible delay.' And I put down at the bottom a place for, typed in, 'H. H. Arnold.'

"We went to Washington to see our immediate boss, General Echols," Harman continued. "He read it and said, 'I suppose you know what you're getting into.' So we went down the hall to see General Arnold. He came out and I told him, 'Good morning' and I tossed this letter on his desk, and he read it, slapped the desk, and said, 'That's fine. Why doesn't somebody else do something for me once in a while?' So I passed him a pen and he signed it."

Arnold asked Harman where he was staying in Washington, then cautioned him: "Not a word of this to anybody." Harman learned later that Arnold went to see Marshall, then both went to the President. That afternoon Harman received a call at the Mayflower Hotel. No names were mentioned, but Harman recognized the voice on the phone, which said, "Be careful what you say. Approved."

The third prototype was used for aerodynamics and systems tests. (Gordon S. Williams)

So was born the "B-29 Special Project," with Wolfe in charge and Harman deputizing. Arnold was anxious to get B-29s into combat before the end of 1943, but when Harman prepared to take the third prototype up on May 29, disaster stared them in the face again.

It began when Harman and his "one-man contact" from Boeing, N.D. Showalter, were experimenting with the ailerons. They planned to approach flying speed, but not fly, to see if their changes had solved the problem of overcontrolling. Harman continued, "So we wound up the engine and got in and poured the coal to it. Of course, it was light weight. Next thing I knew, we were in flight. And then it was just like going down the highway at sixty miles an hour and turning the wheel to the left and the airplane went right instead. Next thing I knew the wingtip was dragging on the runway. I was in a vertical bank. So I gave it full power on the starboard engines and throttled the left-hand engines. The wing gradually came up and kind of went over and we landed on a taxi strip parallel to the runway . . . I had the hell scared out of me."

K. B. Wolfe, who always referred to the B-29 as "this thing," was watching from an office window, and remembered thinking, "My God, we're going to lose the second one!" They "didn't dare" tell Arnold, who found out about the incident long afterward.

It was discovered that the aileron control cables had somehow been reversed, and next day the XB-29 flew again. Harman said, "Boy, I put it through the paces and found out we had a hell of a good airplane, just a tremendous airplane."

The final XB-29, in all her gleaming glory. (Boeing)

On June 27, 1943, Harman flew Wichita's first service-test YB-29, but the engine problems continued, and although corrective steps were taken, the R-3350 would not be ready for combat even when the first B-29s made their long journey to war.

Yet there was simply no alternative, and the problems had to be coped with. There were modifications to engine nacelles and adjoining structures, modification of fuel fillernecks, the addition of bulkheads and ventilation to the leading edge, tightening of the seals in the firewalls, improvements to exhaust shroud cooling — all these and more received top priority.

Major Vic Agather of the project office at Wright Field recalls that there "was probably less military bureaucracy on the B-29, nevertheless it was very difficult to co-ordinate all the problems and take into consideration all factors necessary to get a fix on these problems . . . as the technical problems erupted they were assigned to different groups. We had first priority on everything.

"The source of the engine-fire problem went back to the original design by Wright Aeronautical . . . the concept to design an engine that had less than one pound of weight per horsepower. Consequently original engines had a high amount of magnesium in the crankcase and accessory housing. Over a period of time test engines did perform fairly well on dynamometers, and engine-test stands, but would break up under vibration when moments of inertia were developed, because of the peculiarities of magnesium crystals . . . a redesign of the engine was required, but in no measure were we in a position to change basic design, because of the time factor required to accomplish these changes, and still meet production schedules. Consequently we did patch work and fixes on engine cooling such as ducted baffles, slotted valve adjustment screws . . . and many other changes that used engine oil for cooling as well as increase the air flow around exhaust valves. The engine-fire problem centered around the overheating of the exhaust valves . . . the engine would swallow the valve and in most cases this resulted in an engine fire. If the engine fire could not be contained within the forward section and reached the accessory housing, the magnesium, which burns at extremely

The first of fourteen service-test YB-29s is weighed at the Wichita plant. The airplane was rolled out in April 1943, but did not fly until June. (Peter M. Bowers)

high temperature, would burn through the fire wall into the main spar, and the wing would peel off with the loss of the airplane."

Wolfe's and Harman's "Special Project" was second in priority to only one other, with the seemingly innocent cover name of "Manhattan Engineer District," and in time these projects would come together to change the world. This priority treatment allowed Wolfe to strip his Wright Field office of key people to be his technical staff. He took Jake Harman along as his deputy, and to direct the B-29 crew-training program he chose General LaVerne "Blondie" Saunders, who had commanded a B-17 group in the South Pacific.

Wolfe's plan called for a bombardment wing that would be made up of four combat groups, with a fifth, the 472nd, to remain behind as an operational training unit when the other four had gone overseas. The aim was to make the B-29 command as nearly independent as possible, a kind of aerial task force. Each group would have four bombardment squadrons and four maintenance squadrons. Instructors had to be trained so that they in turn could prepare the combat crews. As a nucleus for the training staff Wolfe procured twenty-five pilots and twenty-five navigators with a wealth of experience in four-engine airplanes and long flights over water.

So in June 1943 Wolfe became the commander of the new 58th Bombardment Wing, with headquarters at Cobb County Army Air Field in Georgia, near the Bell plant. Part of his task was to speed up modifications to the B-29 at Bell, and at Wichita, while maintaining the flight-test program. To hasten this process, Wolfe "borrowed" Colonel Abram Olson's Accelerated Service Test Branch from Wright Field, and sent them to Smoky Hill, Kansas.

The plan for the Wichita operation was that Boeing would collaborate with the Air Force on testing to evaluate the airplane's speed, range, and engine cooling. Boeing ground crews would maintain the planes, and military pilots would school Boeing flight personnel to enable the company to build a staff to fly the B-29s as they rolled off the production lines.

During August and September Boeing's N. D. Showalter worked with Wright Field's people gathering the data they needed. Wolfe returned a lot of the flight-test program to Boeing and, because Wichita's longest runway was not capable of handling high-gross-weight takeoff tests, Colonel Olson took his organization, of by then four B-29s, to Salina.

Olson checked out Colonel Lewis Parker, who took a YB-29 to Pratt Army Air Field, Kansas, and began setting up the 40th Bomb Group. Within three weeks he received three more airplanes for training. Colo-

The first flight-test XB-29 was sent to Salina, Kansas, for some tests which required a longer runway than was available at Wichita. Boeing's N.D. Showalter was the test pilot, and Don Whitworth was test engineer. After water had been added to the bomb-bay tanks the aircraft was taken off at 135,000 pounds gross weight, as part of the program to learn the requirements for B-29 airfields. With the testing completed, they left Salina for Seattle, but were weathered in for three days at Billings, Montana. Whitworth recalled that the crew flipped a coin to decide who would stand guard on the airplane the first night, and although they were to change on the second night, the same man volunteered for duty. Other members of the crew surmised that something was afoot, and went out to the airplane to find the "guard" conducting tours of the airplane for airport personnel at a dollar a head. (Boeing)

This YB-29 went to the 444th Bomb Group for training, then passed on to the Boeing school in Seattle.

nel Alva Harvey took the next three production airplanes to Great Bend, to begin the 444th Group. Harvey had reported to Boeing Seattle as a project officer on the B-29 back in October 1942, and moved to Wichita early in 1943, where "each flight was a thrill in itself . . . if we returned to base with three out of four engines running, that was par for the course."

Colonel Howard Engler took three B-29s to Smoky Hill as the basis of the 468th Bomb Group, and Colonel Richard Carmichael took three more to Walker to build the 462nd. The first B-29 combat command was forming, its group commanders hand-picked by General Hap Arnold.

*   *   *

In the fall of 1943 the Accelerated Service Test Branch at Smoky Hill was flying a pair of YB-29s, and then the Kansas winter set in. There were no hangars big enough for the B-29, so the crews had to maintain the aircraft under miserable conditions. With the 468th Group now sharing the Kansas base, it was decided to move the ASTB to Marietta in Georgia. John Mitchell recalls that it was still cold, and "still no hangars to work in . . . any support we may have expected from the Bell factory proved nonexistent. Bell was trying to build B-29s with former cotton farmers and everything was a mass of confusion. However, with all the obstacles through the winter months, things slowly began to shape up. We were learning the tricks of the trade. Some things were simple once we learned . . . but they were the cause of many hours of frustration until they were mastered."

As the battle with the Wright engines continued, ASTB's veteran line chief, Sergeant Jimmy Graham, partially solved the excessive cylinder-head-temperature problem. There were twelve cowl flaps on the engine nacelles, and ten of them could be opened to a maximum of over seven inches during ground operation. Naturally the maximum for takeoff and flight was much less, as wide cowl-flap openings while in the air resulted in severe buffeting and loss of speed. The long cowl flaps on the early B-29s created a vicious cycle, being so large that if they were opened enough to keep the temperature at an acceptable level, they disturbed the air flow around the nacelle and created excessive drag. Opening them three inches meant a quarter of engine power was used merely pushing air through the cowl. The top two flaps were stationary and could not be opened, and Graham suggested that they be opened about two inches and fixed in that position, and that a couple of inches be cut from the trailing edge of the other flaps so they could be opened farther without interfering so much with the air flow. It was tried on some of the ASTB airplanes and it eased the problem.

John Mitchell adds that they knew the cause of the engine failures was "lack of lubrication to the valves, the stems got too hot and eventually separated from the head. This happened most in No. 3 and No. 16 cylinders. Since these cylinders exhausted to different sides of the engine we became adept in predicting which cylinder was going to fail by observing which side of the engine smoked the most taxiing out for takeoff. Suggestions to the Wright Aeronautical engineers as to the cause and a possible fix by increasing the oil to these cylinders were to no avail. I personally suggested that external oil lines be routed to these trouble areas, as I had noted on Pratt & Whitney engines. The response was that the design of the 3350 was to provide oil to the upper valve mechanisms through the hollow push rods. The fact that not enough oil was getting there didn't seem to interest them, and it appeared we would have to live (or die) with the problem of swallowed valves."

Eventually, crossover oil tubes were fitted, but B-29s would not leave the production lines with these modified engines until toward the end of 1944 . . . the interim was costly.

As all the changes, major and minor, were made, production airplanes from Wichita were dispatched to a modification center begun by Bell at Marietta, or to Wright Field, while some were modified at Seattle and others remained at Wichita. The Accelerated Service Test Branch took a YB-29 to 30,000 feet at 127,000 pounds gross weight, but that test only underlined the fact that the engines were far from ready. Other problems, such as sighting blister failures and a tunnel failure, had to be solved as the tests went on.

                    *   *   *

The composition of the crew to man the most complex airplane ever built had been discussed during the design stages, and a final figure of eleven men was reached. There were a pilot and a copilot, referred to as

The YB-29s contributed extensively to both the training and the testing programs. Once at Marietta they towed a fully loaded air- *plane around the ramps for days to see how much the pavement settled under the weight. (Bowers)*

airplane commander and pilot. In front of them was the bombardier, in the glass nose, and behind them, on the right facing aft, the flight engineer. He handled most of the power plant, electrical and basic mechanical operations to give the pilots more time for flying technique, particularly in the combat situation. Fuselage windows allowed him to visually check the engines. Both pilots and the engineer had a set of throttles at their stations, with the airplane commander having an override control in the earlier B-29s. The turbosuperchargers were controlled by a single dial knob on the pilots' pedestal. The radio operator was on the right side of the airplane, the navigator on the left; in all, six men worked in the forward pressurized section.

Back past the bomb bays in the center section were the three gunners: the right and left blister gunners with their pedestal sights, and the central fire-control gunner with a sight on a ring mount, who sat on a swivel-type stool to reach his top sighting blister. Aft of the gunners, in the same section, was the windowless radar operator's compartment. The pressurized tail compartment was small, and provided only for the gunner who occupied it.

Like all combat aircraft, the B-29 was cramped when loaded for war. Although it was the largest production airplane of all, there was little room to spare, typical of military airplanes. In the nose the bombardier was surrounded by his Norden bomb sight, gun sight, table, and controls. The pilots had their instruments and controls, and the flight engineer had his. There was the radio operator's seat, table, and bank of equipment, the navigator's seat and table. There were clipboards, first-aid kits, oxygen lines, cables, hand fire extinguishers, even an axe. The well of the top turret intruded into the forward compartment, and took up so much space that the navigator's table had to be hinged to allow easy passage past it. In the center section there was the equipment for the three gunners, the upper aft turret well, the radar operator's equipment. Every piece of usable space was utilized . . . in the rear unpressurized compartment there were the auxiliary power unit, the lower rear turret well, provision for aerial cameras, and the tail-turret ammunition cans.

As the crews who would take the B-29s overseas assembled at the Kansas bases, they sometimes saw a Superfortress at close quarters, but rarely. For the most part they trained with synthetic devices and flew Martin Marauders or B-17 Fortresses. Other crewmen were sent all over the country to various schools — Boeing B-29 school in Seattle, the engine course at Wright Aeronautical in Paterson, New Jersey, Minneapolis-Honeywell's Automatic Pilot refresher course, navigation school at Chanute, a self-sealing tanks course at U. S. Rubber in Detroit. . . .

The B-29 was not necessarily a specialist's airplane, but transition was not all that simple at first. Len Grantham, an instructor, recalls that being right up in the nose felt like "sitting on the front porch facing the street and practicing flying the house." There was no fixed horizontal reference, and some pilots used the artificial horizon. A small spot on top of the instrument panel could be used as a horizontal reference for the wings, and the pilot had to move his head to compensate for the frames of the windows as the nose came up. The B-29 required "technique" . . . a runaway prop on takeoff could be controlled by momentary use of the feathering button, a crosswind takeoff with the huge tail was challenging. The B-17 narrowed the gap from basic trainers, but did not fill it.

The year of 1943 was ending, and only one B-29 had flown a long-range mission, and less than seventy men had checked out as B-29 pilots. The Superfortresses were averaging only a couple of hours in the air each day.

Still, the aircraft were rolling out at Wichita, and Bell's first "all Georgia" B-29 had flown on December 20, the first B-29A from Renton taking to the air the same month. Martin at Omaha was getting going, although their operation would not be in full swing until the middle of 1944.

A Place to Go

As the B-29 program followed its rocky road, General K. B. Wolfe faced a second set of problems. In the middle of 1943 the war against Japan had been mainly defensive, and was planned to remain that way until Germany was defeated. Under the circumstances, the results achieved had been remarkable: The Japanese had been stopped at Midway, in the Aleutians, the Solomons, and New Guinea, often with shoestring forces. The only area where they still held the initiative was China. The British were struggling in Burma, and the China situation was approaching collapse. Roosevelt had a "special" feeling for China, a sense of obligation, and this played a significant part in the story of the B-29. The President was anxious to do something positive in the China-Burma-India Theater, feeling it was absolutely necessary that China be kept in the war. At the end of 1943 the B-29 timetable was looking solid enough, and while the Superfortresses would be too late to play a major role in Europe before the invasion, they could lead a strategic air offensive against the Japanese homeland.

The first Renton B-29A leaves the factory for the short barge trip to the airport, December 1943. Renton airplanes were distinguished as B-29As because there was an important structural difference in the wing. At Wichita and the other plants, a two-piece center section was bolted together on the center line, and this was installed as a single unit passing through the fuselage and supporting the engine nacelles. The Renton B-29As used a stub center section that projected a short distance from the fuselage, and each pair of nacelles was fitted to a short section of wing. The outer wing panels were attached at the same point on all B-29s, but the Renton aircraft had a one-foot-greater wingspan. (Bowers)

In the CBI Theater distances were vast, all forms of communication were slow, and the overall situation was poor. Three Allied nations were facing the Japanese with threadbare forces and little tangible success. The Chinese leader, Generalissimo Chiang Kai-shek, had an obvious objective to drive the Japanese out of China, but that was hindered by his perhaps greater concern with keeping his political party in power and staving off the Communists in the North. The British had imperial considerations in India and were more concerned with the reconquest of Burma and Malaya than any ground action in China. General Joseph Stilwell, the theater commander in Burma, had to keep China in the war, but was frustrated in almost every positive move.

From the very beginning, both Britain and the United States had been unwilling to send large forces of troops to China, for sound reasons. The war could not be won there, and the logistical situation was impossible; it was preferable to arm the Chinese through Lend-Lease and send small air forces to the theater. The Japanese had cut the Burma Road in 1942, reducing supplies to China to a "trickle" delivered by air over the awesome Himalaya Mountains. To break the Japanese blockade would require the recapture of northern Burma and the opening of a road through to Kunming, China, or putting massive resources into an airlift. At the beginning of 1943 Chiang Kai-shek had been promised assistance to achieve both goals, but the promises had not really been kept. Stilwell, as his uncomfortable chief of staff, wanted to retake Burma and open a road, but the generalissimo's air leader, General Claire Chennault, believed that a huge airlift and a bigger air force in China were the answers. Stilwell wanted to build and equip a strong Chinese army to drive out the Japanese; Chennault believed he could defend the country with existing Chinese armies by cutting Japanese supply lines.

A conference was held in Washington, and both strategies were presented. Chennault's concept won out, but for reasons other than any abiding conviction that he could keep his promises. Chiang Kai-shek naturally favored the decision, and was "encouraged," a source of great satisfaction to the President and other key men in the Administration. China evoked an almost missionary zeal on the part of her supporters, and the truth of the situation was submerged in a welter of goodwill and wishful thinking.

Roosevelt met with British Prime Minister Winston Churchill at the Quebec Conference in August 1943, and China was again on the agenda. Further commitments were made, but Chiang was asked for more cooperation in return, and plans were formulated for quicker results. Earlier in 1943 Hap Arnold had asked for "an analysis of strategic targets in Japan" that could bring about the enemy's collapse. Morale factors in the United States, China, and Japan were also considered, and added to a hope that the Japanese could be defeated within a year after Germany. Speculating that there would be ten groups of B-29s available in October 1944, and another ten in May 1945, and considering that the existing timetable indicated that no Pacific island within B-29 range of Honshu would be available in 1944, China was an alternative. Political and strategic decisions reinforced the choice.

It was proposed to build a chain of airfields north and south of Changsha, putting most Japanese industry within B-29 range. These targets could conceivably be wiped out in the twelve-month period after Germany's surrender. This plan depended on logistical support via

India, and without interfering with other operations. All supplies would have to be moved by air . . . from Calcutta, India, to Kunming, China, then on to Changsha. Liberators would be converted to transports after the victory in Europe and used at the rate of two hundred per B-29 group.

The combined chiefs of staff referred this plan, "Setting Sun," to their own staffs, who concluded that it was "unfeasible." Stilwell was asked his opinion and he was pessimistic. He came up with an alternate plan, "Twilight," which involved the use of several fields along the Kweilin–Changsha railroad, but as advanced rather than permanent bases; for maintenance and security the bombers would be based in India. The B-29s would carry much of their own fuel, and transports could supply the rest. Worked out by people who knew the theater from agonizing personal experience, "Twilight" trimmed away the more lavish aspects and involved a lesser effort, more time, and less logistical support. The idea of sending the B-29s to India to operate from advanced bases in China would further confuse a command that Arnold, after seeing it firsthand, drily called "somewhat complicated."

Arnold directed a special board to look over an outline plan that generally endorsed the Twilight concept, and in September 1943 he recommended the elaboration of a modified version of it. At the Quebec Conference the joint chiefs had expressed interest in taking the Marianas, a group of islands in the central Pacific, as a naval base, possibly early in 1946. The Air Force suggested that the landings could be much earlier if other islands were bypassed, and the Marianas would yield B-29 bases. Even so, it appeared that for a year China would remain the only place that put Japan within reach of the B-29s. That was perhaps enough to justify the horrendous logistical problems, but it was also powerfully supported by the political factor, the need to strengthen China's morale.

The die was cast. Arnold called Wolfe in and asked him to prepare an operational plan to begin strategic bombardment of Japan with the greatest number of B-29s in the least time. Toward the end of 1943 Wolfe had the fundamentals of his scheme, which was expanded by the Air War Plans Division. It was based on "Twilight" but brought the date of the first mission forward to June 1, 1944. Wolfe proposed to make the operation almost self-supporting by transporting supplies for 100 B-29s in the Kweilin area, with 150 more working from fields near Calcutta. June was too late for the President, who wanted something immediate, so the plan was revised and sent to Arnold on October 11. Wolfe believed he would have 150 B-29s by the beginning of March, and twice that number by

September 1944. Working with those figures, he proposed a B-29 command with two wings of four groups each. Stilwell had to provide bases in India and China and improve transportation facilities.

All the Superfortresses would be based in the Calcutta area and stage through advanced fields around Kweilin. Wolfe believed he could begin about the beginning of April. After three one-hundred-plane missions in fairly quick succession, the B-29s could fly around two hundred sorties per month until his second wing arrived. The B-29s would supply themselves, aided by Liberators until a stockpile was accumulated. Wolfe was aware of the weaknesses in the plan, but thought the gamble was acceptable. As far as the advanced bases were concerned, Stilwell's assertion that fifty first-class Chinese divisions would be needed to defend Kweilin led Wolfe to go along with the alternative, Chengtu, capital of the province of Szechwan, located about two hundred miles northwest of Chungking and four hundred miles from the Hump terminal at Kunming.

Arnold approved the plan in principle on October 13 and added a written note: "I have told the President that this will be started on March 1. See that it is done. H.H.A."

Roosevelt was still dissatisfied. In fact, he was "pretty thoroughly disgusted" with all aspects of the situation, and Arnold's report was "the last straw." Roosevelt failed to see why something could not be done sooner, or why they "have to use B-29s." Arnold replied specifically, noting that only B-29s could strike directly at Japan, so the March and April dates were accepted.

The plan was polished and ready on November 9, with the ambitious title "Early Sustained Bombing of Japan," eventually code-named "Matterhorn." As an American effort, it needed only the approval of the joint chiefs and the President, but due to complications it was four weeks before it was finally accepted, and it was under siege for months. The Navy disliked it because of the priorities demanded by the B-29s, and the Army was chagrined by the diversion of aviation engineers to build the Calcutta bases.

General Haywood S. Hansell of the Air War Plans Division recalls that "the position of air strategists regarding the air offensive against Japan was very weak in November 1943. B-29s were beginning to come off the line, but essential bases had not yet been provided . . . an outline plan was prepared for use of the B-29s from bases to be constructed by the forces of Chiang Kai-shek in China. It was the only way we could find for applying the B-29s, however ineffectively, against Japan proper, prior to the capture of the Marianas."

President Roosevelt acted positively: After being briefed he approved the plan in principle and on November 10 he advised Churchill and Chiang Kai-shek of its outline, and asked for their assistance in securing the airfields.

The Committee of Operations Analysts reported to Arnold on November 11, 1943, on strategic targets in Japan, and these targets would justify Matterhorn's existence. The committee listed six preferred target systems: merchant shipping, urban industrial areas, aircraft plants, ball-bearings industry, electronics industry, and steel production. The steel industry was to be attacked through coke ovens, and the report indicated that two thirds of Japan's steel production could be destroyed by knocking out six coking plants: three on the southern island of Kyushu, two near Mukden in Manchuria, and one in Korea. The coke ovens, very vulnerable to high explosives, were true strategic targets, and were suited to the long-range planning for the war against Japan.

So while the Superfortresses could not take the war to the Emperor's Palace from the Chengtu bases, these "prime economic targets" were well within range and lent a logical base to Matterhorn. However, imminent decisions to accelerate the Pacific war would make the steel targets too deep in the structure of Japan's war production for their destruction to have the desired effect.

Matterhorn was approved at the Cairo Conference in late November, with Chiang Kai-shek in attendance and promising to build the China bases, and the British agreeing to provide bases in India. Wolfe had already sent Colonel William Fisher to China, with the elaborate "cover" of being commander of the 308th Bomb Group, which flew Liberators. Fisher took over the group early in November, and between missions checked out potential sites for the B-29 bases and conferred with air leaders in the theater. His information went back to K. B. Wolfe by normal mail.

The paperwork moved quickly. The 20th Bomber Command, headed by Wolfe and composed of the 58th and 73rd Wings, was activated at Salina on November 27. Wolfe took part of his staff for his higher headquarters, leaving Jake Harman in command of the 58th Wing.

Although no definite decision had been made by the joint chiefs, the President's attitude amounted to virtual assurance. Significant doubts about Matterhorn were swept aside . . . it was under way and rolling.

The argument was not over. The decision to use the B-29s against Japan was never a major issue, but how they should be used caused long, drawn-out debate.

Approval had also been granted for the capture of the Marianas, with B-29s scheduled to be there by December 1944, and there were alternate plans for B-29 strikes from Ceylon and the Aleutians. The Joint Intelligence Committee did not like Matterhorn, believing Chengtu was the worst place to send the new bombers. The Marianas were obviously the best, and they contended that until they were captured, the B-29s should operate from bases in Australia or New Guinea.

In the middle of February 1944, the Joint War Planning Committee still maintained that B-29s operating from Australia against oil and shipping targets, was far preferable to using China. However, a later report, tinged by "decisions at highest level," recommended that Matterhorn receive the first eight B-29 groups.

A firm decision to take the Marianas was reached on March 12, to begin with landings on Saipan on June 15. This schedule, which brought forward the availability of the best base, was the final solution. Matterhorn stood, but with delays accumulating and earlier schedules going out the window, "interim" placement of the B-29s became less and less important. Matterhorn would only get the 58th Wing, which was beginning to move to India. Arnold was not unhappy. The political purpose so close to Matterhorn would be served, and the B-29 would receive an arduous operational test while hurting the enemy.

Wolfe arrived in India in January with the advance echelon of his 20th Bomber Command staff, and early the next month Arnold was advised of "entirely satisfactory" meetings among Wolfe, Chennault, Stilwell, and other key figures, resulting in complete understanding of their various roles in Matterhorn. Chennault was actually not so satisfied: He had written Arnold criticizing the operation. Arnold, however, liked neither Chennault's ideas nor his bold approach.

The B-29 Bases

In the CBI area the airfields had to be made specially for the B-29s. They should ideally have been built by local labor with local materials, but in India both American engineers and American materials were needed to supplement local resources.

Roosevelt was concerned with getting speedy results, but delays built upon delays, and essential features of Matterhorn were being scrapped in the scramble to get the B-29s over Japan.

In India it was best to improve existing airfields to B-29 standards, and southern Bengal was chosen as the rear-base area for sound reasons. It was fairly secure from enemy attack, with port facilities at Calcutta, and by Indian standards a good rail and road system. On the edge of the alluvial plain of the Ganges, around seventy miles west of Calcutta, the British had laid out a number of airstrips to handle Liberators. Wolfe looked over these sites in December 1943 and it was decided to build four fields, each with capacity for two B-29 groups, at Kharagpur, Chakulia, Piardoba, and Dudhkundi. Wolfe chose Kharagpur for his headquarters —it was an important junction and there was a large new building, the Collectorate, nearby. It had been built to hold political prisoners but was destined to become the 20th Bomber Command's headquarters.

Constructing the runways was a major task, and with no heavy equipment yet available, concrete was spread by hand by native workers. Although Washington read reports that work was progressing on schedule, it was a schedule unlike that hoped for, and the fields were not finally completed until September. The bases, including a fifth at Kalaikunda for transport use, cost about twenty million dollars. This was "modest" compared to the cost of the forward bases in China, where five sites for fields had been selected.

China's real strength lay in her huge population, and by the time the fields were completed possibly a third of a million workers had been on the job. While this peasant labor force with its quaint and ancient tools and methods brought bemused admiration, the Americans soon found that the Chinese Government's thinking was firmly planted in the twentieth century. In December Chiang Kai-shek set the total cost of the fields at "over two billion" Nationalist Chinese dollars and asked Roosevelt to guarantee that amount. This was acceptable, but the exchange rate was the rub. An American dollar would buy one hundred Chinese dollars on the black market, but the Chinese had an "official" rate of only twenty to one. The fields were expensive at any price, but at the official rate the cost was outrageous—one hundred million dollars. Stilwell, confiding to his diary, exploded: "My God, fifty million gold to build the fields and fifty million gold squeeze!"

In Washington, Secretary of the Treasury Henry Morgenthau raged about "a bunch of damned crooks" and the wrangle went on for months, with the Chinese refusing to compromise. To keep the project alive, Stilwell had to guarantee payment of the sum demanded, with the exchange rate to be decided later. Work began toward the end of January 1944, with the draining of the first rice paddies.

By March the estimate for the Chengtu fields, including one for a fighter defense force, had risen to nearly four and a half billion Chinese dollars, close to the final figure. Settlement was eventually reached in July and a lump sum of over two hundred million American dollars was paid. This also covered other items, so the true cost of the Chengtu fields will never be known. It was astronomical, but the bases, literally handmade, were completed.

There was a third base area to be used by the B-29s, but there the 20th Bomber Command had no permanent installations. Matterhorn planners had suggested that missions could be flown against oil targets at Palembang, Sumatra, by refueling the Superfortresses in Ceylon. A decision was made to improve the field at China Bay, and American engineers worked with the British to complete a B-29 runway with hardstands for two groups and a fuel-distribution system, and the work was completed in July.

*   *   *

Meanwhile, back in Kansas, the heartbreaking mechanical problems continued. During January the 44th Bomb Squadron had scheduled ten long-range practice missions, but only three aircraft got off the ground and only one completed its mission. Upon landing, that airplane was found to need an engine change.

The last of the service-test YB-29s was with Carmichael's 462nd Group at Walker, and it crashed on January 29; the accident investigation resulted in a toss-of-the-coin verdict: "50 per cent faulty fuel gauges, 50 per cent pilot error."

The B-29s were grounded until a series of modifications could be carried out before they went overseas. While this work was under way, Colonels Lewis Parker and Alva Harvey went to England to look at bombing techniques being used by the Eighth Air Force and to gain combat experience. Both group commanders flew five missions, the fifth being the daylight raid on Berlin on March 6, 1944. Harvey flew with the 100th Group that day, which lost fifteen of its thirty planes; Parker was shot down in a B-17, but survived the war as a prisoner. Colonel Harvey had a "breathtaking nine hours," and soon after was back with his 444th Group in Kansas.

One of the 58th Wing historians reported that morale at the B-29 bases was good, "despite Kansas," but as January ended Roosevelt was prodding Arnold and there were still gunners who had not fired a B-29's guns, and copilots who had not even taxied the aircraft. The crews, sensing that their training period was nearing completion, were worried that it

The first XB-29 worked long and hard; the crews finally named it The Flying Guinea Pig, *with an appropriate painting. The aircraft was fitted with four-bladed propellers by the time this photo was taken, and was still flying in 1947. (Boeing)*

After testing, the first of the fourteen YB-29s was sent to General Motors to be fitted with Allison liquid-cooled engines. It was redesignated the XB-39, and first flew in December 1944. The improvement in overall performance was not great enough to warrant further conversions. (Boeing)

would be rounded out in the combat zone. By mid-January ninety-seven B-29s had been built, but only sixteen of them were flyable. Most headed straight to modification centers from the production lines, some lingering there for up to two months as hundreds of changes were made, including additional bomb-bay fuel cells, new parts for the radar, and the replacement of R-3350-23 engines with R-3350-23A "war engines," with drilled rocker arms and sump changes.

In short, the Army Air Forces did not really have a "combat" B-29, and Arnold did not want to break promises to the President, who had been so scathingly critical about the failure to deliver the bomber by the beginning of 1944.

The principal modification centers were Bechtol, McCone, and Parsons in Birmingham, Alabama, and Bell at Marietta. In the middle of February Arnold flew to the Marietta center, and after being briefed by Bell officials he ordered that seventy 58th Wing men be brought in to break the "Marietta bottleneck." Some B-29s were sent to Martin at Omaha and Continental Airlines in Denver, where a group of Boeing people from Wichita and Seattle were "transplanted." The "war engines" were to be installed at centers in San Antonio and Oklahoma City, under Air Technical Service Command supervision. Arnold wired Wolfe and the commanders in the China-Burma-India Theater that the B-29s would be moving on March 10.

The "Battle of Kansas"

Arnold had decided that the 20th Bomber Command would need 175 B-29s to get their show on the road, and had gone to Wichita to see how that 175th B-29 was coming along. He found its fuselage section just entering final assembly. "This is the plane I want," he said, "I want it before the first of March." The 175th B-29 was rolled out on February 28 and became the *Gen. H. H. Arnold Special* with the 468th Group, but in March 1944 any B-29 could have suitably borne that name.

When Arnold went to Salina on March 9 to watch the first departures, he was livid: They were not ready to leave. Arnold found the entire modification program to be "void of organization, management, and leadership." No one at Salina could tell him if and when parts might arrive for the B-29s, so Arnold demanded a detailed rundown of exactly what the situation was, and that night a chart was prepared that told the sad truth. For one reason or another, not one B-29 was ready to go.

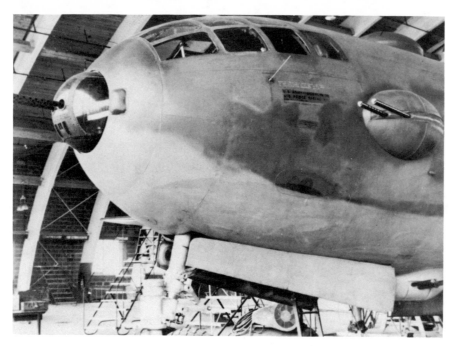

This YB-29 was modified to carry ten machine guns in addition to the normal armament system. Paul Tibbets recalls that the airplane, which had to be flown unpressurized, "was so heavy and cumbersome we gave up on it in a hurry. . . . The purpose of this one test aircraft was to determine the feasibility of a gun-loaded escort to be inserted in B-29 formations." (Bowers)

General Hap Arnold and the B-29 he "wanted," the 175th airplane. (Boeing Wichita)

The twenty-ninth production Superfortress from Wichita, which went to the 468th Bomb Group and subsequently became the tanker Esso Express. *The fact that all the production airplanes were virtually indistinguishable from one another underlines the basic soundness of the design. (Barry Gilkes)*

Arnold gave General Bennett Meyers full authority to act in his name as special project co-ordinator, and the B-29s took priority over everything. Meyers chose a deputy, Colonel "Bill" Irvine, and other technical and logistics experts were moved in.

Ironically, one of the squadron historians in the 468th Group recorded March as a month of "little activity," as most of the air crews were being transported by B-17 to modification centers where they were assigned a certain B-29 being modified. To secure the other modifications needed for combat, these crews ferried the planes from one center to another, piling up some flying time. The 468th historian also noted that the "terrific parties" in places like Atlanta, San Antonio, Birmingham, Seattle, New York, and Omaha "seemed like a dream" a couple of months later. Clay Sandhofer of the 462nd Group remembers having "a chance to visit the plant, see the plane go together, and strut our 'fearless airman image' in front of the assembly-line girls . . . since we got to test and ferry several B-29s from both Wichita and the Martin plant in Omaha, we managed to latch onto the plane that seemed to have least manufacturing defects and above all weighed the least empty on the scales. The difference in weight from one identical plane to the other was unbelievable, apparently caused by allowable commercial tolerances in raw materials and other factors."

While the flight crews were ranging far and wide, the ground crews were trudging through Kansas snow and feeling the bite of cold spring winds, and it soon became obvious that the final work on the B-29s could not be completed with available personnel, and a desperate plea went out to the manufacturers, particularly Boeing, for the loan of experienced production and assembly-line workers. Although it would possibly cost some production, Boeing sent six hundred workers from Wichita to join the all-out effort. Subcontractors were told to stop all else until they had met their B-29 commitments. Planes, trains, and trucks came in droves as the "Battle of Kansas" began.

Most of the work had to be done in the open, in blizzard conditions. The situation of the 40th Group at Pratt was typical: It was five back-breaking weeks of fatigue, confusion, and bitter weather. The group itself was to undertake seven changes and modifications to the planes, while the other forty or fifty were done by modification-center crews. The 40th had to change every engine that was not the "war" model, all rudders that were not the new, strengthened type, all main-landing-gear tires . . . they also had to modify the cowl flaps and make other changes. Their radar section was faced with the task of installing thirty-six AN/APQ-13 sets, and the men were "hampered" by the fact that none had ever installed a set of that type.

The Twentieth Air Force

Arnold really needed no more problems, but everybody wanted the airplanes he didn't have. It had begun as early as March 1942, when General Brereton had staked a claim for them from India, and after the Battle of Midway they were wanted in Hawaii, Harmon needed them in the South Pacific, and the Antisubmarine Command tried for a couple of dozen in April 1943. When the Navy asked for B-29s for long-range patrols, there were signs that the scars of past long battles had not healed — the reply was that "the Army Air Forces will not discuss the allocation of B-29s to the Navy." When General George Kenney arrived in Washington in January 1944, he also "wanted some B-29s," which he knew "were coming available," and explained that with their performance he could destroy the oil refineries in the Netherlands East Indies. Arnold made no promises but apparently told Kenney that if he had a runway long enough to take them by July, he might let him have fifty. Typically, Kenney sent word to begin work on a ten-thousand-foot runway at Darwin, Australia, "with parking area for a hundred B-29s." Whether Arnold was being generous with what he did not have, avoiding a typical Kenney onslaught, or simply echoing the view of some of his planners, is unknown — Kenney would never see a B-29 in one of his units. Then in February General Douglas MacArthur made it plain that he wanted all the B-29s in the Southwest Pacific. Later he modified the request to thirty-five, to hit the oil refineries in the Netherlands East Indies. In the CBI, where the B-29s were going, the problem still arose. Lord Louis Mountbatten, supreme Allied commander in Southeast Asia, had suggested that B-29s might perform long-range reconnaissance and strike missions in his command, but this was almost totally ignored. Considering the situation, this was "impolitic," and caused friction. Mountbatten had been asked to divert a large part of his airfield-construction facilities to provide the airstrips for the B-29s, for operations outside his theater. He "complained to General Hap Arnold a bit" about it when they met, and demanded some return for his outlay, and they came to a "gentlemen's agreement." Mountbatten considered it honored when the B-29s flew a mining mission in August, among others. Finally, Chiang Kai-shek wanted the B-29s to be under a "unified air command," presumably controlled by Chennault, and then later insisted that he himself command the B-29 project.

Arnold was well aware of the effects of "theateritis," a complaint fairly common among theater commanders, and there had already been much "discussion" over the use of the B-29s. Arnold had a unique answer to the problem.

Normally, air forces were assigned to a theater commander, but the concept of strategic bombardment meant its mission might not be related to events at the front lines. Using strategic bombers for tactical purposes interfered with the primary mission, and with operations at very long range, theater boundaries could further impede the B-29s' flexibility. The rivalry, jealousy, and general malaise in the China-Burma-India Theater and the Pacific conflict between General MacArthur and Admiral Nimitz would make it hard to move a strategic bomber force from one command to another. None of the theater commanders had shown a particular allegiance to the doctrine the B-29 represented, and Arnold was not keen to let them have the airplane.

Hap Arnold maintained "it was something I did not want to do" when, after touring the Pacific in the autumn of 1942, he decided to keep control of the B-29s. That was probably hardly the case — while the command was an additional burden, it was also the most illustrious combat command of the war.

It was decided, with the President's approval, that the B-29s would be controlled by the joint chiefs of staff from Washington. Arnold would give "executive direction" for the joint chiefs.

With the unexpected assistance of Admiral Ernest King, it was determined that there would be an "air force, known as the Joint Chiefs of Staff Air Force," which Arnold would command as the agent of the joint chiefs. Arnold would follow specific directives, which he would help to conceive.

All the major decisions governing the use and objectives of the B-29s would be made by the joint chiefs, although theater commanders could divert the B-29s to other use in an emergency situation. With command firmly in Washington, the B-29s could be moved from India to the central Pacific later.

The new Twentieth Air Force was activated on April 4, 1944, with Arnold as commander and each member of his staff doubling in a similar role in the new air force. The working staff was a group of deputies— General Hansell was selected as chief of staff, and Hansell was one of the most articulate exponents of strategic bombardment, an indication of the plans Arnold had for his air force. Hansell, with Colonel Cecil Combs as his operations deputy, would run things. The chains of command rattled from Hansell to Arnold to the joint chiefs of staff.

*   *   *

New planes, new air force, new bases . . . as the crews prepared to go overseas it was amid an air of excited anticipation at the Kansas bases. One 468th Group squadron historian recorded "stuffing empty boxes with liquor and toilet paper and frantically trying to get in the last fling . . . certain members of the squadron had narrow escapes on disposing of their cars . . . it is rumored in some quarters that they were traded for things the boys decided they would miss most."

According to the plan concocted between Salina and Washington, the first Superfortress went to England, partly as an eleventh-hour test of the airplane in long flights over water, partly as a cover plan. The Japanese could hardly be unaware of the unusually long runways around Calcutta in India and Chengtu in China. The cover plan involved planned leaks to give the impression that the B-29 had not measured up, and would be used as an armed transport for Hump flights.

Colonel Frank Cook, former production engineering officer at Wright

The first "all Omaha" B-29 emerges from the Martin factory in May 1944, destined to become Satan's Angel *with the 444th Group. The differences among the aircraft produced at the four factories were hard to define, although maintenance crews felt that* *Wichita aircraft were less prone to trouble than Renton aircraft, and one pilot found a Martin B-29 that was about ten miles an hour faster than any other B-29 he had flown.*

Field, flew the airplane, one of the fourteen YB-29s. His flight plan took him first from Kansas to Miami. Then the YB-29 roared into the night, flew South over the Atlantic for an hour, and changed course, heading North to Newfoundland. From there the Superfortress flew nonstop to Europe at twenty-five thousand feet, and within an hour after landing, a German reconnaissance plane had recorded its arrival. Over the next two weeks, the B-29 was inspected by Generals Eisenhower and Doolittle and high British officials. Cook then flew on to Kharagpur, India, arriving on April 6. His B-29 was the second to reach the theater.

The second B-29 to depart from Kansas left on March 25, with Colonel Jake Harman, and a steady stream of Superfortresses followed as March ended and April began.

The planes were heavily loaded, with an average gross weight of over 130,000 pounds; each carried a spare engine in the rear bomb bay, bomb-bay gas tanks, spare parts, emergency repair kits, documents, and personal equipment.

The aircraft thundered into the night and headed for Presque Isle, their first stop on the road to war.

Into the Cauldron

When the second leg of the B-29s' journey terminated at Gander Lake, Newfoundland, some crews thought they were on the way to England . . . at each terminal they received briefing only for the next leg, not the entire route. From Gander they flew to Marrakech, French Morocco, and from the Newfoundland snow and ice to the African heat; airplane performance began to decrease as the temperature increased. The next leg was to Cairo, then from Cairo to Karachi, and on to the Calcutta bases. On April 2 Colonel Jake Harman landed at Chakulia in the first B-29 in the theater. Harman, who had made the journey in eight days, assumed command of the advance echelon, 40th Bomb Group.

By April 15 only thirty-two planes were at their bases. Except for one 462nd aircraft, which force-landed at Presque Isle, the ocean crossing had been without problems, but then misfortune set in. On April 13 there was a total wreck at Marrakech, then a partial one at Cairo, and a quick succession of five serious accidents, including two planes completely wrecked at Karachi. The B-29s en route were grounded, and Wolfe began an investigation. He advised Arnold that it was "imperative that improved engine cooling be obtained immediately."

The problem was studied in the States and it was determined that the engines were still overheating around the exhaust valves on the rear row of cylinders, leading to complete engine failure. To correct this, fourteen new engine baffles were designed so that cooling air was directed to these valves. Also, the top cowl flaps, originally fixed, were made operable from the cockpit and shortened about three inches. A third important modification was the installation of crossover oil tubes from the intake to the exhaust rocker box of the top five cylinders on both the front and rear rows. While this crash engine-cooling program got under way, the flights resumed, and by May 8 one hundred and thirty B-29s had arrived at the Indian bases.

The heat was unbelievable, and had a drastic effect on the B-29s. The 58th Wing's Jack Ladd recalls making takeoffs in India "when the cylinder-head temperature gauges were against the stops and we did not know how high the temperatures actually were. The streamlined engine cowling was designed for low drag but was too close for adequate cooling, which the Boeing engineers admitted later on . . . the first planes had excessively long cowl flaps to try to cool the heads but if they were opened far enough to cool effectively they created a severe buffet . . . the Chandler-Evans carburetors on these first airplanes were very vulnerable to fires, one good backfire and you usually had an engine on fire. Some engines actually burned off the wing and fell to the ground. The engine-fire stories were not overdone and if anything they were underplayed. I had more two- and three-engine time on the B-29 than I had with all four engines running. It got so I'd tell my flight engineer to keep his mouth shut about how hot they were running. I said I didn't want to know."

Special measures had to be taken—engines could not be kept running in a long takeoff line, and were shut down and restarted on the taxiway just before lining up for takeoff. Sometimes it was necessary to tow the aircraft to the head of the runway and take off immediately. The 462nd Group worked out a standard procedure to keep the engines as cool as possible on the ground—they were started as rapidly as possible, and the flight engineer was given exclusive use of the throttles. The airplanes were operating at very high gross weights, and therefore flying slower, making the available cooling even less effective.

The intense heat of India led to other, lesser problems. The Plexiglas blisters cracked as they expanded and then contracted between ground and high altitude, and large sections blew out. The supply of blisters was inadequate, and old ones had to be repaired. Metal became too hot to touch, and maintenance could only be accomplished during the early morning or at night, with lights that attracted swarms of insects.

Delays in the building program had forced the temporary use of another Liberator field, Charra, where the existing runway was extended by steel mats to cater to the 444th Group's B-29s. To the 444th, Charra was something special. Their history tells that "personnel left Great Bend, Kansas, with the firm belief that no operational base in the world could be as bad . . . we had heard the normal rumors about the large, well-equipped bases being built for the B-29 in England, Russia, China, India, Siberia, and elsewhere." Charra to the 444th was "typically British—scattered all over Hell's half acre—April 12 the first B-29 rolled to a smoking, brake-screeching stop . . . bewildered crews climbed out into the blast-furnace heat and viewed the single short dusty runway, the bone-dry rice paddies, the dark emaciated dirty natives. . . ."

The 468th at Kharagpur found dust and heat their worst enemies, and the greatest topic of speculation became the approach of the monsoons and the rainy season.

On April 24 Colonel Jake Harman flew the first Hump cargo mission to China, landing at Kwanghan, the advance base of the *444th Bomb Group. Even at this early stage, the new bombers were being dubbed "C-29s."*

On April 24 Wolfe, Saunders, and Harman made the first flight over the Hump in two B-29s, landing at Kwanghan, but in early May, with his B-29s on hand or momentarily expected, Wolfe was still faced with the daunting task of accumulating a stockpile in China before he could send out his first mission. "Matterhorn" was in danger, because the Japanese could not fail to be aware of the plan.

The transportation difficulties started at the factories and depots, air bases and seaports in the States, and continued along the long road to India. The critical stage of the supply route was the final one, India to China. The distance was not the problem, as a cargo-laden B-29 could easily fly the twelve hundred miles from Kharagpur to Hsinching in five or five and a half hours, but the true barrier was the Hump. From India the B-29s crossed the Brahmaputra River and the Himalaya foothills, then faced the Hump, where seemingly harmless flocks of clouds were broken by the stark, jagged peaks of the world's highest mountains. Wild river gorges lay far below, and pillars of clouds sent trickles of moisture across an airplane's windows, which turned to ice in seconds. Over China the terrain was unchanged, more clouds forcing a continuous high altitude; then lakes and waterfalls, a treacherously beautiful landscape, appeared below, and the sheer mountains gave way to the hills, many covered by an amazing pattern of terraces, and soon the plane was roaring across the great Chengtu plain.

Wolfe was battling to establish his forward base, and stockpiling in China was running well behind schedule. The commanders in the theater had accepted Matterhorn without enthusiasm and viewed the plan rather darkly, irrespective of the assurances they had received that the B-29s would not gobble up their jealously guarded shares of Hump tonnage and air transport. Matterhorn would allegedly sustain itself by drawing on its B-29s and a backup of twenty Liberator transports; this of course never happened, even from the beginning. Air Transport Command was asked for help, and this caused anger among other organizations. Wolfe's force was considered as "an interloper with specious claims of independence and a habit of sponging."

A directive of March 5 ordered the B-29s to fly a shakedown mission out of India and a mission from China during April, and three more in May. These missions would never be flown, as the B-29s straggled in and the supply buildup in China lagged. Using the Superfortresses on the transport run would shorten their combat lives, but this misuse was an integral part of the Matterhorn scheme. Wolfe and the planners in Washington knew this from the beginning, but the overall appeal of the plan and the way it solved some prime problems outweighed this. From the outset the logistical system was just about breaking down entirely. One promising stopgap measure was that twenty-two tons of fuel had been hauled in May by B-29 "tankers." Early in the month a 40th Group B-29 had been stripped of armor plate, all guns and related equipment except the tail turret, and some of the radar equipment. An additional tank was fitted in the rear bomb bay, to make a total of four bomb-bay tanks and a gas capacity of over eight thousand gallons.

With its cleaner lines and lighter weight a tanker could offload considerably more fuel than a combat B-29 with the same capacity, but the results were in excess of expectations. A tanker could average less than three gallons consumed en route for every gallon delivered, while the combat planes were burning five gallons for every one. At the end of May it was decided to make more tanker conversions, and eventually every squadron in the wing contributed an aircraft . . . they had names befitting their role, such as the 468th's *The Gusher* and *Esso Express,* or the 462nd's *Petrol Packin' Mama.*

Washington queried the stripping of the B-29s, but they could be

The first tanker, from the 40th Group, taking off from Tezgaon, India, on May 14, 1944. (Howard Levy)

Hump Happy Pappy, *the original tanker conversion, survived to return home late in November 1944. (Fritz Lindgren)*

reconverted in a week, and without the necessary fuel stockpile in China there was little need for combat B-29s anyway.

Chennault later accused the Bomber Command of continuing a "Pentagon standard of living," and told Arnold that under the "deplorable conditions" he could not be held responsible for defending the China bases and considered himself "at the mercy of Wolfe, who controls the purse strings." In actual fact Wolfe was living on a shoestring, not tightening purse strings—for his B-29 groups there were no PX supplies, no shipments of clothing and, probably worst for morale, less than a quarter of the mail taking up cargo space. Even so, Wolfe would have difficulty mounting one major mission, and combat missions naturally meant less transport missions.

There was improvement as the command learned more about the B-29 and a lot more about the air-transport business, but the B-29 crews still lacked training in crucial areas, including gunnery, visual and radar bombing, rendezvous, and high-altitude formation flying. Wolfe felt his first mission should be flown at night, but Arnold insisted that it be a daylight precision raid. So Wolfe began a short but intensive training program, and even on the Hump run the B-29s started flying in formation, a gas-guzzling way to make up for lost time.

During April and May the Japanese launched a huge ground offensive, Operation *Ichi-go;* one of its prime objectives, it was learned later, was to "forestall the bombing of the Japanese homeland by American B-29s from bases in Kweilin and Liuchow." Japanese intelligence had cleverly and quite accurately predicted much about the B-29; they were aware before the war of work on a "super bomber"; then in the spring of 1943 they learned of the crash of the prototype. The investigation branch of Japanese air headquarters was slowly picking up information, but the matter was considered so urgent that they decided on a novel approach. The investigation branch attempted to put themselves in the position of the Boeing designers, working on a "super" version of the B-17. Taking into consideration all the known factors, they matched their estimates against fragments of intelligence material, and came up with a quite accurate prediction of performance. By March 1944 they were quite confident that they knew what to expect. They knew the airplane would require very long runways, and they knew where very long runways were being built.

The Japanese also studied the production probabilities and believed that the Americans would have two hundred B-29s by the end of March 1944. Opinion varied about when they would begin combat operations,

Major George Weschler of the 25th Bomb Squadron leads the 40th Group's B-29s out on their first combat mission, June 5, 1944.

but May or June was the widespread belief. The main assault of *Ichi-go,* with four hundred thousand troops, was launched on two fronts during the last week of May.

On June 4 Stilwell decided to use his emergency powers to give tonnage guaranteed to Matterhorn to the Fourteenth Air Force, despite a personal belief that it might be wasted due to the rapidly deteriorating situation on the ground in China.

Shakedown

While Matterhorn was considered almost a shakedown operation, it had a shakedown of its own — the flight to the theater, weeks of flying supplies over the Hump, and a combat mission to Bangkok on June 5. The target that day was the Makasan railway shops, and the mission was flown from India to preserve the precious fuel in China. It was a two-thousand-mile round trip, and the Japanese defenses were real enough, but would not be savage.

Gross weight at takeoff was around 134,000 pounds, and this was too much for the 444th's runway at Charra, so that group staged in equal elements from the other three fields.

A dawn takeoff was set to avoid the blistering ground temperatures, and ninety-eight B-29s were airborne in a little over an hour. Tragedy struck when Major John Keller's 40th Group B-29 was midway through its takeoff run. The nose wheel lifted, and stayed in the air during the rest of the run, as the tail skid banged the ground several times. The plane was airborne after seven thousand feet and looked all right, but then the left wing dropped, leveled, dropped again, and kept slipping until the huge bomber hit the ground. It cartwheeled, exploded, and burned. Everyone was killed except the copilot, who was too badly injured to give a comprehensible report of what had happened.

Fourteen B-29s aborted and others did not make the target, which was obscured by heavy overcast. On the way home many of the aircraft were critically short of fuel. At the 468th's base the rains were just clearing as the B-29s returned. Captain Robert Darden in *Lethal Lady* came in with two engines out of gas, and a third quit as soon as his wheels touched the ground. Darden cleared the runway with the power from his remaining engine.

The trip home proved far more dangerous than the time over the target. Major Donald Malone's aircraft had engine trouble and was running low on fuel leaving the target. He made for Kunming, the nearest friendly airstrip, but his tanks ran dry sixty miles out. Ten of the crew jumped and were brought to safety. Another B-29 crashed during an emergency landing at Dum Dum, twelve landed at wrong B-29 bases, thirty more landed at other fields. One was heading for Chittagong when the engines died, and Captain John Sanders of the 40th Group eased her down onto the smooth sea. Air-sea-rescue Spitfires were at the ditching in a few minutes, and nine survivors were promptly picked up. Sanders and his engineer searched for the other two crewmen, but could not find them, and they were not aboard the hulk of the B-29 when it floated ashore the following day.

Another 40th Group plane had fuel-transfer-system problems. The pilot and radio operator were killed during their ditching, but ten others got out, all injured to varying degrees. Eight spent the night in two life rafts, and midway through the next day picked up the other two, who were floating with just their Mae Wests and an empty oxygen bottle. The ten went through another day and night of agony before being washed ashore and eventually picked up.

The mission was completed "without fanfare" and was considered an operational success, although five B-29s were gone, and the bombing, which was credited to B-24s at the time, was "spotty."

On June 6, before all his B-29s were gathered in their rightful places, Wolfe was urgently advised by Arnold that a Japan mission was required to ease pressure in China and support an "important operation" in the Pacific—the landing on Saipan on June 15. Wolfe replied that he could get fifty planes over Japan by June 15, five more if he could have an extra five days. This was not good enough, Arnold insisting on at least seventy B-29s. Wolfe accelerated Hump missions and cut the fuel ration to the fighters defending the forward area to a potentially dangerous level.

Eight thousand gallons of precious gasoline burn up as this 462nd Group B-29 is incinerated. A flight engineer was trying to fix a fuel leak in the bomb bay when a spark set off a puddle of fuel that had formed under the airplane. The crew escaped, but there was no way to save the B-29. (Marvin Hooker)

The aptly named Bella Bortion, *from the 468th Bomb Group.*

Target: Japan

The first Japanese target was the Imperial Iron and Steel Works at Yawata, which the press would enjoy calling "the Pittsburgh of Japan." It was the most important single objective in Japan's steel industry, and although Hansell of Air War Plans had a preference for Anshan in Manchuria, Yawata's priority held.

The B-29s began moving forward over the Hump on June 13, and seventy-nine made it after one plane and crew were lost en route. Major Douglas Hatfield of the 468th tried to make the crossing on two successive days but aborted both times. Finally his ship, the ninth Bell aircraft, ended up with three engine changes and the unanimous selection of the name of *Bella Bortion* by the crew. Major John Millar, a Cobb County boy, saved the honor of Georgia when he took the tenth Bell B-29, which he called *Georgia Peach,* on the Yawata mission.

The B-29s came in from India ready for battle, requiring only gasoline in China, and each plane carried two tons of bombs. The planners, believing the B-29s could not make the journey to Yawata in formation, had finally ordered a night mission with planes bombing individually. A couple of pathfinders from each group were to go out a few minutes in advance of the main force to light up the target.

It was one of the significant bombing missions of the war. By the big day there were eight generals in the Chengtu area, plus eight war correspondents and three news photographers. Wolfe had been grounded by Washington, but Blondie Saunders was flying, and all the press men were riding in the B-29s.

The 462nd's Old-Bitch-U-Airy Bess *is readied for Yawata. Radioman "Sandy" Sandhofer, leaning out the copilot's window to check the antenna of the radar interrogator set, explained the naming of the airplane: "Be it the enemy or its own crew, it would contribute to the obituary column one way or the other. . . . Bess was a bulldog I once had as a boy. I never mentioned this to the others, however; they just seemed to go together. Thurm Sallade, the crew wit who also doubled as bombardier, came up with the spelling." The painting was done by tail gunner "Big Red" Arents, standing second from the left. (Bernard Hoffman,* Life*)*

The final briefings were held on the morning of June 15—briefings based on a 1928 ground plan, a photo taken the same year on the ground, and a few undated pictures. Colonel Richard Carmichael told the 462nd Group that it was just another routine problem with about four minutes' work at the end. After briefing, the crews had lunch and went to their planes for last-minute preparations. Operations Jeeps dashed from one B-29 to another collecting loading lists and forms.

Takeoff began a few minutes early. Two of the groups got off about on schedule, but the other two were slow. At 1624 hours China time Colonel Howard Engler of the 468th took off in *Lady Hamilton,* with General Saunders aboard. Fourteen more of the group's airplanes followed, but the next faltered and crashed into a rice paddy off the runway, engulfed in flame as the left wing hit the ground and broke away. The whole crew got out before she exploded, with some minor burns and cuts. The 468th got three more B-29s up after the fire had died down.

Finally, sixty-eight B-29s were airborne. To conserve fuel the bombers headed toward Japan individually at between eighty-five hundred and eleven thousand feet to get over mountains a couple of hundred miles east of the bases. These were "inaccurate" on their maps, often higher than indicated, and this was dangerous, as the planes had to cross them on instruments. A few breaks in the cloud helped every airplane get past this first obstacle. The B-29s droned over mile after mile of small, rounded hills, each covered by a perfect pattern of small farms, as dusk began to close in on them.

The B-29s had little trouble following their course, and about twenty minutes before midnight the signal "Betty" was flashed from *Lady Hamilton;* Betty was the name of the wife of Colonel James Garcia, the command's intelligence chief, on the mission as an observer. The word meant that the first bombs were tumbling toward Yawata.

The target was perfectly blacked out, alerted long before. Lieutenant Tom Friedman, flying with Captain Jack Ledford's 40th Group crew, had known they were expected. Friedman was flying in the newly created position of radar countermeasures observer, in the windowless, crowded radar compartment. His search gear was mounted in three racks at the front of the compartment. Friedman remembers, "I was preparing to monitor one frequency range with an occasional foray up to a higher range to see if the Japs were using any German-designed equipment.

"A small electric motor swept the receiver back and forth across the band while I listened with earphones for the first sign of enemy activity and tried to assume a comfortable position on my 'seat' — the chemical toilet. Radar countermeasures equipment had been installed at the last minute, after the B-29 had been completely designed, so it had been necessary to make certain compromises. Naturally the RCM observers were forced to endure numerous wisecracks about the appropriateness of their position!

"Finally the receiver whipped by a whining signal and I flipped off the motor and tuned the station in manually. A half minute's work with the

Case Ace, *from the 462nd Group, taxies out on her way to Japan. (Bernard Hoff-man,* Life)

analyzer revealed that the station was of the early-warning type. We had been detected, well back of the China coast and several hours from the target. It remained to see what use the Japs would make of this advance information. As we neared the coast other signals came and increased in strength . . . a glance in the radarscope showed the mainland of China receding . . . at the initial point the radar activity of the Japs reached a high level and signals were starting to crescendo until my earphones were whining as if a thousand devils were screaming in unison at us. It was an eerie feeling to know that far below our every move was being carefully watched on scopes and plotting boards. . . ."

The correspondents gave lively accounts of the battle that night over Yawata, but it was not a hot fight. Sixteen fighters were sighted, but only three fired, and they hit nothing. The flak was heavy but inaccurate, although it did damage six B-29s. The searchlights were active and annoying, but they did not work well with the flak guns.

Again the road home was rough for some, routine for others. *Life* photographer Bernard Hoffman, flying in the 462nd's *King Size* with Major

Edwin Loberg and his crew, reported, "At 5:00 A.M. the next morning the bombardier was fast asleep over his bomb sight . . . the engineer opened a can of pineapple and was passing it around. . . ." Shortly after dawn they were back on the ground, to a breakfast of potatoes and eggs.

Colonel James Edmundson brought *O'Reilly's Daughter* home with sixteen hundred gallons of gasoline left, but three of the 468th Group's planes did not return—one, carrying *Newsweek* correspondent Robert Schenkel, had crashed and was located the next day, but all on board were lost. Another had crashed into a mountain two hundred miles north of Chengtu, where the entire crew was buried by the Chinese. *Limber Dugan* went down in the target area.

The most vivid account of the mission was brought back by *Time*'s Harry Zinder, who flew the mission with Captain Robert Root of the 444th Group. Their No. 3 engine quit around dawn, and Root chose to land rather than cross the mountains to Chengtu. He put the B-29 down on a grass field just inside friendly territory, where they were met by Chinese troops. An officer said, in an "amazingly offhand way," that he would get them fifteen hundred gallons of fuel, tools for repairs, and level a takeoff strip. However, after going over the plane the crew found it was beyond repair and prepared to destroy it. They did not have to. Two Japanese fighters rolled in and peppered the wings and fuselage; then more fighters and six bombers came along. After the fighters had finished shooting up the field the bombers droned over, taking their time to reduce the B-29 to a burning pile of twisted metal. Before the crew left the field Root looked at the remains of his plane and muttered, "Those goddamn bastards, they'll pay for it. They'll pay for it."

The forty-seven B-29s that had reached and bombed the target fitted well with Wolfe's prediction, but in all the mission had cost seven B-29s and fifty-five men, and the Japanese had made little contribution to those losses. Luckily the enemy did not attempt to hit back at the China bases, where Wolfe had to borrow fifteen thousand gallons of fuel just to get his Superfortresses back to India.

Target photos taken a few days later revealed that the bombing damage at Yawata had not been significant—only one hit had been made on Imperial's complex of shops, and that was not on the coke ovens. Yawata was important mainly because it was the first time the B-29s had attacked Japan.

Irrespective of results, it was a notable mission, and the joint chiefs introduced the Superfortress to the public with carefully worded statements that appeared in the press alongside the more strident accounts of the correspondents. General George C. Marshall said that the attack "introduces a new type of offensive against our enemy. It also creates a new problem in the application of military force. Because of the enormous range and heavy bomb load of these Superfortresses, far exceeding that of previous strategic bombers, they can strike from many and remote bases at a single objective. The power of these new bombers is so great that the joint chiefs of staff felt that it would be uneconomical to confine the Superfortress organization to a single theater. These bombers, therefore, will remain under the centralized control of the joint chiefs of staff with a single commander, General Arnold, acting as their agent in directing their bombing operations throughout the world."

Hap Arnold followed up with: "The use of the B-29 Superfortress in combat brings actuality to an Air Forces plan made years in advance for truly global aerial warfare. . . . I assume the heavy responsibility for its employment under the joint chiefs of staff with full confidence in its potential use . . . this mighty weapon advances the bomber line a long way. The Superfortress is not going to win the war by itself, nor has anyone thought it would do so. It will, however . . . prepare the way for ultimate decision by our well-established team of land, sea, and air forces. The employment of the B-29 is just beginning. It goes directly into battle from the production lines, and we have a lot to learn before its full power may be developed. Consequently, the frequency of its use will be carefully determined for some time. From this circumstance, let our enemies take what comfort they can while they can."

The generals had just about covered all the bases.

Meanwhile, back in the theater, the crews had been unhappy to learn that the mission had been announced while they were still over enemy territory, but one statement infuriated them. Representative Joe Starnes had told the House, "It is now officially confirmed that American Superfortresses flying from remote bases have successfully bombed Tokyo in a very heavy raid. It can be safely assumed that these were the new B-29s. It may be safely assumed that these planes approached Tokyo at an altitude of more than thirty thousand feet and a speed of more than three hundred miles per hour with the heaviest bomb loads and the greatest armaments of any airplanes in the world."

Home newspapers were sympathetic about Starnes' Tokyo gaffe, one noting that Tokyo was synonymous with Japan to many Americans. Less understanding was *The Command Post,* published in the theater, which headed its editorial "Now who talked?" Referring to Starnes' "babblings" and safe assumptions, it demanded an answer to the statement that he had "been advised from a good source." Some hours later the War Department officially announced the target, unmentioned in earlier communiqués, but ignored Starnes' statement. The Japanese made hay with it in their propaganda broadcasts, implying that the Americans were being fooled by their own government.

So ended Yawata, the first B-29 mission to the Japanese homeland.

*　　　*　　　*

Wolfe was advised two days later that he must increase pressure on Japan, irrespective of his fuel situation. Arnold wanted a major daylight attack on Anshan, some harassing raids, and a big strike against Palembang from Ceylon. Asked for an estimate, Wolfe's reply was not encouraging. Nonetheless, Arnold directed a fifteen-plane night mission during the first ten days of July, a one-hundred-plane mission to Anshan between July 20 and 30, and a fifty-plane attack on Palembang as soon as China Bay was ready. Wolfe was urged to step up operations of both his B-29s and transports over the Hump. Washington was using stateside B-29 performance as the yardstick, which Wolfe thought was not realistic. He spelled out the conditions necessary to meet the latest demands— more Superfortresses and a share of Air Transport Command Hump tonnage. His plan for Anshan, made out on June 30, consisted of fifty or sixty B-29s, not one hundred.

Arnold received the plan the next day, and Wolfe was packing his bags within a week. Leaving Blondie Saunders temporarily in command, Wolfe farewelled his staff with a few insights into the problems he had faced: "You tell General Arnold you can get fifty aircraft, he says, 'Fine, now get a hundred.' When you tell him you can do something in a week, he says, 'Fine, do it tomorrow.'" Wolfe knew this kind of pressure worked to a degree, and without it his command might have done less, but while the impossible simply took a little longer in other theaters, in Wolfe's theater it was often just impossible.

Arnold had given Wolfe one of the best jobs of the war, but perhaps later doubted his judgment, saying, "With all due respect to Wolfe, he did his best, and he did a grand job, but LeMay's operations make Wolfe's look very amateurish" . . . a comment that seems to lack a degree of fairness.

II

The CBI: Harsh Realities

With Wolfe gone, Saunders took over and faced the same daunting problems, although the real trouble now was the shortage of B-29s, because July was an excellent month on the Hump run. One 58th Wing tanker flown by Captain Miles Thomas established a record of over 4,000 gallons of gasoline delivered to China; with 6 bomb-bay tanks and 60 5-gallon cans stowed in the tail, she was flown in with a crew of 7 and a ton of general cargo, a total weight of around 137,000 pounds. The tanker was from the 462nd Group, and named *Hobo Queen* . . . she was also the only YB-29 in the theater, the old stager that had flown the feint to Europe back in March.

Washington was promising more airplanes, but with the tanker conversions Saunders was still scratching to get a major mission together. The first July strike, a night raid on various Kyushu targets, was flown as planned, with eighteen B-29s. This time the radio code word, sent as the first planes were over the target, was "Lolly," the name of the wife of Colonel Kenneth Gonseth, 58th Wing communications officer.

Getting one hundred combat B-29s for a mission to Anshan was Saunders' real problem; he had the numbers, but getting them over the target was a challenge to his maintenance organization. To help the situation Saunders wanted to stop B-29 transport operations ten days prior to the mission, so that aircraft not making it over the Hump the first time could be repaired and try again. Sending the B-29s to China so early was a risk, but Washington went along with the plan. Also, the promised replacement aircraft were beginning to arrive. Toward the end of the month the groups were receiving new B-29s, with improved engines and increased fuel capacity due to the installation of four additional tanks in the center wing section, and Saunders had over one hundred planes at the forward bases by July 29.

The primary target that day was the Showa Steel Works at Anshan, and the aiming point was a battery of the fragile coke ovens. Overnight rain turned the Kwanghan runway into a bog, and the 444th Group could not get off on time, but by ten o'clock in the morning their strip was dry enough for their planes to take off. They were five hours too late for Anshan and bombed a secondary target.

The other three groups put up seventy-two airplanes. One crashed minutes later, but sixty reached Anshan, where conditions were nearly perfect. The first wave dropped just off the aiming point and the target became shrouded in thick, swirling smoke, dirty black and sickly yellow. The Japanese put little vigor into their defense.

The only combat loss was Captain Robert Mills, in the 468th's *Lady Hamilton*. Losing power in No. 2 engine, Mills chose the last resort target, the Chengsien railroad yards. Already hurt by flak, the B-29 was attacked by five fighters, one of them an American P-40 with Chinese insignia, which shot out another engine.

Mills ordered the crew to bail out, and eight survivors reached Chengtu a month later, after walking out of occupied China with the help of guerrillas. The Chinese also helped save another plane, which force-landed near Ankang—it was on the ground for five days while an engine, tools, mechanics, and spare parts were flown in.

Another B-29 that failed to return was Captain Howard Jarrell's 462nd Group plane. Hit by flak turning after the target, with No. 3 engine smoking and feathered, and No. 4 losing oil, he had no chance of reaching a friendly base. His navigator gave him a heading for Vladivostok in the Soviet Union, about 450 miles away. As the crippled B-29 crossed the Soviet border, Yak fighters surrounded her and fired across her nose. The crew was surprised by the "welcome," but the pilot of one of the Yaks eased up alongside and indicated to Jarrell to land at an airfield near Tavrichanka. The airfield was too small for a B-29, but Jarrell, with no option, just managed to get the plane down safely. The crew was met by armed Russians and soon found they were being treated like prisoners. They would never see their B-29 again, but Russian engineers would . . . it was the beginning of a Soviet strategic air force.

Although the Anshan mission had not gone off like clockwork, it was encouraging. The bombing appeared to be good and there were hits and near misses on several batteries of coke ovens.

The fifth and sixth Matterhorn missions were flown on the night of August 10, one to Palembang in Sumatra and the other to Nagasaki in Kyushu. This was the most complex mission yet, and once again the operational success was more impressive than the results.

Rapid changes in the Pacific and the destruction of Japanese shipping had diminished the importance of the Pladjoe refinery at Palembang, and the command would have willingly canceled the mission, but Washington wanted it. They had directed a daylight attack with over one hundred B-29s, but with only the British China Bay field available in Ceylon, that would mean staging in waves, which could be courting disaster. Washington "relented" and ordered a strike by fifty planes.

The final plan was for a night radar attack, and part of the force, briefed by Navy mining expert Commander Kenneth Veth, was to mine the Moesi River, channel of all Palembang's exports. The British wholeheartedly supported the mission—while fuel and construction costs at China Bay were charged to Lend-Lease, the British turned over the base to the Americans and even shared their whiskey rations with the visitors.

On the afternoon of August 9 fifty-six Superfortresses, fourteen from each group, landed on the strip at China Bay. The approach was spectacular: The B-29s soared over the mastheads of capital ships of the Royal Navy, *Illustrious* class aircraft carriers and *King George* class battleships, and the captured French battleship *Richelieu*.

The final briefings were limited to an hour on the morning of August 10 because the small base theater had to be shared for the individual group briefings. Takeoff was scheduled for the late afternoon, and the 462nd's lead plane was first off. Fifty-four B-29s were airborne, one turning back with engine trouble to be repaired and sent out again within a couple of hours.

The 462nd's mining crews were experienced teams. Colonel Richard Carmichael was flying as airplane commander, with the plane's usual pilot, Major Conrad Kolander, flying in the right seat. Also aboard was Commander Veth and the group navigator, Major Ed Perry.

Perry remembered that at the initial point they descended to one thousand feet altitude, and although the planning had allowed for radar bombing, visual conditions were very good: "Tall trees along the river really highlighted the water surface, with the trees quite dark and the river surface shimmering from the rays of the moon. I moved to the front of the cockpit and sat piggyback on Red Bell, the bombardier, with my legs each side of him. From this position I could reach the release button if it became necessary for him to man the forward gun sight and I could also help in the direction of the aircraft along the river."

The B-29s growled through the soft darkness. Carmichael's release points were farthest along the river, and closest to the land targets being attacked by the other groups. Perry continues: "Red and the gunners did some low-level strafing of boats along the river as we went upstream to our release points. Since we were the first aircraft we had the element of surprise in our favor. The tail gunner did report some ground fire at us after we had passed the ground positions.

"As we approached the scheduled release area for our mines we saw a large ship, presumably a tanker, in the channel. Red released one mine before we reached the ship, strafed the ship as we passed overhead at no more than 350 feet altitude, and released the second mine just beyond the ship. The tail gunner reported both mines entered the channel."

They were unable to close their bomb-bay doors on the lead plane, and one engine was needing a richer mixture than usual. After attempts to close the doors manually they were still unable to get one side all the way up. Carmichael's B-29 was first out of China Bay and last back, taking about nineteen hours to complete the mission.

Colonel Alfred Kalberer, the deputy group commander, had flown over the area for years as a KLM pilot, and knew precisely the location of a fuel dump at one of the airports. With this in mind, he had loaded an extra five-hundred-pound phosphorous bomb, which he intended to drop on the fuel dump. Unfortunately, when the mines dropped the bomb went with them and sank to the bottom of the Moesi River.

In *Old-Bitch-U-Airy Bess*, K. D. Thompson and his crew, had thought they had fuel for seventeen hours, thirty minutes less than the flight plan called for. They were willing to try it, but removed all unessential equipment from the plane before they left China Bay. Their mining had been "dead accurate," and the flight engineer, Sergeant Vaughan Plevan, was carefully maintaining the cruise control. Radio operator Clay Sandhofer remembers, "The transfer of fuel was arranged between him and Major Thompson, so that the best balance was had and the aircraft was 'on the step.' This gave the best fuel economy. Unfortunately, after fifteen hours into the mission we could not transfer the fuel from one of the bomb-bay tanks. This was serious and of great concern as we had no way of removing the fuel from the rear tank. Something had gone wrong. Furthermore, we could not salvo the tank for some reason . . . as a result additional weight was added with a loss of usable fuel . . . we became badly unbalanced because of the added gas weight in the back of the aircraft. As we were burning fuel the aircraft was getting lighter in the nose.

"One hour from Ceylon, now believe me, we had passed our original flight plan of seventeen hours. We were convinced that we had to ditch and planned to do so. To keep the aircraft from losing control, Major Thompson had the crew in the rear come up forward. All eleven members crowded into the nose compartment. Although dangerous for a ditching, it did put the aircraft 'on the step.' We cut the engines to minimum rpm's without losing the cylinder-head temperature and managed fuel as best we could. We discussed cutting one engine so we could run the other three at a slightly more efficient speed but no change was made. . . .

"We made a straight-in approach, almost a dead-stick-landing approach, since we were in deadly fear of losing the engines and we didn't feel we could depend on them with full flaps and landing gear down. We landed at a high rate of speed, exactly nineteen hours from the time of departure. As we began to taxi off the runway, the engines began cutting due to lack of fuel."

The bombing mission to Palembang was marred when a flare B-29 miscarried, but thirty-one planes bombed by radar or visually.

The dual strike had been code-named "Boomerang," and the round trips of around four thousand miles indicated that there might have been some courtship of Lady Luck in the name. Only one B-29 was forced to ditch, and the intricate rescue precautions saved all the crew except a gunner killed during the water landing.

The ends did not justify the means, and the 20th Bomber Command recommended that China Bay be discarded as a staging base. The cost of developing it for just one mission was "a glaring example of the extravagance of war."

* * *

Saunders' August capability had been boosted by additional Hump tonnage and the halving of the effort out of China Bay, and he proposed for the balance of the month a small night incendiary attack on Nagasaki, on the tenth, a big Yawata attack ten days later, and another maximum effort against Anshan at the end of the month.

His Nagasaki mission had been flown the night of August 10, synchronized with the Palembang strike. Washington had been anxious to see the results of incendiary missions against Japanese cities, and that night two dozen B-29s were over the target. Results were hard to estimate, but intelligence reports suggested they were nothing spectacular. The 462nd's *Missouri Queen,* on the way home with Captain Stanley Brown,

Colonel Winton "Wimpy" Close's Big Poi-   *Bomb Group, in addition to a couple of*
son *reached India on April 13, 1944, and*   *dozen Hump flights. (Howard Levy)*
flew both the June missions with the 444th

became lost after mechanical trouble and, almost out of fuel, put down at
Hwaning the next morning. The field was held by the Chinese, but within
easy reach of three enemy airfields. The B-29 was stuck in mud at the end
of the strip, and the Japanese were able to knock out two engines by strafing. American fighters flying cover shot down three fighters and tore up
one of the Japanese strips, while fuel, parts, and mechanics were flown
into Hwaning. *Missouri Queen* was stripped and patched up. The Chinese
jacked her out of the mud and inched her along the strip, sinking over
four thousand railroad ties into soft spots to provide a short runway.
Twelve days after she landed, *Missouri Queen* was flown to Chiung Lai
with a crew of four.

Matterhorn was beginning to feel pressure from the deteriorating tactical situation in China, with Chennault asking for attacks on Chinese
targets. Saunders, consulted by Arnold, did not wish to comment on the
strategic merits of Chennault's requests, but naturally any diversion
would disrupt the main thrust of the B-29 effort. When his second
request was turned down, Chennault suggested that the B-29s should ei-

ther divert from steel targets or get out of China. For the present, Saunders' orders held, but the situation was bad. Some of his staff were in favor of using B-29s only at night, as bomb tonnages on the long daylight missions had been low. Others wanted to convert more B-29s to tankers, get plenty of fuel over the Hump, then sprinkle the tankers among fully armed B-29s on night missions. However, the Anshan mission of July 20 had fostered optimism about daylight precision bombing, and Saunders sought permission to make the August 20 Yawata mission against the Imperial Iron and Steel Works a daylight strike. Washington was "delighted with the change."

The bomb load would be light, but Saunders created a new policy: He set a minimum bomb load of one ton, and allowed the groups to assign individual loads according to the efficiency of each plane and crew.

On August 20, three groups got off from China without problems, but the eighth 462nd aircraft, Captain Miles Thomas' *Starduster*, failed to gain enough speed to become airborne. Running out of airstrip, and traveling too fast to stop, Thomas jerked up the landing gear and bellied her in. Another B-29 clipped *Starduster*'s tail and knocked a chunk off it when, by late afternoon, it was possible to get eight more planes up and over the wreck by lightening their loads. These were joined by five aborts from other groups and went to Yawata for a night attack.

The B-29s airborne for the day mission headed for Yawata. Sixty-one planes dropped on the target, but intense flak shot one down and damaged eight. The fighter opposition was considered moderate but accounted for three more Superforts.

The 468th Group had put two dozen B-29s over the target, and four did not return. *Reddy Teddy* was hit by flak. *Gertrude C.*, flown by Colonel Robert Clinkscales, had just released her bombs over the target when a Nick fighter came at her head on. Sergeant Shigeo Nobe of the 4th *Sentai* had already radioed to his formation that he was going to ram, a spontaneous decision. The Nick's right wing smashed into the B-29 just outboard of No. 1. engine, and lodged there; the rest of it catapulted in flames over *Postville Express'* right wing. *Gertrude C.* burst into flames and disintegrated. Pieces of her smashed into Captain Ornell Stauffer's *Calamity Sue*, shearing off the vertical stabilizer, and she spiraled down out of sight. Nobe and his crewman had destroyed two of the new Superfortresses in the first recorded ramming. The fourth 468th loss that day was *O'Reilly's Daughter*, with Colonel William Savoie and his crew. Messages were received later in August that the wreck of *O'Reilly's Daughter* had been found on the northeastern coast of China, and Savoie and three of

Starduster cracked up on takeoff for the   *B-29 taking off over her clipped her high*
daylight mission to Yawata, after the pilot   *tail with its nose gear. (Marvin Hooker)*
jerked the gear up at 120 miles an hour. A

his crew finally made it back to India in the middle of November — they
had bailed out over occupied China after two runaway props refused to
feather. Some of the crew had jumped over the Yellow Sea and were
never found.

Major Gus Askounis, piloting *Windy City,* ran out of gas approaching
the 468th's field . . . No. 4 engine sputtered out and the crew was alerted.
No. 2 and No. 3 failed, and the order to jump was given. Five men in the
back of the B-29 bailed out, but the nose wheel would not function, and
the people up front had to make a gear-up, dead-stick landing as No. 1
engine went out.

The 40th Group also had a hot time. One of their aircraft was
unreported after leaving the target, but it was later learned that it went
down and the entire crew was buried by the Chinese. Major Richard
McGlinn had an engine shot out over the target, waved good-bye, and
headed North . . . his B-29 crashed in the foothills of the Sikhote Alin
Range, east of Khabarovsk in the Soviet Union. The crew had abandoned the plane and wound up in the same Tashkent detention camp as

Captain Jarrell and his crew. Captain Boyd Grubaugh's B-29 also failed to reach home, but a couple of days later it was learned that he and most of his crew had bailed out and all but three were safe.

The 444th's *Flying Stud* caught fire and went down seventy-five miles from home after her crew got out safely; another of their B-29s crashed on landing, killing all but one man; and another was missing after it had reported reaching friendly territory. The 444th considered all their losses "operational."

On the way from the target Colonel Richard Carmichael's 462nd Group B-29 was attacked from below by a fighter and hit at the same time from above by an aerial bomb. The aircraft was on fire, but before it went out of control and crashed to the ground eight parachutes were seen. Colonel Carmichael, the group commander, was among the survivors, and he was an important prize for the Japanese. He recalls that he was in Kempei Tai headquarters in downtown Tokyo for six weeks, and that the Japanese were mostly interested in the composition and disposition of the immediate B-29 threat rather than any longer-term aspects. He got "a lot of questions about our bases in India and China. My navigator, Ed Perry, was flown to China for detailed questioning about bases. I remember being kicked around at Ofuna, the Navy camp near Yokohama, for not knowing why General Hansell was called 'Possum.' "

Carmichael was tried as a war criminal for having "indiscriminately killed civilians at Yawata," but he survived to lead B-29s again in another war.

On the night of August 20 the later force of ten B-29s reached Yawata and all got back, although one crash-landed in China.

The strike photos of the daylight mission showed hits on two coke ovens, but Japanese records indicate that the damage was not serious. The American losses were: four B-29s in combat and ten to other causes.

Plans for the next mission, to Anshan, were approved on August 29, the day Major General Curtis LeMay took command of the B-29s in India. LeMay had taken a B-17 group to England in 1942, and his work on improving bombing, in particular the idea of lead crews, had brought him promotion and the command of a wing. Reflecting on his new command, LeMay acknowledged that he had "never been able to shake off the idea that General Arnold himself never believed that this would work." It was "Arnold's dream of a strategic Air Force come true," but with overtones of a nightmare.

LeMay insisted on flying at least one mission with his new command, and that was grudgingly approved. He chose the second Anshan strike.

Saunders, pressured by Washington over the amount of B-29s he was putting over the target, had introduced a policy of sending every B-29 that could fly. That policy, and maintenance improvements, paid off on the second Anshan mission. Over one hundred B-29s took off from the China bases on September 8, and ninety-five reached the target, where the weather was good and they inflicted significant damage on the Showa plant.

This spurred the Japanese into their first retaliation. The two groups of fighters defending the forward bases in China were capable of thwarting any daylight attack, but had no night fighters. Apparently helped by ground signals from fifth columnists, Japanese bombers struck just after midnight, but only slightly damaged one B-29.

Regardless of the success of the Anshan mission, LeMay revised the command's tactical doctrines and began a thorough training program. He did away with the four-plane diamond formation that had been used, and introduced the twelve-plane "combat box." He also wanted "synchronous bombing," with both the radar operator and bombardier following the bomb run, and visibility determining who would take over in the criti-

A camouflaged 40th Group B-29, behind the enemy lines in northern China. Battle damage to two engines forced her to land following the Anshan mission of September 8. The airplane took off later, with three good engines and the fourth running on seventeen cylinders. (Ira Penn)

The 468th's Postville Express *established a record for a combat B-29 when she* poured 2,600 gallons of fuel into the China tanks.

cal seconds before bombs away. The 40th Group historian called LeMay's arrival "a turning point."

On September 5 LeMay ordered each group to select lead crews, and a week later a school was set up at Dudhkundi. The eleven-day course at "Dudhkundi Tech" was strenuous. Also, classes were begun in target identification, navigation, bombing, gunnery, and other subjects at the bases.

LeMay quickly became aware that the greatest B-29 effort was "in bringing in gas to those Chengtu strips," but he had promised Washington a one-hundred-plane strike and chose to finish off Anshan. In the morning of September 26 the mission was airborne. At the target a cold front had moved in, completely cloaking it. The B-29s bombed by radar, but photos revealed no new damage at all. That night some enemy bombers hit Chengtu and damaged five B-29s, two of them seriously, but there were no Superforts lost to any cause.

In Washington, General Norstad underlined that silver lining, telling the press that a one-hundred plane, no-loss mission "would be a remarkable record on a bombing mission of any type, and this is all the more remarkable when applied to the B-29, which is still relatively experimental. . . . Every plane that left the ground returned safely . . . no mechanical failures or maintenance problems."

The third Anshan attack brought Matterhorn's first phase to an end. The April 1944 schedules, which looked realistic in Washington, had

The 462nd Group produced some of the most outstanding and unusual artwork to adorn their B-29s. Nightmare *flew with their 771st Squadron. (Harry George)*

been reduced to reality by the theater; coke and steel targets should by this point have been destroyed. The ledger hardly balanced: Only two missions, the first two Anshan raids, had been truly successful, and the Japanese steel industry had not been significantly hurt. From the beginning the B-29 project had been experimental, the 20th Bomber Command's own historian describing it as "a great combat testing laboratory."

The command continued to struggle against the problems it faced. A "radical revision" of the groups' structure, involving three squadrons of ten aircraft each and the merging of the maintenance squadrons with the bomb squadrons, had been approved before the B-29s even flew their first mission, but its realization had lagged. LeMay was finally able to obtain a directive to make the changes on September 20. They involved disbanding the sixteen maintenance squadrons, and one bomb squadron in each group. The new organization also discarded the concept of doubly trained crews who were able to complete first- and second-echelon maintenance on their planes. That idea had proved valuable, particularly during emergency landings at remote fields in China, but the time factor in training the crews was prohibitive. A B-29 gunner could be trained in five weeks, but if he was to double as an electrical specialist his training period would total nearly ten months.

LeMay's command had obligations that indicated that it would have to step up transport missions, but Arnold had insisted that the combat B-29s must not be worn out on the grueling Hump flights. Tonnage had fallen away in August, but in September, with the B-29s again flying transport missions, and with the aid of C-109s flown by B-29 crews who had Liberator experience, the situation got better. LeMay was advised on October 17 that "it would be desirable to get you out of the transport business," and in November the combat B-29s were again taken off the Hump flights. In December the tankers were withdrawn and sent back to the States. The plan for Matterhorn to be self-sufficient had finally been abandoned.

Change of Direction

The tenth mission was not run until October 14, but LeMay had decided to accelerate operations, which would generally be heavier and more destructive. As the B-29s in the Marianas got closer to their first mission, the importance of the Chengtu bases diminished proportionately. By September Arnold was considering the transfer of the B-29s from India to the Marianas, which had always been a Matterhorn contingency.

The 462nd's Rush Order *was a Bell B-29-10, the first production batch with the new four-gun top turret. She got her name because the group received her on October 11, 1944, and she was able to fly both the Formosa missions — the first only fifteen days after she left the production line in Georgia.*

The October 14 mission was in support of General MacArthur's campaign in the Philippines. His decision to go into Leyte on October 20 had brought this initial "Pac-Aid" mission forward, and on September 22 the joint chiefs had advised the various theater commanders of the outline plan for supporting the Leyte operation. The B-29 contribution was planned as two closely spaced large missions against Okayama or Formosa, plus very long-range reconnaissance as requested. These B-29 missions would tie in with fast carrier strikes. The Navy strikes were very successful, but Okayama needed more attention if it was to be useless to the enemy as a staging field to the Philippines. LeMay put more than one hundred B-29s over the target in good weather; they bombed well and the damage looked so heavy that LeMay thought a second major effort would be unnecessary. To "police" Formosa he sent two groups back to Okayama on October 16 while the other two hit individual targets, the 40th's mission being flown the following day. These Formosa missions were less successful, although results at Okayama were excellent—the Japanese considered it was "the first case of major damages suffered by land installations . . . as a result of B-29 attacks."

During the summer of 1944 opinion in Washington had moved from steel toward the aircraft industry as the most lucrative Japanese target. Although Arnold was impatient, the priority could not be changed immediately, but LeMay was told to be ready for a possible switch in objectives that would give top priority to aircraft plants at Omura, Mukden, Watanabe, and Okayama. These were not the most important aircraft plants, but were the best within range of the B-29s flying from Chengtu. LeMay was advised of the change in target systems on October 11, and the best target was the Omura Aircraft Factory on Kyushu, manufacturing Petes, Zekes, and the new Grace. The first mission was flown with good results on October 25, when fifty-nine B-29s bombed the target, and Omura would be hit five times before the B-29s left China.

LeMay was unhappy with the slow pace of Matterhorn operations, and the performance of the crews. He decided to run a series of "training" missions from India that would be less demanding than the Japan or Manchuria raids but that would give the crews the kind of comprehensive experience the slow tempo of missions from China denied. The first of these missions was to Rangoon on November 3, and the bombers carried maximum bomb loads to the target, the Malagan railroad yards. The roundhouse was the aiming point, and it was demolished. LeMay was unusually lavish in his praise, calling it the B-29s' "first job of precision bombing."

The 468th Group's lead ship, seconds before bombs away over Haito, Formosa, on October 16. (Ray Tolzmann)

Hoodlum House II *of the 462nd Group, back from Omura on October 25.*

More good news was in store. At the end of October Arnold had suggested that the mauling suffered by the Japanese Fleet during the battles in the Philippines had made Singapore a juicy target. LeMay's operations staff was doubtful about a daylight mission of almost four thousand miles, but Washington wanted it, and seventy-six B-29s took off on November 5.

The primary target was the largest Singapore dry dock, the King George VI Graving Dock. The first Superfortresses were over the target early in the morning, and the lead bombardier, Lieutenant Frank McKinney, laid a 1,000-pound bomb within 50 feet of his aiming point, the caisson gate. The bombardier two planes back put one alongside. Then the bombardier in the 468th's *Mary Ann* hit the aiming point, which measured about 30 feet by 150. This was the kind of bombing that the Super-

Captain Ira Matthews takes the 40th Group's Eddie Allen *to Rangoon on November 3, her fourth mission. The B-29 was "bought" by Boeing Wichita employees with bond purchases during the Fifth War Loan.*

The Eddie Allen *went on to Tinian, and had bombed targets in seven countries before she was so badly damaged over Tokyo on May 25 that she was sent to salvage.*

fortress had been created for. The strike photos showed water rushing into the dock, and it would be useless to the enemy for months. The dock took other hits, and so did a freighter lying in it. The defense was weak, but the long journey took its toll of two B-29s. *Lethal Lady*, flown by the 468th's commander, Colonel Ted Faulkner, crashed into the Bay of Bengal and no trace of the plane or crew was ever found. *Raidin' Maiden*, with Captain Charles "Doc" Joyce and his crew, barely made it. When Joyce asked his navigator how long it would take to get home, the answer by then was about twenty minutes. Joyce asked his flight engineer if they could do it, and he answered, "I think it'll be a tie."

Ten minutes dragged by and *Raidin' Maiden* was nearing the coastline when an engine sputtered and ran smoothly, then started sputtering again. The flight engineer, Flight Officer Charles Passieu, was juggling

Captain Weston H. Price and the crew of the Gen. H. H. Arnold Special. When she force-landed in the Soviet Union it gave that country a second complete B-29, an airplane they had unsuccessfully tried to obtain through Lend-Lease. The Soviets faithfully duplicated the Superfortress, naming their version the Tupolev Tu-4. Production began in 1945, and by 1950 a large number of the bombers were serving in Dalnaya Aviatsiya, the Soviet strategic air command. (Henry J. Stavinski)

the remaining fuel among the engines. Then the field was about twenty-five miles ahead; *Raidin' Maiden* was at nine thousand feet. They lowered the gear and flaps and then the bad news came: "No. 3 is out." "There goes No. 4 too." The B-29 dropped its right wing, and the pilots grabbed her and got her level. "No. 2 is out," called Passieu. "No. 1 is just about gone." The B-29 was still above seven thousand feet when Joyce ordered the crew to jump. Everybody from the forward section bailed out except Joyce and Passieu, and they thought they were the only two in the plane. When Joyce got the B-29 safely through a dead-stick landing, the rest of the crew, who had not heard the order, scrambled from the back of the airplane.

Omura was next on the target list, and on November 11 nearly one hundred B-29s were airborne. Late weather reports warned of turbulent conditions and clouds at the target, so the formation was ordered to attack the last-resort target, Nanking. Less than half received the changed order, and approaching Omura they were scattered by winds and clouds. The twenty-nine planes that got through could not see the primary target, and the turbulence complicated radar bombing. The Japanese put up little defense, but the weather contributed to the five B-29s lost or missing, and there was no new damage to the target. One of the losses was the 468th Group's *Gen. H. H. Arnold Special,* with Captain Weston Price. Over the target Price reported he was low on fuel and heading for Vladivostok. Approaching the Soviet Union he transmitted the international signal for "friend," but anti-aircraft fire began to burst near the B-29. Fighters then boxed her in and shepherded her to the field at Vladivostok. Price and his crew joined the growing B-29 contingent at Tashkent.

The next Omura mission, flown ten days later, was similarly expensive and unproductive. Originally planned to coincide with a carrier strike and the first B-29 mission from the Marianas, it was flown on November 21 due to delays in the Pacific and the fact that weather looked favorable that day.

The capricious weather again ruined the planning. Sixty-one B-29s bombed the primary target by radar, but there was confusion when two formations were badly scattered as they attempted to change lead planes for the bomb run. The flak was inaccurate but the fighter opposition was moderate to strong, and more aggressive than usual. One 462nd B-29 was shot down and crashed into the bay, and another B-29 simply disappeared. An aircraft of the 444th was hit in the CFC compartment over the target, apparently by a rocket. Its gunnery system was wrecked, one gunner was killed, and another was blown out through his blister. The tail gunner was seriously wounded, and above him the rudder was so badly damaged that the controls had to be roped down for the pilots to keep the B-29 level and on course. They made it back to a crash landing at Ankang. Later, Captain John Dunn's *This Is It!,* hit by an empty shell case in a nacelle over the target and unable to feather the engine, and with damaged aileron controls, attempted a landing after dark at Ankang. Dunn could not hold the B-29 on the wet-grass strip, and *This Is It!* careened into the other damaged 444th Group airplane. Dunn and three others in the nose of *This Is It!* were killed in the crash.

The 40th Group's takeoff had been hampered by dust, and visibility for

One of the 444th's B-29s crosses the Hump, cloaked by clouds, on the way to Omura.

the last planes taking off was only a quarter of a mile. The dust clouds churned up by the engines clung to the noses of the B-29s, wet with condensed moisture. Twenty-one of their aircraft made it to the primary and twenty bombed through the cloud cover. One of their aircraft was hit by fighters over the target and the bombardier was killed and the copilot wounded. The B-29 got as far home as the approach to the strip when fuel shortage forced the surviving crewmen to bail out. They all jumped safely.

Last Resort, piloted by Major Donald Roberts, headed into the Japanese defenses, and far below and a little to their left they could see the buildings of Omura. The bomb doors popped open. At that moment three fighters dived directly at *Last Resort*. Their attack was crisscross fashion, with two coming from one side, one from the other. The B-29 was raked from wingtips to tail. Almost immediately three of the four engines were knocked out, and the flight engineer's instruments went dead. Miraculously, nobody was injured, but *Last Resort* was slipping into a steep glide as the bombardier salvoed the bombs. A quick survey showed that fuel tanks were pierced and the prop dome knocked off one engine. Alone below the other B-29s, *Last Resort* was a sitting duck, and the fighters did not miss the opportunity. Every turret on the B-29 was firing. The flight engineer coaxed one engine back to life, but on only two the B-29 was still sinking toward the Yellow Sea. The fighters swarmed in. The gunners claimed three and sent a couple more away smoking, until at last the others gave up the chase. The copilot took over the controls while Roberts and the engineer "punched buttons" to keep the precious two engines alive, and the crew began stripping the plane. Over occupied China the gasoline was almost gone and they had been flying on two engines for nearly eight hours when they sighted a little landing field at Laohokao, China. After a ticklish landing they began patching up *Last Resort,* and learned from Chinese at the field that parts had been salvaged from another B-29 that had crash-landed nearby earlier; for the rest, they used baling wire and tape. The Chinese rolled in drums of fuel, and next day *Last Resort* climbed off the short runway and headed for her base.

The Soviet Union claimed yet another B-29 that day, the 468th's *Ding How.* Lieutenant William Mickish headed her for Vladivostok, and the crew spotted the *Gen. H. H. Arnold Special* on the ground below. At five hundred feet, with his wheels down, Mickish was told by a gunner that flak was firing at them, then during the approach six Yaks fired warning shots across the B-29's nose. Now the Soviets had three B-29s, and pieces of a fourth, and four crews. The crews were released through Iran early in 1945, but the B-29s were never returned. Arnold felt that the treatment of his crews, like "captured enemies, certainly not as allies," was "inexcusable."

Strike photos showed no additional damage to the Omura factory area on November 21, and five B-29s had been lost to enemy action.

Later that week another training mission was flown to the Bang Soe marshaling yards at Bangkok, with good results. Then on December 7 the B-29s flew a maximum daylight mission to Mukden, Manchuria. Over ninety B-29s reached the target, where ceiling and visibility were unlimited, but the intense cold frosted the windows, causing great difficulty to pilots, bombardiers, and gunners. Ten planes bombed early, hitting a rail yard nine miles short. The Japanese were again aggressive. Three rammings occurred, but only one was considered intentional. A Nick bored in on the 468th's *Windy City II* and one of the gunners set fire to the Nick's right engine and blew pieces off the canopy. Going down, the Nick managed to pull out and slip up under Captain Roger Parrish's *Gallopin' Goose.* Streaming smoke, the fighter rammed the tail of the B-29, tearing most of it off. There was one parachute sighted as *Gallopin' Goose* went straight down. Major Hatfield and his crew in *Bella Bortion* had a close

Over Mukden the freezing cold had made it impossible to use the forward gun sights or to see the target, but there was further danger. Captain Frank Martin of the 468th Group was bringing in his B-29 low on gas, with the nose glass completely iced up. The B-29 dropped down from about forty feet and the right wing sagged, hit the ground, and the plane swerved off the runway and broke in two. Two of the crew were slightly injured.

Captain Roger Parrish (standing on the left), and his crew ten days before a Japanese fighter rammed them right over Mukden, Manchuria.

shave when a Zeke barely missed and destroyed itself on their No. 1 prop. The 462nd's *Old-Bitch-U-Airy Bess* was badly shot up—Sergeant Vaughan Plevan was killed by a fighter attack, and the spent incendiary shell fell into radioman Clay Sandhofer's pocket.

On December 14 the B-29s went to Bangkok to destroy the Rama VI railroad bridge, a vital rail link, but not a target for B-29s. One formation, discovering heavy clouds at Bangkok, diverted to the Central Railroad station at Rangoon and bombed with fine results. However, tragedy struck this 40th Group formation. Back at Chakulia the first indication that something was wrong was a cryptic message from Colonel James Cornett, leading the formation:

TARGET SECOND BOMBED VISUAL 11 PLANES UNOBSERVED 0444 PLANE NUMBER 831 726 457 MISSING DAMAGED AND IN FORMATION CHT 508 407 729 589 537 BAILED OUT 100 MILES WEST OF TARGET 574 REPORTED 3 INJURED INCLUDED 225 LEFT FORMATION UNABLE TO CONTACT APPARENTLY OK PRESENT POSITION 19'13"93'00" SIGNED CORNETT TROUBLE PLENTY

Twelve 40th Group planes had taken off; eleven went to Bangkok. There were neither fighters nor flak, so two runs had been made before the decision was made to turn back to Rangoon. A perfect bomb run in clear weather at twenty thousand feet was made. Then the ice-blue sky simply erupted. Only two 40th B-29s returned to Chakulia—four landed at Chittagong, another at Cox's Bazaar, but four were lost. One, never positively identified, hurtled earthward sheathed in flame. Two others disappeared in the explosion. A fourth was so badly damaged that the crew, after flying about one hundred miles, had to bail out. Of the surviving planes, all were damaged to some degree, and the navigator in the lead plane had been killed by a bomb fragment.

The 40th Group bombardier conducted an investigation. All that could be assured was that a bomb or bombs had exploded below the formation right after bombs away. The B-29s had been carrying a mixed load—twelve one-thousand-pound bombs and six five-hundred-pound bombs—but the danger of bombs colliding in midair had been considered minimal, and the nose fuses were removed from the bigger bombs as an added precaution. Several flak bursts were seen just before bombs away, and it was felt that the most logical explanation was that flak had detonated the bombs. However, nobody ever really knew what had nearly wiped out a squadron.

The thirty-three B-29s attempting to bomb the Bangkok bridge failed.

The Burning of Hankow

General Chennault had spent six months urging a B-29 strike against Hankow, which was the major supply area for the Japanese forces in China. The city had been bombed twice by a few B-29s as a last-resort target, but Arnold had rejected Chennault's requests because the target could be hit by the Liberators. However, when the Japanese began a drive from Liuchow with Kunming as the possible goal in November, General Albert Wedemeyer, who had recently replaced Stilwell, strongly supported the idea of an all-out Hankow attack. LeMay was unwilling to agree, and an order from the joint chiefs confirming Wedemeyer's authority was needed before he did.

The mission was planned as a massed strike by B-29s, B-24s, B-25s, and P-51s, and LeMay flew to Kunming to finalize the plan with Chennault, who urged him to use only incendiaries and drop them from twenty thousand feet to improve accuracy.

There were political overtones to massed incendiary bombing, as President Roosevelt had often denounced the indiscriminate killing of civilians. That attitude was able to be modified after the German attacks on English cities, and scientists had reported late in 1943 that incendiary bombing of Japanese cities was "one of the outstanding opportunities in all history to do the greatest damage to the enemy for a minimum of effort . . . effect on the Japanese war effort of a national catastrophe of such magnitude, entirely unprecedented in history."

LeMay went along with Chennault, except that every fifth plane would carry high explosives. The target was the extensive dock and warehouse area along the Yangtze waterfront. The operations officers, with a northerly wind predicted, planned to minimize the effects of smoke by meticulously planning bombing sequence from south to north with four formations.

Eighty-four B-29s bombed Hankow, but the mission did not go according to plan. A few hours before the takeoff Chennault had asked for the schedule to be brought forward forty-five minutes, but a communications failure resulted in some of the B-29s being out of place.

Even so, the strike was eminently successful, with great fires sweeping along the three-mile waterfront. Hankow was in flames for three days, and the dock and warehouse area was reduced to ashes. The success of the mission added weight to arguments for more fire bombing, and in

Captain Robert Berman's Bengal Lancer *undergoes last-minute preparations for the December 18 Hankow mission.*

both Washington and India there was support for stripping the B-29s and sending them in on night low-level fire missions.

The Superfortress engine problems still plagued LeMay, and by December a hundred or more modifications had been made. With another Omura mission coming up, he decided to use only B-29s with fully modified engines, but then, to round out his formations, he was forced to use the aircraft with older engines, although losses had been attributed to them on several occasions. Even though the B-29s had stopped over in China after Hankow, only three dozen got off for Omura the next day. Less than half bombed the primary target, unsuccessfully.

On December 21 Mukden was the target for forty B-29s, but two formations dropped their bombs early, missing by between four and nine miles. Once again frosting conditions made it difficult to see the lead bombardier's drop, and there was a heavy and effective smoke screen over the aircraft factory. The Japanese fighters were up and they were vicious. A 468th Group B-29 was rammed and a wing was beginning to fold back as the doomed plane disappeared from sight. Another ramming attempt only destroyed the fighter when he tried to pull over a B-29's wing after apparently changing his mind. The 462nd's *Wild-Hair*,

With her tail markings and belly band   *Major "Blackie" Blackwell, the 678th*
denoting her role as a lead ship, this 444th   *Squadron commander.*
Group plane was flown to Hankow by

with Captain John Campbell and his crew, was hit by an aerial phosphorous bomb just before reaching the target but remained under control until ten or eleven parachutes were seen.

Very Long Range Reconnaissance

When the B-29s went overseas, little preparation had been made for photo reconnaissance, and it was sorely needed, both in advance of B-29 missions and to assess the results.

In the early days some help was provided by other agencies in the theater, but there was much to be done that was beyond the range of other aircraft. Wolfe had a few B-29s modified as photo-recon planes simply by removing the lower forward turret and replacing it with a camera installation.

Meanwhile, back in the States, work was proceeding on a special model of the Superfortress, the F-13, with Wright Field and Boeing leaning on

The 462nd Group's Wild-Hair *went down during the December 21 Mukden mission.*

the experience of the planes modified in the theater. An original mid-1944 plan was that the F-13 would be unarmed except for the tail turret, with the radome moved forward to the lower forward turret well, where it could be completely retractable. The side sighting blisters were to be replaced by flush windows, resulting in a very clean, very fast airplane. Eventually stripped F-13s did reach the combat squadrons, but not until toward the end of the war. The first F-13 was converted at the Denver Modification Center, and assigned purely for training, to be passed down from squadron to squadron as they went overseas.

The combat photo planes had a busy time. The first crashed on the first Yawata mission, but another went along on the second Anshan strike, made runs over North China, and flew the long Palembang mission. The "Photo Joes" looked for possible airfield sites on Okinawa during the summer of 1944, and went back there to gather pictures prior to carrier strikes. They covered northern Luzon in October, at the cost of two B-29s but getting prints to General MacArthur "with the developer solution on them hardly dry." One 468th Group "Photo Joe" flew three

of these secret missions in October, but on the way back from the Philippines on October 20 Captain Paul Lindke and his crew became lost . . . at
night, in fog and out of gas. They crashed and died on the roadway between Pengshan and Hsinching.

During that last week of October, Major Harry Allen formed the Photo
Reconnaissance Detachment of the 20th Bomber Command, later designated Flight "C," 1st Photo Reconnaissance Squadron. The detachment
was activated at Hsinching, the forward base of the 40th Bomb Group.

Until the first F-13As began arriving in December, the unit used the
modified combat B-29s, but by the end of the year they had four F-13As,
all Renton aircraft—*Brooklyn Bessie, Double Exposure, Under-Exposed,* and
Quan Yin Cha Ara.

At the end of December and in early January the photo Superfortresses had two important tasks: They combed the island of Kyushu to
locate every enemy airfield and record the movements on them, and they
also worked closely with the Navy, reporting all shipping sighted during
the long flights to the Japanese homeland. During December the unit's
four F-13As and nine B-29s flew twenty-two missions. On January 5 the
combat "Photo Joes" were returned to their various groups, and the unit
received an additional F-13. Continuing to support the Luzon invasion,
they scouted Formosa and acted as weather planes as LeMay's B-29s
struck the Formosa targets, directing the bombers to visual targets.

On February 2, 1945, the flight suffered its first loss, when Captain Arthur Humby's *Brooklyn Bessie* went down. The flight engineer, Jim Morrison, recalls that the plane was "afire over North China when the order
came over the intercom to bail out. I quickly left my station and dove out
the forward hatch . . . I landed on the crest of a foothill about a thousand
feet high. The surrounding country was absolute wasteland with no sign
of trees or undergrowth."

Morrison could not see any of the others' chutes, and when he stood up
he collapsed—his left foot was broken. Then he heard voices close by,
and saw a group of men in Japanese uniforms.

"With gestures I attempted to let them know I was willing to surrender," Morrison said. "The largest of the group directed four of the men
to advance. They stationed themselves behind other rocks and aimed
their guns at me. The leader advanced and started searching me. He
asked to see my pistol. After examining it he returned the gun. . . .

"I took a chance and brought out my American-Chinese dictionary.
After looking at it, the leader took my pencil and methodically wrote 'B-
29' on the flyleaf."

Chat'nooga Choo Choo *won't you choo choo me home.... This 468th Group B-29* *flew three photo missions in November 1944, including one to Singapore.*

One of the first F-13As to reach the 1st Photo Squadron: Double Exposure's *copilot was named Art Double. (James Morrison)*

Morrison learned that the men were Communist guerrillas, dressed in stolen Japanese uniforms. He was carried on the back of one of the group, and later that afternoon they reached a village. The rest of the crew of *Brooklyn Bessie* was there.

The 1st Photo received word that the crew was safe about two weeks later, but it was over three months before Morrison finally got back, after traveling more than a thousand miles through enemy territory.

When the 20th Bomber Command left the theater, the F-13s began photomapping southern Manchuria, Korea, and central and northern China. During March and April the F-13s continued their work, the last Superfortresses in China. Then on April 10 they moved back over the Hump to Dudhkundi, and began to prepare to move to Guam.

*   *   *

As 1944 drew to an end, the older combat crews were beginning to grow more and more concerned over replacements. There were plenty of rumors but no policy, and the crews needed a goal to work toward. While it could be argued that with only a dozen missions at the most for any one crew, and seven months in combat, their concern was premature, they had combat-tested the B-29, and the majority of their missions were far longer than any flown in other theaters. Their time over enemy territory was greater, and each mission from China involved the round trip over the Hump. They wanted something real to aim for—a number of missions or combat hours.

When the older B-29s began going home at the end of the year, brief hopes were dashed when it was learned that they would be flown by Air Transport Command crews. The 468th was sending home *Pioneer* and *Lassie*, and the morning after the transport crews had taken over, it was noted that *Lassie* suddenly wore five freshly painted Japanese flags and three additional bombs on her nose. The group history notes that "there was much stirring on the line, and the photo-lab cameramen immediately called to record this blasphemous deed. A gasoline rag was immediately applied and the honor of *Lassie* restored."

New Year, Old Problems

A Bangkok training mission began the year of 1945, followed by more strikes in support of operations in the Philippines. The situation in the

The 468th Group tanker Camel Caravan had been flown to the theater by General "Blondie" Saunders and was the first B-29 to reach the forward bases in China. In the first few days of October she flew three consecutive Hump trips in four days. She was flown home by Major Jack Ladd in December 1944, after a grand total of forty-seven missions and after Ladd had said "good-bye" by buzzing the control tower from fifty feet.

Toward the end of 1944 the older B-29s began going home, but their duty was far from done. This old 444th Group plane was stripped and sent to the B-29 Transition School at Maxwell, where over seven hundred B-29 crews were trained. The old

Superforts, still with the red dust of the CBI in them, were a tangible link with the future — particularly when a large battle-damage patch was right by a trainee crewman's position.

Pacific had firmed up as first Nimitz, then Admiral King, agreed to forget any invasion of Formosa and launch operations against Iwo Jima and Okinawa after MacArthur had secured Luzon. The B-29s would add their weight to all these operations. The 20th Bomber Command was to hit Formosa as MacArthur moved North, and provide reconnaissance on call.

Luzon was a major operation, beginning with landings at Lingayen on January 9. Originally scheduled to hit North Formosan aircraft installations, which proved to be unsuitable targets, LeMay set up precision strikes against the Tachiarai Machine Works on Kyushu as primary visual target and Omura as primary radar.

With cloud cover over both targets, twenty-eight Superfortresses bombed Omura, but the attack did not divert the Japanese from their severe mauling of MacArthur's forces. Pounded by kamikazes, which he believed were coming from Formosa, MacArthur asked for B-29 strikes on the airfields there. Arnold and LeMay agreed, and two missions were scheduled. Weather kept the B-29s down on January 8, but the next day a weather B-29, out an hour in advance of the main force, selected Kiirun, where the Superforts bombed with unobserved results.

After this, the B-29s went back to India for another Singapore mission. Once again Japanese cripples had gathered there, and two docks, the King's Dock and the Admiralty IX Floating Drydock, were selected as primary targets. Twenty-seven planes divided their effort between the two without scoring, and another formation bombed other targets, on January 11. Two B-29s were lost.

LeMay sent all his fully modified planes back over the Hump for a double strike against Formosa, and on January 14 fifty-four aircraft pounded Kagi while twenty-one struck other targets. Weather caused a day's delay; then on January 16 the primary visual target, Shinchiku, was open, and the last of the "Pac-Aid" strikes was flown. The B-29s, although "miscast," had added their weight, and the kamikaze situation eased in Lingayen Gulf. The Shinchiku strike was also the last B-29 mission from the Chengtu bases.

*   *   *

LeMay knew that the whole Matterhorn plan was "basically unsound" and justified only by the lack of appealing alternatives. Back in September 1944 he had raised the question of resurfacing the Chengtu strips and was informed that he would be in the theater nine months more.

The 40th was unloading frags from a B-29 on January 14 when a cluster broke and one or more bombs fell on the cement "doughnut" and exploded. The B-29's bomb bay caught fire, and the crash crew and everybody else in the vicinity tried to put the fire out, even though the airplane was still loaded with bombs. Before they could control the fire, the bombs began exploding. The airplane was demolished, and Last Resort *was so badly damaged that she had to be salvaged. Four other B-29s were also peppered by fragments. When the explosions began six men were killed either in or near the aircraft, and a seventh died later.*

When he was asked if he wanted more B-29 groups he flatly declined the offer. The situation in China was always bad — the political corruption and military ineptness of the Chiang Kai-shek government was becoming increasingly obvious. The Chinese were showing no desire to fight, and the Japanese halt in December was more due to weather and strained supply lines than the Chinese "counterattacks" faithfully repeated from Chinese sources by stateside newspapers. The theater commanders considered the B-29s a burden, and the joint chiefs, at Arnold's suggestion, agreed with Wedemeyer's request to get them out of China to give him more bases and supplies to try to save his own situation.

From India the B-29s could conduct limited operations, providing bombing, mining, reconnaissance, and any jobs for Lord Louis Mountbatten's Southeast Asia Command that were being done by Liberators—the Liberators could then go over the Hump to help in China. Meanwhile, the Superfortresses would get ready to move into bases in the Marianas around April.

Planning for evacuating the China bases had begun in November at group level, and on January 27 the forward detachments had pulled out.

LeMay had gone ahead to the Marianas to a new command on January 18, and there was a feeling that the B-29s in India were in the minor leagues. LeMay's successor was General Roger Ramey, who had been serving as chief of staff to General Hansell on Saipan.

There were few industrial targets within range of the Indian bases, and shipping in harbors seemed the most profitable target. At the end of January the B-29s began a campaign that took them back to Rangoon, Bangkok, and Singapore, and new targets such as Saigon, Cam Ranh Bay, Phnom Penh, and Penang. Some were bombing missions, some were minelaying, and some definitely seemed to be "a task thought up chiefly to keep the boys busy." Singapore was the only really good B-29 target, but it was not always "on limits."

A number of the strikes might have been dubbed training missions, but any training was geared to the type of operations expected in the Pacific, not in Asia.

The B-29s had only flown the one aerial minelaying mission, back in August, but mining by Liberators had placed a greater burden on ports out of B-24 range to the east and south. These crowded havens were within the range of the B-29s. This, plus the influx of warships battered in the Philippines, convinced Ramey to begin a limited mining campaign during the full moon at the end of January.

The first effort was a double mission on the night of January 25; two groups laid six mine fields at Singapore, while the 462nd Group sent planes to Saigon and Cam Ranh Bay.

During the next full moon, at the end of February, a dozen B-29s went back to Singapore to mine the Johore Strait, which the Japanese had swept so carefully that traffic had only been stopped for a couple of weeks. Again the job was done well and without loss. On February 28, at Chennault's request, twelve B-29s flew to China for a mining mission to the Yangtze River. For the full moon in March, the B-29s mined the Yangtze again, and Saigon, Cam Ranh Bay, and Singapore as well. No B-29 was lost on any of the mining missions, and the experience was a valuable fund for the 313th Wing, training as a specialized mining unit in the Marianas, to draw on.

This fearsome dummy cannon was fitted to a 462nd Group aircraft when the 20mm gun was removed. Tail gunner "Big Red" Arents explain it this way: "The 20mm cannons were stinkers . . . jammed up very readily and then were utterly useless. . . . One crew built themselves this fake gun of sheet metal. It weighed very little and followed the movements of the machine guns.

The Japs must have thought this 'gun' was some new development because they would send fighters up that would fly level with the B-29, just out of range, and appeared to be attempting to get pictures of the thing. All the crews got a big bang out of the antics of the fighters trying to figure this monstrosity out." (L. J. Arents)

During the breaks between the full moons the B-29s ran other missions. On February 1 they flew a maximum effort against Singapore, when nearly seventy bombed the primary target, the Admiralty IX Floating Drydock, at the navy yard. Large enough to handle any battleship, the drydock was sunk by the British early in 1942 and then refloated by the Japanese. A number of hits and near misses were scored on the drydock and a ship in it. The ship burned and sank, and recon photos later showed the drydock down at one end and sinking slowly until it apparently settled on the harbor bottom. Enemy fighters shot down one B-

The 468th Group heading for Rangoon on February 11, 1945.

29 and mauled another so badly that it cracked up on landing, but this was a cheap price for another outstanding strike against Singapore.

Plans were being rushed for another attack when Ramey was informed that Lord Mountbatten had directed that the B-29s not attack naval installations at Singapore and Penang. This saving of valuable facilities was probably fair in the long term, but at the time it puzzled the command, justifiably proud of the great work they were doing. Ramey asked Washington for guidance and was told to stick to other targets while the Navy looked into the matter. Ramey then flew to Kandy for a conference with Mountbatten and was given as first priority some targets in the Kuala Lumpur area. Second priority consisted of some Singapore targets, but carefully clear of the King George VI Graving Dock, some other docks, and heavy machinery.

The B-29s were divided between Saigon and Bangkok on February 7; the Saigon primary target was the navy yard and arsenal, which next day was also declared off-limits.

On February 11 the storage dumps at Rangoon suffered the first of a series of attacks. Major Charles "Deacon" Miller, pilot of the 444th Group lead plane, *Deacon's Disciples*, was right on target, and oil and ammunition went up in fountains of multicolored fire. But it was something of a comedown for the B-29s to be blowing up ammunition dumps or pecking away at Japanese soldiers in barracks, even though the crews were bombing well and American losses were light.

The rest of the February and March missions were against Singapore. The last maximum effort, an incendiary attack by over one hundred B-29s, was flown on February 24. They hit the Empire Dock area, "the only suitable target free of stipulations left" in the theater. They went to Singapore again on March 2, and then flew two missions against oil-storage installations there. The first, flown on March 12, was poor. For its last missions, the 20th Bomber Command flew a series of mining and bombing missions on March 28 and 29. At best, destruction of the targets would cause the Japanese "some inconvenience," but it was time the

The Singapore flak on February 24 found its mark on the 444th Group's Male Call, *flown by Captain James Williams. Five of the crew were injured by gunfire.*

The 444th Group flies its last mission from the CBI, as mines tumble from the lead plane over Singapore on March 28. The 444th historian noted, "The prime purpose had been achieved: to battle-test the B-29." When they had arrived in the theater no- *body really knew the range, bomb load, speed, or characteristics of the B-29. The 444th took its share of the credit for proving that "a B-29 could be raised from the ground twice in one week without the aid of jacks."*

crews in the 58th Wing learned something about the new tactics Lemay was using from the Marianas. The B-29s went in at altitudes as low as five thousand feet, individually. And that was it for Matterhorn.

*   *   *

An advanced echelon of the 58th Wing had flown out via Luliang, China, on March 20. Each group sent four of its most experienced crews on ahead, and they would be attached to the 313th Wing on Tinian. The 444th sent Captain John Siler and *Princess Eileen IV* and three others to the 6th Group, the 40th's *Smilin' Jack* was one of four going to the 504th Group, and the 505th would get *Ramp Tramp II* and three more 462nd airplanes. The 468th was sending *Belle Ringer, Million Dollar Baby II, Rushin' Rotashun,* and Major James Pattillo's *Bengal Lancer* to the 9th

The shooting-star motif that identified 468th Group B-29s. The color of the insignia identified the squadron. (Harry George)

The tail of Belle Ringer, with the Billy Mitchell flag. Originally designed by General Mitchell for use aboard his yacht, the flag was awarded monthly to the group that performed best, with the group that won it three times retaining it. The 468th gained it on August 27, 1944. (R. Wallace Teed)

Group. Pattillo recalls that they "went out ahead of the main force because the Bomber Command had to get some of its staff officers to the Marianas so they could become familiar with the field then being built on Tinian to receive the 58th Wing, make the necessary operations, logistics, armament, ordnance, communications, and intelligence arrangements to permit the 58th to resume combat operations as soon as possible. . . . Bomber Command headquarters sent along about four passengers per airplane, which were such people as assistant wing bombardier, navigator, communications officer, key noncoms, and other staff specialists, and gave them the usual instructions: 'Get the hell out there, and have all of the problems solved *before* we arrive.'

"On the way to Tinian we left Kharagpur about 8:00 A.M. and landed at Luliang around noon on a beautiful sunny day. We had chow, napped, and by five-thirty had the airplane preflighted and were awaiting our appointed time to start engines. Several of us were standing near the nose wheel of the airplane watching some P-38s shoot landings . . . friendly fighters always fascinated B-29 crewmen, because we never had any to help us but, subconsciously, wished that we could. A P-38 turned from his base leg to final approach at about eight hundred feet, straightened out momentarily, and suddenly spun in, 'right there in front of God and everybody.' We could see no reason for this. The weather was perfect, there were no other airplanes near him, and yet all at once everything was so quiet. There was no question but that the pilot was dead. It just reminded us of the futility and waste of all our China experiences. There being no crash equipment on the field, there was no reason to try to save the pilot as the airplane disintegrated the instant it hit the ground. We had seen enough accident remains that they were no novelty. We quietly looked on in disbelief, then crawled aboard, fired up, and taxied out. In spite of the enthusiasm and tireless energy we put forth operating into and out of China, it had often seemed like just one big heartbreak after another. This P-38's spinning in seemed the appropriate, dismal note on which to close that chapter. . . ."

Arriving over Tinian, *Bengal Lancer*'s crew peered down at their new home. Below were small green islands with their natural contours permanently changed by the requirements of a strategic air war. Pattillo was "all but shocked by the activity down below. Having spent the best part of a year in India and China, where everything was so primitive and all of our equipment and supplies had to be brought over vast distances and with such great effort, and then suddenly seeing below us what looked like Times Square. Eight to ten landing ships were lined up side by side along

Satan's Angel, *the first Omaha B-29,*   *in a midair collision over the Bay of Bengal*
never made it to the Marianas. She was lost   *on March 25, 1945. (Jack McKenna)*

the beach working cargo, more ships seemed to be standing by, waiting to
get to the beach; lights all over the place as if there were not a Jap within a
hundred thousand miles, there were paved roads, and trucks, Jeeps,
weapons carriers, and other GI vehicles moving *all over* the place in
heavy, well-ordered traffic, with lights on as if there were no war anywhere. One felt a sudden surge of enthusiasm (which I had not known
for months), and the feeling, 'Jesus, I'm back with my *own kind*. I'm *home*
again, so now let's get organized and *get on* with this war!' . . . From now
on, all we had to do was bomb."

The main movement of the four B-29 groups from India took place
between April 20 and May 1. Ramey went along as commander of the
58th Wing, while the 20th Bomber Command would go to Okinawa to
provide control for the 316th and other B-29 wings planned for that
island.

The strategic results of B-29 operations from Chengtu were not
decisive factors in the defeat of Japan. If the campaign is summed up in
terms of Yawata, Anshan, and Omura the results of the ten missions
hardly justified the cost in B-29s and crews expended there.

Arnold's staff had seen China as the only area from which the doctrine
of strategic bombardment could be followed at the time, and acted accordingly. The Strategic Bombing Survey was emphatic that these B-29

operations were "a tremendous shot in the arm to the Chinese people," and that the B-29s should take their share of the credit for stopping the total collapse of Chinese resistance.

In Szechwan Province the Chinese seemed to take a personal interest in the B-29s, and their friendliness was noted by unit historians. That friendliness was underlined by the aid given to downed B-29 crewmen in enemy territory. Although the Communist Chinese were denied the kind of American assistance given to Chiang Kai-shek, they also readily assisted American airmen, and LeMay established a solid working relationship with General Mao Tse-tung.

The B-29s could also be credited with causing the Japanese to send fighters from other areas to intercept them. As far as a combat test of the Superfortress, the achievement was significant—a tougher test could hardly be imagined.

While the B-29s may well have been used more effectively during the period, it would not have been in the role envisioned for them. Arnold's unstinting allegiance to the strategic doctrine, primary mission of the B-29, would lead to the great achievements from the Marianas.

Matterhorn had produced neither early nor sustained bombing of Japan, and the cost of the limited results was extremely high. Lord Mountbatten later wrote: "They did excellent work . . . particularly in the long-range mine-laying, which I specially called for, against such distant targets as Singapore, Saigon, and Cam Ranh Bay."

So the B-29s were leaving, as much to the relief of the commanders in China as to the crews.

While some may have seen in India the romance of Omar Khayyam or Kipling, the 444th Group's unit history took a more jaundiced view—of those who would remember the B-29 groups fondly it suggested that "the robber bands who pilfered our guns and ammunition will always be grateful to the 'Sobs' who furnished them a means of livelihood beyond their wildest dreams. . . . Ali, who lives alone in the mountains of Assam, is thankful for the salvoed bomb-bay tank in which he makes his home. The chief of an Indian village in Bengal is thankful for the rupees he got from the Americans who accidentally destroyed half his tribe. He hopes the 'Iron Bird' will come again. . . . The people most happy to have known the Americans, though, are the owners of Carews Distilleries. 'Carews Booze for Combat Crews' was their slogan. . . ."

On May 4, 1945, the 468th Group filed its last morning report in India. The B-29s were going to the Marianas.

III

The Marianas: Frustration and Failure

The Marianas lie some fifteen hundred miles from the heart of Japan, the volcanic peaks of a gigantic mountain range rising almost six miles from the ocean bed, a range literally forming a series of stepping-stones to Japan.

Saipan, invaded on June 15, 1944, has an area of seventy square miles and is hilly and rather bare, except for the pines in the hills and along the coast. Tinian is smaller, green, and flat. The largest and southernmost island, Guam, is tropical with palm trees, high mountains, and tangled jungles full of towering mahogany trees.

These three islands would become the bases of a gleaming horde of B-29s, an air armada unlike the world had ever seen.

Back in the middle of April 1944, General Arnold and Admiral Chester Nimitz, commander in chief of the Pacific Ocean Area, had reached agreement that a group of officers should go to Hawaii, where they could provide Nimitz's staff with an outline of the requirements for the B-29s in the Marianas, and help form the plan. General Walter Frank was chosen to head this vital mission, and Arnold reminded him to be diplomatic—the construction and defense of the bases was the Navy's responsibility, as was the provision of supplies. Frank was to describe exactly what was needed, but carefully avoid giving any impression of demanding how the needs should be met.

Many subjects, from weather information through to ordnance, had to

101

be covered, but there was such a fine working relationship established that Frank's report would be the "veritable bible" for B-29 planners.

To prevent any conflict or interference between the forces of Nimitz and the Twentieth Air Force, which both operated under directives from the joint chiefs, local authority would rest with Nimitz or his area commander. Accepting this provision, Arnold wanted "a strong hand" to be there to deal with and negotiate priorities in areas such as construction and shipping. A new Army Air Forces headquarters was established in the central Pacific, and General Millard Harmon was selected to head it. It was one of the most complicated and difficult jobs of the war: Harmon had to deal with four major headquarters: Arnold in Washington, the 21st Bomber Command, Nimitz at Pearl Harbor and Guam, and the Army at Fort Shafter on Oahu. Directly responsible to Arnold, Harmon was ultimately designated as Twentieth Air Force deputy commander, but, more importantly, he received authority to deal directly with Nimitz. When Harmon reached Hawaii, the Twentieth Air Force had a man on the spot who could reach the highest commanders.

Stiff enemy resistance in the Marianas disrupted the original timetable. The delay at Saipan was minor, but on Tinian and Guam it ran to a month. The plan to use Guam as a fleet base and Nimitz's forward headquarters also pushed the B-29 bases down the priority list.

Seeking to make the best of a bad situation, Harmon inspected all three islands in August 1944 and suggested a revision of plans to Nimitz. Harmon's engineers discovered new factors, including the fact that the site of one of the two planned bases on Saipan was not suitable for Superfortress operations. Also, Tinian was capable of supporting more B-29 runways than the four originally planned. Harmon felt that delays on Guam could be balanced by dropping the second Saipan field and operating four groups from the two runways at Saipan's Isley Field. Only on Saipan was the schedule even partly met. The construction of Isley Field was accelerated as aviation engineer battalions, working day and night, extended the strip and widened it. The runways and key roads were topped with asphalt from a plant mostly constructed with salvaged Japanese material. It was tough for the engineers: Tropical rain teemed down for most of July and August, and the roads from the coral pits became so bad that equipment and men had to be diverted to build a hard-surfaced road from the pits to the airfield. Japanese air raids and the hard coral formations, requiring dynamiting, added to the problems.

The first B-29 reached Saipan on October 12, 1944. Four Thunderbolts met her as she approached, and the gleaming giant gave her new

The payoff: Joltin' Josie *arrives on Saipan. (Robert Meiborg)*

base a salutary buzz job before pitching up and out into the traffic pattern.

She was *Joltin' Josie,* commanded by Brigadier General Haywood S. "Possum" Hansell, already a veteran of the B-29 program, and Major Jack Catton of the 498th Bomb Group. Hansell had possibly done more than anyone to perfect the plan for the B-29 attacks on Japan. As Arnold's chief of staff he had directed the operations of the B-29s in India from Washington. Now, with XXI Bomber Command, he would control the operations from the Marianas at close hand.

Joltin' Josie's arrival was only a token of the success of the plans to operate B-29s from the Marianas. She had landed on a field that was barely fit for minimum operations, and the other B-29 fields were months short of completion. Still, compared to China and India, there was reason to be optimistic. From these islands the B-29s could reach every important target in the Japanese homeland, and the supply situation simply had to be superior.

On October 20 Brigadier General Emmett "Rosie" O'Donnell arrived

The B-29 generals. On the left is "Rosie" O'Donnell of 73rd Wing, on the right "Possum" Hansell. The man in the center, General Millard Harmon, deserves a good deal of the credit for the realization of the Marianas plan. When he took command of the Army Air Forces in the Pacific Ocean Area in August 1944, the use of future B-29 units had been uncertain. Two new wings, the 315th and 316th, were definitely planned for the Philippines as the 22nd Bomber Command, but Harmon, convinced that the Marianas and Ryukyus were the only suitable bases, persuaded Arnold to defer a final decision. The plane in the background is, fittingly, the 497th's Pacific Union.

on Saipan to set up his 73rd Bomb Wing headquarters. Behind him, B-29s were strung out all the way back to the States, and keeping up a constant flow of Superforts would turn into the first big problem.

As the B-29s gathered on Saipan, the 73rd Wing began to take shape.

Activated nearly a year before, its crews were well trained by wartime standards. Their new B-29s had better engines and other improvements and in general had benefited from the 58th Wing experience. "Rosie" O'Donnell's wing was composed of four groups: Colonel Stuart Wright's 497th, Colonel Wiley Ganey's 498th, Colonel Samuel Harris' 499th, and Colonel Richard King's 500th.

Of necessity, much of the 73rd Wing's training had been at the crew level, with little unit training. Soon after arriving on Saipan O'Donnell began a solid training program, which included general theater indoctrination, formation flying, communications, rendezvous, and missions against targets that were mildly defended by comparison to the main islands of Japan.

For the first shakedown mission of his new command, Hansell selected Truk, where there were about forty guns and a few patched-up fighters. On October 18, with B-29s still coming in behind schedule, he put up eighteen aircraft from the 497th and 498th. The general was going to fly with Jack Catton's crew again, but when trouble developed during the run-up the general quickly moved to another aircraft, which would take over the lead. Hansell's luck was not good that day: Fifteen minutes from the initial point, the top blister on the B-29 blew, injuring the central fire-control gunner. The aircraft was forced to abort, and Hansell watched his first mission disappear into the distance. It was also his last chance to personally lead his B-29s. His successor as chief of staff, General Norstad, soon brought down a regulation forbidding Superfortress commanding generals from flying over enemy territory. Fourteen B-29s went on to bomb the Dublon submarine pens at Truk with indifferent results: The 497th put about half their bombs in the target area, while the 498th performance was about half that again. It was not too bad as a training mission, and a few rounds of flak and a very cautious Zeke added some color.

Eighteen bombers from the two groups went back to Truk two days later, but with even less success. On November 2 they returned for a third time, briefed for radar bombing, but this again emphasized that there was much to learn. Two of the three squadrons mistook thunderheads for the initial point, which was a small island, and the bomb bursts were so far apart that it was not possible to prepare a bomb plot.

O'Donnell decided to try the B-29s against a warmer target, Iwo Jima; during the third Truk strike the Japanese had strafed and bombed Isley Field, and though they had done no damage it was assumed that the raiders had staged through Iwo. The B-29 targets were two airfields, and

The 869th Bomb Squadron, led by Dauntless Dotty, *holds tight formation during an early shakedown mission.*

the mission was planned to give experience in both daylight visual bombing and to test the facilities for night returns at Isley. Although successful as a training mission, the Iwo strike again yielded little result. A second attack three days later was also fruitless.

On the last of the training missions O'Donnell sent the 500th to Truk for its first taste of combat. Their eight B-29s found good weather over the target and were more accurate than their predecessors, but still only rated a "fair."

Some crews from every group except the 499th had now flown over an enemy target, and the next time the B-29s left Saipan they would be going to Japan.

*   *   *

The logical choice for the first mission target was Tokyo. If the strike went well, there would be psychological effects in both Japan and the Allied nations, and it was also logical due to knowledge gleaned from intensive study of Japan's industries.

Months before, General Arnold had asked for a report based on two projections: one, that the war could be won by the forces of naval and air power alone, or two, by those means plus an invasion of the Japanese home islands. The report reached his office a couple of days before *Joltin' Josie* touched down on Saipan.

If the war was to be won without an invasion, which seemed doubtful at the time, the report recommended attacks on Japanese shipping, including a heavy mining campaign, the aircraft industry, and Japanese urban industrial areas. The recommendations covering the second possibility, invasion, were similar, but the order and emphasis were changed. Six cities were named for area attacks: Tokyo, Yokohama, Kawasaki, Nagoya, Kobe, and Osaka. However, these attacks were only to be begun when they could be delivered in force over a short period of time. Believing an invasion would be necessary, the joint chiefs favored the latter set of recommendations, and this guided Twentieth Air Force target selection.

As an important and vulnerable target, Japan's aircraft industry was attractive, and this target system assumed top priority. From the very beginning, four companies had dominated the industry: Nakajima, Mitsubishi, Kawasaki, and Tachikawa. Among them they produced more than two thirds of the aircraft built by Japan during the war. Clustered in and around the big cities of Tokyo, Nagoya, and Osaka, these were juicy targets for the B-29s.

When Hansell and O'Donnell had completed their shakedown missions, the Twentieth Air Force and the joint chiefs, through Arnold and Norstad, moved in. Hansell received his first target directive on November 11, which gave his primary mission: the destruction of the Japanese aircraft industry's engine, assembly, and repair facilities. Targets for precision bombardment were listed in order of priority.

The Twentieth had a secondary mission, to support planned Pacific operations, with targets to be selected in Washington, and Norstad indicated that there would also be test incendiary attacks against urban and port areas.

For the first Tokyo mission the primary target was Nakajima's Musashino plant. This was Target No. 357, described like all the others in a special target-information sheet. In 1944 Nakajima was manufacturing 30 per cent of Japan's aircraft engines, and this target was considered second only to Mitsubishi Heavy Industries in the field. At the edge of a dense suburb in northwestern Tokyo, Nakajima's plant was about ten miles from the Emperor's Palace, in the village of Musashi. Actually the target was even more important: It had been thought that the nearby Nakajima plant at Tama was separate, but in fact they had merged late in 1943. The Musashino plant was a single-story steel-truss structure covered with wood, but the Tama section was a multistory building of reinforced concrete. Musashi, as the Japanese called the merged plants, produced more than a quarter of all engines for Japanese combat aircraft, and six important assembly plants were partly or totally dependent on their engine production. With a priority second only to Mitsubishi at Nagoya, the destruction of this target was expected to have quick and substantial results.

While the B-29s were preparing to hit Japan, many were decorated with lavish artwork. This is Major Clarence Fowler's Joker's Wild, *and the artist is a Marine named Bud Sprenger. He is actually applying underwear to the previously nude figure on the airplane. (USMC)*

Another Sprenger paint job was Captain Pershing Yon's Coral Queen. *Sprenger was in the 3rd Battalion, 10th Marines, and his art background was with the Curtis Candy Company, where he had been a sign painter. He painted a handful of the early 497th Group aircraft, and got about $175 and whiskey for each job. (USMC)*

Some of the best art in the 498th Group was the work of Corporal Guillermo Hernandez, a mechanic. He painted Fay, The Wichita Witch, Antoinette, *and* Lass'ie Come Home, *as well as decorating the 874th Squadron officers' club in similar vein.*

Fay, *before Hernandez had completed her nose painting. In the background is* Lady Mary Anna. Fay *disappeared without a trace on March 24, 1945, but* Lady Mary Anna *survived to be sent to the States as war weary in July.*

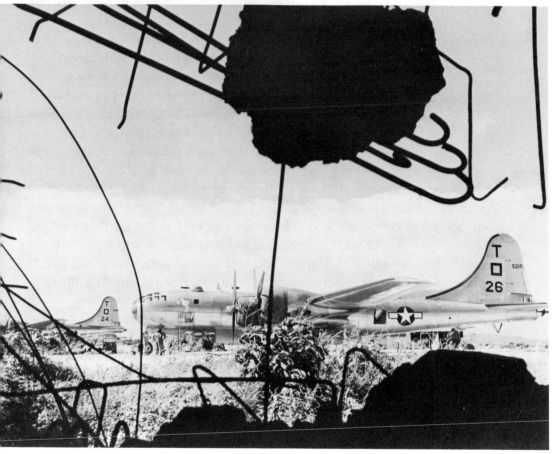

First over Tokyo

On October 19 Captain Ralph Steakley of the 3rd Photo Reconnaissance Squadron had been sipping a drink at the officers' club at Salina, Kansas, when he was told that he was flying out the next day. With another F-13A Superfortress crew, Steakley reached Saipan on October 30, the advance guard of the squadron that would provide Hansell's photographic coverage of Japan. After two days of briefing, Steakley took off in the very early morning of November 1, bound for Tokyo.

By the time the F-13 reached its first landmark, Mount Fujiyama, the crew were at their battle stations, wondering exactly what to expect. Theirs would be the first American aircraft over Tokyo since Doolittle's raiders back in 1942. The weather was clear, and their arrival apparently came as a complete surprise. Slipping along at thirty-two thousand feet, they saw the streets of Tokyo surging with activity. There were no fighters when they arrived that afternoon, just some scattered bursts of flak. For thirty-five minutes the Superfortress crew stayed over the east end of Tokyo Bay as its cameras recorded the secrets of the factories massed along the shore from Tokyo to Yokohama. Lieutenant Charles Hart, the photo-navigator, looked down at the clear outline of the city. He could see the racetrack, the stadium, the Nakajima aircraft factory. Some fighters "buzzed around" the camera plane, but did not come within range.

As soon as the plane landed on Saipan the film canisters were rushed away for processing, and the photos were a revelation. The prints showed crowded factory districts, airfields dotted with planes, and thousands of dwellings. In one, the moated Emperor's Palace was clearly visible.

The F-13s flew two more missions that week. Fighters and flak were ineffective against the photo planes. On November 7 one hundred fighters were airborne but only two were able to get within a thousand yards of the high and fast F-13. On November 10, Captain John Garvin and his 497th Group crew took *Skyscrapper* over Tokyo to gather weather information and check the altitude and accuracy of Japanese flak response. By November 11 Hansell believed he had learned enough secrets about his first target. He had sent Arnold his plan for the first mission, code-named "San Antonio 1." It was a daylight visual bombing attack from thirty thousand feet by ten or twelve squadrons, each with nine to eleven airplanes carrying five thousand pounds of bombs.

Washington had estimated Japanese homeland fighter strength at over

Captain Ralph Steakley and Tokyo Rose. *(Barry Gilkes)*

eleven hundred in mid-October, six hundred at the beginning of November. The Japanese Imperial general headquarters had made a key decision to wage their all-out, decisive battle on Leyte, sending reinforcements to the Philippines at the expense of other fronts and the defense of the homeland. The 73rd Wing's field orders indicated that up to five hundred fighters in the area could be sent up against the B-29s, but actual strength was less than four hundred.

The photos had shown that intense flak could be expected in the Tokyo and Tokyo Bay areas, on the Chiba Peninsula, and along Sagami Bay. Knowledge of enemy radar was vague, and after a debate between Harmon and Hansell over countermeasures, Norstad decided that they should send out "ferret" missions before the strike, and have a few F-13s drop "window" around Nagoya on the day of the first mission as a diversion. Using jamming transmitters was deferred until radar operators were better trained, and to avoid giving incentive to the Japanese to improve their radar network. Air-sea rescue precautions would be elaborate. There was a sense of great anticipation on Saipan as November unfolded.

Hansell wanted to get the B-29s over Tokyo as soon as he could, but did not wish to send less than one hundred. He also hoped to co-ordinate the mission with a carrier strike, which should dampen the fighter defenses. If the B-29s went over on November 17, Hansell would have his one hundred planes, and while not enthusiastic, Norstad agreed with

The silver horde gathers on Saipan. The B-29s were prime targets, but the Japanese were unable to take full advantage of the fact.

The 73rd Bomb Wing took over this Japanese building for their operations building at Isley Field. The base was named for Navy Commander Robert Isely, killed making a strafing run two days before Saipan was invaded. Although an early misspelling of his name has been perpetuated, and official histories call the base "Isley Field," it is interesting to note that the name is spelled correctly on the sign on the operations building, and was spelled correctly in most early 73rd Wing records. (Larry Reineke)

Tokyo bound: Armorers lead belts of machine-gun ammunition into the 497th Group's Our Baby.

the timing. The heavy Navy involvement in the Philippines forced Nimitz to hold off the carrier strike indefinitely, so the B-29 mission was set up as an independent operation.

At the wing briefing Colonel Bryon Brugge rose, and indicated the target with a pointer. It was a dramatic moment. Brugge's remarks were few, and he then handed the stage over to the various briefing officers. The primary target was the Musashino aircraft plant, with the urban and dock areas of Tokyo as the secondary, but the weather would play its own crucial part in this mission, a harbinger of things to come.

On the momentous day, the Marines had made certain there could be no possibility of a tipoff from Japanese holdouts on Saipan by conducting a "rabbit hunt" around the runways, which netted them over two hundred killed.

On the hardstands the tension that had built up was accentuated when the takeoff was put back an hour. Sheets of rain drummed against the glistening B-29s as the crews hunched under the wings or in shacks and trucks. By the time the downpour began to ease and the gray clouds were breaking up, a Jeep was already dashing from plane to plane, passing the word that the mission was canceled.

The rest of that long day was sunny and clear, and there was a feeling of disappointment. The next day the same thing happened, and Hansell, who had seen the havoc weather could cause in Europe, was anxious. In Washington, Arnold and his staff were impatient.

Finally it was Friday, November 24, 1944. For the first time in a week the day dawned sunny and bright. There were a few misty clouds over Mount Tapotchau, which the rains had turned to bright emerald green. Shortly before takeoff time the ground shook as hundreds of engines turned over and warmed up. Clouds of dust surrounded the dispersal areas. Along the runways Jeeps and trucks formed grandstands for the big show. Among them were ambulances and crash trucks, their crews equipped with metal cutters and other emergency equipment in case of a mishap.

The F-13s were to enter the Japanese radar screen as the first of the bombers came in from the southwest, and about ten minutes before the scheduled takeoff of the first bomber a photo plane thundered down the runway. Across the strip was a line of dump trucks hauling coral, which an unwary guard had allowed to begin their laborious crossing. The trucks, close together, were crawling across the center of the runway, blocking it. The pilots in the F-13 saw the trucks in the half light in disbelief. They began to haul the plane up two thirds along the runway. The F-13 was ten feet off the ground, that was all, and cleared the trucks by a few feet.

The taxiways at Isley were jammed with B-29s, nose to tail. All Saipan was throbbing to a sustained throaty rumble, like distant thunder, only louder. The constant noise was punctuated by a stronger roar. *Dauntless Dotty*, with General O'Donnell and Major Robert Morgan, was at the head of the runway at full takeoff power. The long, black-topped surface disappeared over the slight hill in the distance as the pilots released the brakes. The gleaming B-29 sped down the runway, watched by hundreds of anxious eyes. The wheels lifted from the ground and she was flying, after using every inch of the strip. Then *Dauntless Dotty* dissappeared

Lucky Lynn *and Captain John Brewster's* *field, of antennas for radar counter-*
Bad Brew, *both with artwork by Lin* *measures operations without disturbing the*
Decker. *The cover plates on* Bad Brew's *pressurization of the nose section, or requir-*
nose are for the easy installation, in the *ing any cutting of the skin.*

momentarily as the pilots dropped down to skim the water and gather air speed.

Major Joe Baird was off in *Pacific Union* a minute later.

Lucky Lynn roared out across the coral shoals, fifty feet above the water, and Captain Len Cox relaxed and fell into a little ritual. He happily chanted "Hubba hubba hubba . . . chop chop chop chop chop." Back in the waist his crew was already settling down for the long flight — one was reading *Crime and Punishment,* another Steinbeck's *Pastures of Heaven.*

The original plan had called for five combat groups of two squadrons each — two squadrons from the 497th Group, two from the 498th, followed by a composite group composed of a 497th and 498th Group squadron, with two squadrons from the 499th and two from the 500th taking off from the second runway.

In the 498th Group's *Long Distance* the takeoff was over, and Major Walter Todd yelled to his flight engineer, Lieutenant Milan Kissinger, "I'll give you a dollar for every gallon over a thousand we land with." Kissinger thought Todd was making a pretty safe bet, but had nothing to lose. About an hour out from Saipan the lead ship of the second combat group, *Lady Eve*, with Major Russell Cheever and the group commander, Colonel Wiley Ganey, aborted, and Todd took over the lead.

Back in the lineup of thundering B-29s still on the taxi strip, Lieutenant Ray Ebert, bombardier in *Fickle Finger*, was watching the spectacle. Although it was a court-martial offense, he was determined to keep a "blow by blow" account of this mission in his diary. At five minutes after six his airplane commander, Captain James Lampley, cut the engines because there was trouble up ahead — *Shady Lady* had misjudged a corner and slewed off the runway into the mud, blocking the strip for over an hour.

The 499th and 500th groups completed their takeoffs while the composite group awaited its belated turn. Then finally these last 497th and 498th B-29s were on their way.

Up ahead in *Lucky Lynn* somebody had brought out a box of food, and there was griping when it was discovered that the Thanksgiving Day turkey sandwiches had apparently already been eaten. The gunners turned the switches on their control boxes on; the amplidynes, supplying working power to the turret-drive motors, made their coffee-grinder sound, and the guns rattled as they were tested. The tail cannon jammed, and the gunner, Sergeant Bill Stovall, left his lonely compartment to get a screwdriver. His only company back there for the longest part of the mission would be a harmonica, a girl's picture, and a pair of panties.

In *Fickle Finger* Ray Ebert was meticulously keeping his log: "Hell we

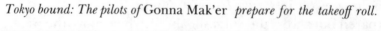

Tokyo bound: The pilots of Gonna Mak'er *prepare for the takeoff roll.*

are now over the Blue Pacific, Tokyo bound. Have to excuse the pen-
manship the air is terrifically rough. Because of our delay in takeoff our
group will be the last ones over the target. It is not an enviable position . . .
temperature outside is 30°C at one thousand feet we are practically
melting inside the ship . . . the entire distance thus far has been a series of
thunderstorms, sure hope the target is clear . . . we also have our bombs
all autographed . . . Mikie, Eve, Dotty, Roselle, Bunny . . . the crew
members are saving the safety pins from this first load . . . well we are getting nearer to the Jap homeland on the greatest history making flight of
the war. Just hope we don't become a part of it. We have been joking and
having a lot of fun in the plane but confidentially I think I'll be a wee bit
scared. Major Morgan's outfit should be hitting the target in about one
hour we are keeping the radio tuned in in hopes of hearing their results.
Our cumulus clouds have now dissipated and according to weather there
should be a cold front moving down to Japan. Wonder with what feeling
Myra will receive the bombing news. It will reach her by radio long before
I am ever able to mention it in my letters. Wonder if she'll realize I'm on
it."

In the 498th's *Long Distance* they had been traveling at five hundred
feet for several hours. Major Todd crawled back to the gunners' compartment to shake hands with the crew members and then went back up
front with the parting words, "I'll be seeing you." The navigator fired a
flare as the signal to the formation to begin climbing. Todd prepared to
pressurize the aircraft, and the flight engineer gave the no-smoking sig-

Tokyo bound: A 499th Group B-29 takes to the air.

nal and began to transfer fuel. Mild vibration rippled through the aircraft as the guns were tested. The bombardier removed the inch-long safety pins from the bombs.

Lucky Lynn's crew was passing the time with a lot of cigarettes. The B-29 had been named after Len Cox's daughter, born just before the crew left the States. Cox told the crew to put on their flak suits, and a few minutes later the navigator, Lieutenant Jack Ehrenberg, was on the interphone: "Navigator to all gunners: We've sighted Japan."

Towering through the wispy clouds was the initial point, Mount Fujiyama, snowcapped, its peak sparkling in the early-afternoon sun.

Lieutenant Al Hansen, the bombardier, was watching the clouds. *Lucky Lynn* was more than five miles above Japan, and Cox warned him not to point the guns straight ahead, in case they iced up.

Ehrenberg called Hansen: "You should be able to see a town underneath us now, Hansen. . . . Flak at eight o'clock, low. . . . Fighter at three, low." Cox and Ehrenberg had both flown in B-17s with the 91st Bomb Group from England, and were old hands.

The people up front in *Lucky Lynn* saw two sticks of bombs fall from *Dauntless Dotty*. Hansen casually said, "Bombs away," and *Lucky Lynn* lifted a little and seemed to gain speed. Off her wing Captain O'Neal Archer in *Little Gem* moved closer, and a line of flak bursts that had been feeling for her burst harmlessly to one side. Far below, Japanese fighters were circling as they groped for altitude.

Lieutenant Sam Wagner's B-29 was holding an outside position in the formation. Right after leaving the target a Tony came in on his tail from the right. Three B-29s fired on it, but Wagner's gunners did not. The fighter was also not firing, but crews on other B-29s watched in horrified fascination as the Tony wobbled through the air and smashed into the tailplane of the Superfortress. Both aircraft, the huge B-29 and the little fighter, slowly spiraled. There were no parachutes, and those who saw the collision believed it was unintentional. A few moments before, another fighter had raked Wagner's plane with gunfire, the only possible reason for the lack of return fire from the B-29.

Long Distance barged through squalls, each punctuated by a rainbow at the end, then was above the clouds as Fujiyama appeared. The radio operator picked up a musical program on a Tokyo station. As the B-29 turned from the initial point, a fighter headed straight at the B-29, came almost within range of the bombardier's guns, then zigzagged away.

Making the long, sweeping turn from Fujiyama to Tokyo, the rugged hills below melted into rice paddies and small villages. Ahead of *Long Dis-*

The Heat's on, *flown by Lieutenant Wayne Dameron, passes over Tokyo, more than five miles below. (John Mitchell)*

tance, the first formation of B-29s had reached the target and dropped their bombs, about three minutes ahead of the 498th Group. Over Tokyo the formation closed up. The bombardier, Lieutenant Roman Pucinski, searched for a break in the clouds and pressed the release as one appeared. The bombs were swallowed in the clouds, but a minute later Tokyo was again visible and they could see smoke and fire. Fighters were on their tail, trying to reach them. The fighters' attempts seemed "feeble and fluttering"—only one gained enough altitude, and it stayed out of the tail turret's range. Flak blotched the sky, but most of it was wide. As *Long Distance* left the city and skirted Tokyo Bay, visibility was perfect and the crew could see the Imperial Palace. She would make it back to Saipan with fourteen hundred gallons of gas left, meaning a four-hundred-dollar windfall for Lieutenant Kissinger.

As the last B-29s were going over the target, Ray Ebert noted in his diary, "When we reach the target it will be 10:00 P.M. in Gresham Wisconsin and I can't help but wonder what Myra will be doing while her old man is up here with the crap scared out of him. We can expect fighters at any time. Here I am all dressed up in a big bulky flak suit ready to make that run on the target. At 1330 we received a message that A-26 went down at 1250. . . . It sure is a funny feeling to know that in a few minutes we'll be looking into the hungry jaws of Death."

After ninety minutes Ray Ebert was able to return to his diary to report: "My Hell what we just came through. We hit the target about 1415 but golly what took place before and after. The flak was so heavy I think a man could have gotten out and walked home on it. I may be exaggerating a little but fighters were buzzing around us like flies. Just after leaving the target a burst of flak caught us just aft of the camera doors and nearly turned us over. Vahey's mask was torn loose by the blast and we depressurized so fast I'm sure there must be a few popped ear drums in the crowd. When the pressure seal broke our cabin temperature dropped from +20 to −37 and I'm shivering so bad I can hardly write. I didn't think to bring winter flying clothes. Don't know how many ships we lost in the melee. . . . I have a camera in our ship and I was supposed to take four impact shots but became so excited I took 83. . . ."

En route to the target 17 B-29s had aborted, and 6 more were unable to bomb due to mechanical failures. The weather had complicated matters, a 120-knot wind giving the B-29s a ground speed of about 445 miles per hour. The target was almost completely submerged in undercast, and only 24 B-29s bombed the Musashino plant. The others dumped their bomb loads on urban and dock areas or bombed by radar. Back on

3¢

DAILY  NEWS

Copr. 1944 by News Syndicate Co. Inc. NEW YORK'S PICTURE NEWSPAPER   Trade Mark Reg. U. S. Pat. Off.

 3¢

Vol. 26. No. 132   New York, Saturday, November 25, 1944*   20 Pages   2 Cents IN CITY LIMITS | 3 CENTS Elsewhere

TOKYO ABLAZE AFTER RAID

— Story on Page 3

Strasbourg Conquered; Allied Artillery Blasts Rhine Forts

— Story on Page 2

Packing For Trip To Tokyo

Trouble — tons of it — is readied for Tokyo as ground crewmen prepare to load bombs aboard Dauntless Dottie, B-29 Superfortress in background. Dottie led the armada of planes which ripped the Jap capital. The big plane, in which Brig. Gen. O'Donnell had his command post, was piloted by Major Robert Morgan, who also piloted the immortal Memphis Belle. Returning crews reported seeing violent fires consuming the great Musashina aircraft factory. This was the first air raid on Tokyo since Doolittle and his men went over in April, 1942. —Story on page 3; other pictures in center field.

(Associated Press Wirephoto)

The kind of publicity that was never encouraged by the 21st Bomber Command.

Saipan, the intelligence officers figured that about 125 fighters had tangled with the B-29s, a mixture of Tojos, Zekes, Tonys, Nicks, Irvings, and some unidentified planes. The expected savage fighter response had not eventuated, and the B-29s claimed 7 as destroyed.

Air-sea rescue precautions paid off when Captain Guice Tudor of the 499th Group ran out of fuel and ditched; his whole crew was picked up by a destroyer.

The strike photos revealed that only 16 bombs had hit the target, although after the war it was found that actually 48, including 3 duds, had landed in the factory area.

As often in the B-29's short career, the intangible results were the most important. They had paraded over the toughest target area of Japan without excessive losses, and the Japanese knew they would be back.

*   *   *

The first Tokyo mission set the pattern of the new command's endeavors for the next three months. The attacks were high-altitude, daylight precision strikes against the Japanese aircraft industry, in strict accordance with Army Air Forces doctrine.

With only minor damage resulting from the November 24 mission, Hansell intended to get the B-29s back to Musashino quickly, in a similar attack. Hoping to take advantage of any uncorrected weaknesses in enemy defenses, he chose November 27.

That day eighty-one B-29s were airborne, but nineteen aborted and the others dropped on secondary targets when they found Musashino totally blanketed by cloud. A B-29 from the 500th Group was lost with its entire crew after ditching on the way home.

The two Tokyo attacks, although not truly effective, aroused the Japanese. They raided Isley Field in small but effective heckling attacks.

John Mitchell of the 3rd Photo Squadron recalls, "It was thought they had no means of sending planes, especially fighters, over in the daytime . . . their nearest bomber base was Iwo Jima. There was a small island, Pagan, only some one hundred miles away, but no one paid any attention to it, probably only a few soldiers there with no means to threaten all our power on Saipan. About noon November 27 changed all those ideas. I stepped to the door of the orderly room to look over toward the motor pool—over by the mess hall the men were lining up for the noon meal. I paid scant attention to the two fighter planes I saw making a sweep over the ridge and heading toward our area. Just a couple of Navy boys I thought, pulling a buzz job before landing. But then one plane banked slightly and I saw the big rising sun emblem on the side of the fuselage at the same instance I saw the winks of light as his wing guns opened up. As I made a leap for the switch to turn on the air raid alarm I remember seeing the little puffs of dust in front of the orderly room as the slugs tore into the ground. The first two Zeros swept past to be followed by another pair. I turned the switch off—if people didn't know there was a raid on now they would never know—and went outside to see what was going on. People were running from the tent area toward the trees and brushy area that we used as an air raid shelter. . . . As I looked toward the flight line I could see one of the Zeros making a run down the line of parked B-29s. On the far end of the field I could see smoke boiling up from burning planes.

"The Zero completed his run down the flight line, banked sharply and reversed course and headed again for the camp area. He was bearing down directly on me but this time the gun emplacement to the east of our area opened up and I could see the tracers tearing into him. He slowed, wobbled a bit, then smoke and flame poured from his fuselage. I saw he was going down and I thought if he hits and bounces he will come down right on top of me. It took me two jumps to be through the orderly room and hit the dirt on the other side where I could look back through the hut and see what happened. The Zero staggered and then, engulfed in flames, hit the ground and exploded."

In all, seventeen Zekes had raced in over Isley, and all but four were shot down by antiaircraft fire. Later, near Pagan, the Thunderbolts picked off another, and one more as it landed. The other two were never sighted and were presumed to have ditched. Although probably wiped out, the Zekes had achieved some success: The 497th's *Skyscrapper* was blazing furiously, a 499th Group B-29 was a burned-out wreck, and two 498th Group aircraft would never fly again.

Before it crashed into the ocean one burning Zeke had skimmed across the beach so low that the heat burned some men in foxholes. Another Japanese pilot had bailed out just before his plane crashed, landed, and started shooting . . . a black Marine shot him dead. Another parachuted from his riddled plane over Tinian.

Hansell said that he had "no comment." The defense of the island was not the responsibility of the Twentieth Air Force. However, he had warned at a press conference prior to the first Tokyo mission that the enemy could be expected to react violently. The night attacks had caused little damage, but Hansell was now worried enough to move some of his

During November the Japanese raids were a costly nuisance. This 499th Group airplane was completely destroyed during the November 27 raid. (Richard Morgan)

planes from Isley to Guam. He was also planning joint air and sea strikes against Iwo Jima, where his B-29s could help remove the thorn from their side.

Hansell also notified Washington that he planned maximum strikes against the top-priority targets whenever weather allowed visual bombing and he could put up sixty planes. When weather was bad or he had thirty or more B-29s on hand he would launch raids against secondary targets. The B-29s would also fly nightly weather-strike missions.

Isley Field was a more likely place for a B-29 to be destroyed than the icy skies over the Japanese Empire. Partly to relieve congestion there, and partly to keep pressure on the enemy, Hansell sent out a thirty-plane radar night mission on November 29. The results against the dock and industrial areas in Tokyo were again "negligible."

The next big daylight mission was run on December 3, against the Nakajima plant at Ota, northwest of Tokyo. The weather looked bad, with the possibility of high winds over the target. With this in mind, it was decided to send the bombers to Musashino again, where they might find clear weather. Eighty-six took off, and all but ten reached Tokyo to find good visibility but high winds. The planes that bombed visually got poor results, and six B-29s were lost. One of these was the 500th Group B-29 with Major Robert Goldsworthy and the 500th's commander, Colonel Richard King, as well as Colonel Bryon Brugge of 73rd Wing headquarters. Goldsworthy and his crew planned to name their plane *Rosalia Rocket,* and were making a final choice of the luscious pinup that would

Captain Ed Campbell and his crew cleaning Special Delivery *of the 497th Group. Washing a B-29 with gasoline increased indicated air speed by three to five miles an hour, a lot on a fifteen-hour mission with maybe three hundred gallons' gasoline reserve.*

accompany the name. Before bombs away the B-29 was attacked by fifteen fighters, which hit the left inboard gasoline tank so badly that fuel sprayed all over the aircraft and the entire ship began to burn. The enemy fire also destroyed the electrical system. As the B-29 rapidly dropped from thirty-two thousand feet the crew began bailing out. Colonel King counted at least eight or nine other chutes as he floated down. Landing in an open field he discovered he was burned on his hands and face; some civilians quickly found him and not only handcuffed him but also bound him with the shroud lines of his parachute. Brugge and eight others of the crew who bailed out did not survive the war, but King made it, along with Robert Goldsworthy, who remembers months in solitary thinking of the Saipan mess hall. While some of his luckier fellows complained bitterly about that mess hall, Goldsworthy would have gladly traded his "dab of rice."

On December 3 Lieutenant Donald Dufford of the 498th was rammed in No. 3 engine by a Tony, which cartwheeled and struck another fighter. Both went down in flames, while Dufford flew the damaged *Long Distance* home safely. It soon became obvious that the collisions were not damaged fighters, but were intentional rammings. Without an efficient turbosupercharger, Japanese fighters were virtually incapable of effectively engaging the B-29s at their bombing altitudes. Early in November, when increasing B-29 raids became a certainty, extreme measures were decided upon. The 10th Flying Division, responsible for the defense of the Tokyo-Yokohama area, ordered formation of special flights in each of its groups for ramming attacks. The policy was extended to other divisions covering the homeland: the 11th, defending Osaka, Kobe, and Nagoya; and the 12th, charged with the defense of northern Kyushu. In the 10th and 11th divisions the special units were called *Shinten Seikūtai* (Heaven-shaking Air-superiority Unit).

The ramming aircraft were lightened by stripping them of radios, armor, sometimes even armament and fuel-tank self-sealing. Even so, the *taiatari* (body-crashing) attacks were not considered suicide, and the pilots could and did survive the attacks.

*   *   *

Early in December nightly Weather-Strike Missions against the Empire began. The missions had a dual purpose, as the name implied. The crews collected data on cloud cover, temperatures, and barometric information, as well as dropping bombs—usually incendiaries. The 497th Group was given the first mission, to be flown on December 6. The first of three B-29s scheduled that night found Tokyo brilliantly lit—"just like flying over New York," reported Colonel Robert Morgan. The second B-29, Captain O'Neal Archer's *Little Gem*, bombed through clouds and got the best precision-bombing results so far obtained at Tokyo. The third plane did not reach the target. These little missions were valuable, and during the month the 497th dispatched three planes nightly, except for a few instances when weather was too bad to permit the flights, until December 19, when another group took its turn.

On December 7, in the very early hours of the morning, low-flying enemy bombers strafed Saipan. Half an hour later, another thirteen arrived. The antiaircraft gunners got six, and ships offshore knocked down a seventh, but three Superforts were destroyed, three were seriously damaged, and a score more were slightly damaged. The next day B-29s took part in a combined attack against Iwo Jima.

Hansell was obligated to support Pacific operations, in particular those leading up to the Mindoro invasion scheduled for December 15. According to the doctrine, this support could best be given by striking a major industrial objective, and the choice was the Mitsubishi Aircraft Engine Works at Nagoya. This target, still enjoying top priority, lay some two and a half miles from Nagoya Castle, in the northeastern section of Japan's second city.

The 500th's Tokyo Local *was lost over Nagoya on December 13. After turning away from the target she dropped out of formation with one engine windmilling and another belching smoke. She made it out across the enemy coast and ditched, but Captain Charles Grise and his crew were never found.*

The mission was flown on December 13, and Hansell was able to get ninety B-29s on the way, most carrying high-explosive bombs but with one squadron in each group loaded with incendiary clusters. Sixteen turned back early, and another three bombed targets of opportunity. The enemy put up some "lively" resistance, which cost four B-29s. This mission was the 73rd Wing's introduction to "Flak Alley": Forced to fly North up Nagoya Bay toward the city, which was at the end of the narrow bay, the B-29s flew through co-ordinated heavy flak from both sides of the bay. Fighter opposition was also extremely heavy, and the crews thought Nagoya was "a bitch."

The mission showed improved bombing, and while this was enough cause for optimism, if the intelligence officers had had access to the full story they would have been even more pleased. Officials at the plant itself estimated that the attack cut their monthly production capacity by a quarter, and after this mission they began a program to transfer equipment underground.

Five days later the B-29s were on their way back to Nagoya, this time to the Mitsubishi aircraft works, target No. 194, a huge assembly plant that received most of the engines produced at the target they had hit last time. The Mitsubishi complex, built on reclaimed land in the northeastern corner of Nagoya Harbor, was large and conspicuous, an excellent target for visual bombing and, due to its position close to the waterfront, also good for radar bombing.

Ray Ebert was flying that day as bombardier in the 497th's *Ponderous Peg,* and again his diary tells the story:

"0730: Here is your little reporter again with on the spot coverage.

Over Nagoya on December 13 the 497th's Texas Doll *was badly damaged: A 20mm shell crashed through the nose, killing the bombardier, and another shell blew a hole in the rudder and the tail compartment, wounding the gunner. (Edward Prunuske)*

This 499th Group B-29 was ditched on December 13, at night. It was a good water landing and the entire crew got out into three life rafts. The bombardier had been pitched through the nose but was not injured. Cold and sick, they drifted all night, and the next morning their B-29 was still floating nearby, even though one bomb-bay door was open when they ditched. Some of the crew went back aboard and picked up extra equipment. By midday on December 14 they were spotted by a Navy Catalina, and late that afternoon a destroyer picked them up. The destroyer tried to sink the B-29 with gunfire, but it was not until a shot hit the wing tanks that the big bomber slowly turned on its side and disappeared beneath the water. (USN)

ASql Morgan just taxied by so we are about ready to start engines—we will be tail end Charlies again today. 0736: Started engines. 0739: Taxiing. 0757: Ready for takeoff. 0759: Airborne. 0820: Test fired the guns, let's hope that's all we'll need fire them. Walling is flying *Dixie Darlin'* today, we have *Ponderous Peg*. 0937: Just saw a Pilot's Halo ahead of us—we should have good luck. 1110: Just had a report ASq31 weather ship is missing. Another 870th Squadron plane. 1230: Well we are in our climb and will be at the target in about two hours. Don't have much to do

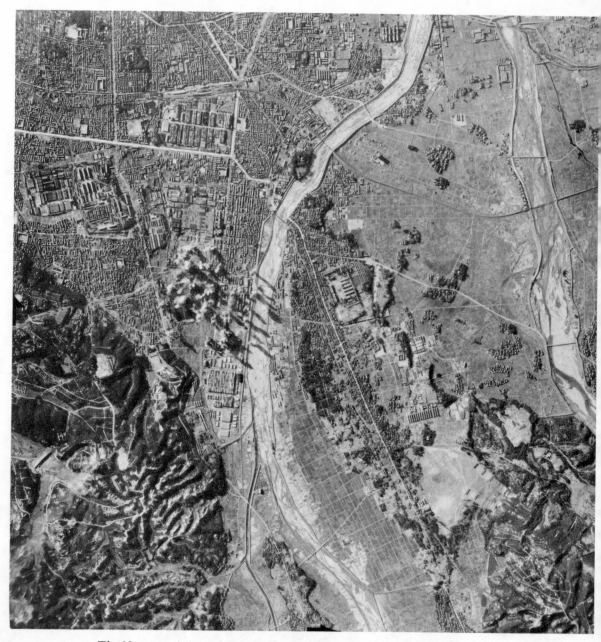

The Nagoya mission of December 13 cost four B-29s, but the bombing was good. This strike photo was taken from the 497th's Shady Lady. (Reineke)

right now so will write a letter to Mikie. 1300: One of our ships aborted don't know who it was yet. 1330: The lead element is not filled so we're trying to jockey in there. 1404: Another ship just turned back. Now we are six. Strike report from 869th Squadron came through—Primary Radar Nine—Goody, 1415: Now there are only five of us left, the Japs will have a chance to shoot the shit out of us. 1430: Just test fired our guns and three turrets are jammed. Frankly I'm getting scared. There aren't enuf other ships to give us adequate protection. 1545: Can see the coast of Japan, this is it for better or for worse. 1630: That's finished again no casualties in our ship—don't know how the others fared. Our bombs were away at 1542 . . . had a chance to shoot today but I'm afraid I missed him. Our bombs hit the target dead center. At the time of bombs away it was 0042 Monday morning back in the States. Wonder where Mikie was."

The abort at 1300 was the plane Ebert had flown overseas in, *Dixie Darlin';* it turned back in the vicinity of Iwo Jima and nothing was ever heard from it again.

The official report read that only sixty-three B-29s bombed the primary target, where cloud cover was heavy, and most bombed by radar, adding to damage caused by an earthquake eleven days before. In spite of this, production loss only ran to about ten days' work.

Mitsubishi's engine works at Nagoya were again the target four days later, but this time it was a daylight incendiary mission. Washington had wanted "test" incendiary raids, and Arnold's headquarters were convinced that the Japanese cities were extremely susceptible to this form of attack. As early as November 11 Washington had directed that trial fire missions should be flown before mass attacks on six selected cities. Incendiaries had been used on other missions, but Washington felt too much use was being made of high-explosive bombs, with fairly limited effect. Norstad asked for a major incendiary strike against Nagoya as soon as one hundred B-29s could be used. This was an "urgent requirement" for planning purposes. Hansell made strong protests: He had "with great difficulty implanted the principle that our mission is the destruction of primary targets by sustained and determined attacks using precision bombing methods both visual and radar." Now, as this was "beginning to get results" on the aircraft industry, pressure to use his B-29s for area bombing threatened to negate that progress. Norstad seemed sympathetic, advising Hansell that the aircraft industry was still accorded "overriding priority," and this test fire raid, he repeated, was only "a special requirement resulting from the necessity of future planning." Hansell agreed to schedule the mission as soon as possible. This promise was made on December 21, three days after LeMay's B-29s had put a large section of Hankow, China, to the torch.

On December 22 Hansell could only find seventy-eight B-29s, which did not fulfill Norstad's request, and the mission was flown as a daylight

Captain Howard Clifford's The Dragon Lady *was rammed by a fighter over Nagoya on December 22; the attack sheared the top* *off the tail. Clifford made it back to Saipan, but the airplane never flew combat again. (Reineke)*

precision attack. The weather was foul, and only forty-eight B-29s bombed the Mitsubishi plant, by radar. The 498th Group's performance that day was typical of the problems that bedeviled Hansell. One of their squadrons had four of nine aircraft abort, and the leader of that formation decided less than an hour from the target that there were too few aircraft to justify proceeding. Based on what appeared to be misinformation from other crew members. he made two complete turns to allow what was reported to be a straggler to catch up, although the five-aircraft formation was reasonably intact at all times. During the second turn the formation broke up because of complete confusion as to what was happening. The other two 498th Squadrons, one with six aircraft, the other with seven, proceeded to the target, but the second of these formations followed a course well west and north of the initial point. They dropped

Ponderous Peg's luck finally ran out on February 25. At fifteen hundred feet, in perfectly clear conditions, another B-29 crashed into her from slightly above and behind. Ponderous Peg *appeared to dis-integrate and crashed to the water, exploding and sinking almost immediately. The other B-29 appeared to recover momentarily, then it too went down. Both crews were lost. (Reineke)*

by dead reckoning, and while no photos were available, an analysis of radarscope photos indicated that their bombs fell forty miles to the left of the target and thirty miles short.

Perhaps the greatest boost to morale from this mission was provided by the 497th's Major Fred Trickey, in *Ponderous Peg* that day. Hit by fighters near the target, the right inboard engine began giving trouble during violent evasive action. They feathered the engine and fought their way out, beginning the long trip home on three engines. Getting close to Iwo Jima, the right outboard engine caught fire, and a stream of flame licked back as far as the tail. The extinguishers took care of the fire, but the engine was gone. They thought they would have to ditch, as *Ponderous Peg* wallowed and dropped away to one side. They started throwing equipment overboard, and after losing thirteen thousand feet were able to level off at seven thousand. Trickey and the pilot, Lieutenant Keith Whitaker, did a beautiful job of fighting the lopsided pull of the two engines on their left wing. Their landing was perfect, and a B-29 had made it home with two engines gone.

The last mission for the year was yet another trip to target No. 357,

The Wichita Witch, from the 498th Group, was destroyed during the last major Japanese attack on Saipan, on Christmas night in 1944.

Musashino at Tokyo, on December 27. By any "reasonable standards" the mission was a failure. Slightly over half the Superforts bombed the primary and again inflicted minor damage. The mission was bad from the beginning for the 498th Group: One plane lost an engine on takeoff, attempted to jettison its bombs, struggled to regain altitude, but ditched in the strait between Saipan and Tinian. Only three crewmen were rescued. And it got worse. All three losses that day were from the 498th. One was *Uncle Tom's Cabin,* with Major John Krause. Leading the third element of a tight formation of nine planes on the run from Mount Fuji to Tokyo, *Uncle Tom's Cabin* was singled out. A minute before bombs away a fighter raced in, head on and slightly high, with its guns winking. His fire blew the top blister away, probably killing the CFC gunner. The fighter kept coming, and its wing tore the B-29 open like a knife from the nose to the leading edge of the wing, killing or wounding the pilot, engineer, and radio operator. The three-foot-wide gash spewed a great sheet of brilliant flame, and parts and equipment were flying out of the stricken B-29. For thirty seconds she held formation before dropping out, losing speed and altitude so quickly that the other B-29s could not slow down enough.

Lieutenant Philip Webster in *Pocahontas* left the formation, turning back to intercept the fighters and cover the crippled bomber. The fighters came from every direction. About a minute after the first mortal attack, *Uncle Tom's Cabin* was reportedly rammed again from the right, which smashed away an engine and part of the wing. The B-29 was at twenty-eight thousand feet and going down quickly when another reported ramming occurred. The Superfort still refused to die—it went into a spin, recovered, and took up a parallel course below the rest of the squadron, but thirty fighters were still after her. Finally, about seven minutes after the first attack, she went out of control and plummeted straight down. There were no chutes, and minutes later a column of smoke rose from the ground a few miles northwest of Tokyo Bay. Other planes confirmed that at least nine fighters were shot down by Krause's crew.

Webster shook off the fighters, continued on to the target, and ultimately got *Pocahontas* home on three engines. The third loss that day was *The Heat's On*, ditched with the loss of all but four men after the fuel-transfer system failed.

The test incendiary mission that Washington wanted was run on January 3, when nearly one hundred B-29s took off to strike Nagoya. They were carrying a mixed load of bombs—incendiary clusters fused to open at eight thousand feet, and a fragmentation cluster that would burst open a thousand feet below the release altitude. Less than sixty planes hit the primary target area, and although there were fires there was no conflagration. Later in the day, other B-29s were sent to the target, their bomb bays full of frags to kill the firemen at their work.

Pocahontas was a lucky airplane, and built one of the most impressive records in the 498th Group. She made the first Tokyo mission, and the last mission of the war—a total of fifty-six. (Prunuske)

Blister gunner James Krantz dangles from American Maid, twenty-nine thousand *feet over Japan. Krantz, previously a ma-* *chinist, had developed his safety rig from an old parachute harness. It worked. (Reineke)*

In Captain John Bartlett's *American Maid* the left blister gunner, Sergeant James Krantz, was wearing a special safety belt he had designed, after seeing what happened on a previous mission when a top blister blew. He knew his blister was "plenty big enough" for him to go through. In the target area the B-29s were hit by up to one hundred interceptors, including Nicks, Irvings, Tonys, and Tojos. *American Maid*'s tail gunner, Sergeant Donald Wilson, got a confirmed kill on a Japanese fighter, but a few minutes later, during the bomb run, he was in trouble. He was shooting at one fighter when another slipped in from above. Two cannon shells slammed into the B-29. One hit in front of Wilson and over his head, and the other hit right behind him, driving a chunk of shrapnel into his chute pack. At the same time a smaller-caliber bullet tore one of the fingers from his left hand.

Krantz was never sure exactly what happened: "It might have been the release of pressure from the hits in the tail position," he said. "Or maybe one of the shell fragments or a piece of flak hit my blister. Anyway, the whole blister blew out and I followed it right out, head first.

"One minute I was at my station and the next I was flying through space. The first thing I felt was a terrific jerk as my belt caught me by the shoulders. I managed to jam my left foot in the edge of the blister hole as I went out. My other foot and my head were hanging down. I bounced once against the side of the plane as the wind hit me. My .45 fell out of its holster and the wind peeled off my gloves and tore away my oxygen mask just as if it hadn't been fastened on. The cold was terrific. For a second there I was sort of dazed, but I wasn't too scared . . . I can remember struggling against the wind to get back in. The next thing I knew, I was inside the plane and the copilot and CFC man were giving me oxygen."

Krantz did not get the whole story until later. He had been "dangling like an old rag," but most of the crew were too busy to get to him immediately. The first ones were the copilot, Lieutenant Franklin Crowe, and Sergeant Alvin Hart, the CFC gunner. Crowe leaned out and grabbed at him, but the only thing he could get was the shoulder-holster strap. He tried to pull Krantz in, but couldn't. After a few more agonizing minutes, the bombardier came back to help, and among the three of them they somehow turned Krantz around and grabbed one of the straps of his safety harness and got him inside the plane. He had been out there for about fifteen minutes, buffeted by the freezing slipstream.

All the way home to Saipan Krantz was given morphine and plasma to stop him from going into shock. His shoulder was dislocated and his hands had been badly frostbitten, but he was one of the lucky ones.

Less lucky that day was Major Barney Hurlbutt and his 500th Group crew. Returning crews reported that a damaged fighter had slammed into the aircraft in the vicinity of the No. 3 engine. The B-29 lurched but stayed under control before it peeled from formation and lost altitude, going into a flat spin and crashing into the ground south of Nagoya. No chutes were seen, but the tail gunner was found safe in a Japanese prison camp after the war.

The fighter that slammed into Hurlbutt's plane was not damaged. Lieutenant Minoru Shirota, pilot and writer, had meticulously planned his heroic death. Six miles below, on a rooftop, one of his friends had filmed the scene. His sacrifice made the newspaper headlines next morning.

The lucky and the luckless . . . the Nagoya mission had cost five B-29s, but part of the crew of the 497th's *Jumbo* was found by Captain Lampley's crew while they were taking *Gonna Mak'er* on a test hop and undertook an unauthorized search for their squadronmates. They found a life raft containing the airplane commander, Captain Howard Clifford, and three

The 499th Group's Wugged Wascal *near Fuji on January 9, with Captain Kimmel Murphy and his crew. A few hours after this* *photo was taken she crashed into the sea, less than seven hundred miles from Saipan. (Reineke)*

Captain Walter "Waddy" Young and his crew bringing the art on their plane to life. On January 9, Waddy's Wagon *was flying in No. 2 position when the No. 3 aircraft,* Miss Behavin', *was rammed.*

Young radioed to the formation leader to "slow this formation down; I'm going to ride herd on Crowell." Both planes disappeared into the clouds, then Young radioed that he was ditching.

others, and the tail gunner was found the next day. Five of the eleven crew had been saved.

As an incendiary test, Nagoya was not conclusive, but it did give the Japanese a false impression that their fire-prevention methods and equipment were adequate.

On January 9 the B-29s took off in the middle of a rain squall as Hansell returned to precision bombing. Again the target was Musashino, and wind whipped the formations so badly that only eighteen of the more than seventy B-29s bombed the primary target. Six planes were the cost of yet another ineffective mission to No. 357, and half the losses were from the 497th Group: Major Joe Baird and his crew, Captain Walter Young in *Waddy's Wagon,* and Lieutenant Ben Crowell in *Miss Behavin'*— over the target Lieutenants Sukeyuki Tange and Shoichi Takayama of the 244th *Sentai* had slammed their Tony fighters into Crowell's B-29, wrecking it. Tange had sacrificed his life, but Takayama survived. Search crews went out the next day to look for survivors of ditchings, but all they found was a nacelle door four hundred miles from Japan.

A mission to the Mitsubishi factory at Nagoya, target No. 194, was flown on January 14, but again the results were not good. Yet another B-29 proved how much punishment they could take and still get home: The 498th's *Lass'ie Come Home*, flown by Lieutenant Wagner Dick, had a back-firing engine over the target. Then a fighter set fire to another engine, which burned for fifteen minutes. The radio and the oxygen system were shot out, three crewmen were wounded, and the center section of the B-29 was afire. Captain Tom Kuenning tried to maneuver his B-29 to give some protection, but lost *Lass'ie Come Home* in the overcast. Dick fixed the engine fire by diving the B-29 and blowing it out. The malfunctioning No. 4 engine had lost most of its power, and the prop was windmilling on the shot-up No. 1 engine. The fighters were able to casually rake the B-29 with gunfire from one end to the other. It took both pilots all their strength to keep her on course, and it felt as if the aircraft were falling to pieces.

Dick said, "The right gunner reported he had been hit. I told one of my men to give him first aid but he too was wounded and fire had broken out in his compartment. We were then at about twenty-three thousand feet and the oxygen system failed. The CFC gunner reported he was wounded. Major Hugh Mahoney, an observer, crawled all over the plane helping with first aid. Someone said something about ditching the plane and Mahoney said, 'Don't talk about ditching — *Lass'ie*'s going home.'

"Kuenning's plane covered us and the Japs were not coming in any more. He really saved our lives. Our radio was shot out. I didn't know it then but our rudders were held on by only one strand. Without oxygen we were forced to drop to about nine thousand feet and lost Kuenning in the soup. The No. 4 engine picked up some power in the lower altitude, off-setting the drag of the windmilling No. 1. Then No. 3 started leaking oil. The No. 2 was hit by flak fragments but was undamaged. Sparks flew from the windmilling prop and the hub became so hot from friction that it glowed in the darkness. The left gunner said he thought it was the moon coming up when he saw the reflection of the white-hot glow. Halfway home the propeller flew into space. Shortly afterward the plane broke out of cloud, and the navigator, Lieutenant John Prince, made his first celestial fixes and announced in pleased tones, 'We are halfway home already — we ought to make it after all.' The engineer transferred the fuel from the useless No. 1 into the tanks of the good engines to get just enough gasoline to get home. The fuel system fortunately was about the only undamaged part of the plane."

As *Lass'ie Come Home* limped through the darkness, three men on Saipan had not given her up. They were Major Tom Kuenning; Colonel Boris Zubko, the 874th Squadron commander; and Major Edward Lass, who named the plane and flew her on her early missions. She made it, so badly damaged that she would never fly again.

*   *   *

Following the Nagoya failures the crews were informed that they would have ground school eight hours a day, five days a week, and that a mission would not count unless 40 per cent of the bombs fell within the target area. Ray Ebert drily noted in his diary, "At this rate we will be here for the duration."

Lass'ie Come Home's survival on January 16 was partly credited to a bottle of Canadian Club whiskey, the "Dissolution of Evolution," which was carried in the airplane. When she staggered back to Saipan, so badly damaged that she could never fly again, the bottle was taken to the squadron commander's office and "fittingly interred." (Prunuske)

An attack on the Kawasaki Aircraft Industries Company, flown January 19, was a bright spot in this "litany of failure." Near Akashi, a village twelve miles west of Kobe on the Inland Sea, this plant built Nick and Randy fighters and engines for the Oscar, Frank, and Tony. Hansell got sixty-two B-29s over the target, where the weather was good. The lead bombardier was the 497th Group's Captain Bill Duffield, who won a "handful" of Distinguished Flying Crosses for accurate bombing. There were no losses, and intelligence officers believed that 38 per cent of the roof area of the target showed major damage. The results were much, much better. Every important building had been hit, and production was decimated by 90 per cent. Kawasaki dispersed the machine tools to other plants. This was the first truly successful 73rd Wing strike, and it had been flown strictly according to the doctrine Hansell championed. Yet his time had already run out, and on the following day he was succeeded by General Curtis LeMay.

The decision could not have been easy for Arnold, who had rewarded Hansell's brilliance, diligence, and loyalty as his top planner with the most important bomber command of the war. But Hansell was not getting the B-29s over the target, and Arnold was becoming progressively disenchanted. The arduous battle to keep the B-29s away from the theater commanders, the staking of his own prestige on this first truly strategic bomber—and the results were just not coming. The reasons mattered little. Arnold decided to give LeMay the job.

Late in December 1944 Hansell had released a statement that included the words, "We have not put all our bombs exactly where we wanted to put them and therefore we are not by any means satisfied with what we have done so far. We are still in our early, experimental stages. . . ." The three major targets had been damaged, but "not destroyed by a damn sight," as Hansell reportedly told war correspondents. The official statement annoyed Arnold, particularly the part about "early, experimental stages." Less than two weeks earlier, a newspaper story out of LeMay's command in India had asserted that "the experimental phase of B-29 operations is over."

General Lauris Norstad arrived on Guam on January 6, and LeMay flew in from Chengtu the next day. As Hansell told his public-relations officer, Colonel St. Clair McKelway: "LeMay is coming here to take over this command. I'm out. . . ." It was a difficult situation—Norstad and Hansell had worked together for years, both involved in the development of the doctrine that had so far failed. Norstad's mission, to relieve Hansell of perhaps the best job in the Air Force, was not a happy one. Norstad

The doctrine of strategic bombardment was personified by this strike on the Kawasaki plant at Akashi. The photo was taken from the 500th Group's Fancy Detail. (Reineke)

said to Hansell: "LeMay is an operator, the rest of us are planners. That's all there is to it."

LeMay took General Roger Ramey, Hansell's chief of staff, back to India to take over the 20th Bomber Command, then arrived back on Guam to assume his new command on January 20. With him he brought a small group of officers, a Lucite name plate, a walnut tobacco humidor, a letter opener made from a B-29 throttle, and a leather folder containing pictures of his wife and daughter.

The strain showed on Hansell. Before dinner on his final night McKelway recalled that Hansell had two glasses of sherry instead of one, and sang, to guitar accompaniment, "Old pilots never die, never die, never die, they just fly-y-y away-y-y."

LeMay kept in the background, saying little, until Hansell left. During the farewell ceremony LeMay smoked his pipe, hiding it in his pants pocket when the band played "The Star-spangled Banner."

Before leaving the Marianas, Hansell wrote a ten-page letter to Arnold that drew attention to the relative performance of the 58th and 73rd wings, which he felt made his B-29s not "look too bad." He felt his major challenges were implanting a belief in precision bombing by daylight, improving the "deplorable" bombing accuracy, reducing the number of ditching losses, improving air-sea rescue, and reducing the abort rate, which had topped 20 per cent and was a real problem. The 73rd Wing Abort Board considered such "questionable" aborts as, in one case, a copilot's "severe headache." Morale in the 73rd was low.

Hansell believed he had driven his crews too hard, and his letter was a blanket answer to any criticism of his command, spoken or unspoken. Hap Arnold was an impatient man, and Hansell had not been getting the results he expected, the results he demanded.

Hansell never considered switching his B-29s to medium- or low-level bombing. He states, "My operations were in daylight, since the targets required precision bombing and our radar bombing equipment did not, at that time, permit night or cloud-cover bombing. Our force, operating alone and unescorted, took advantage of all their technical superiorities in order to overcome Japanese fighter opposition. The margin of Japanese fighter performance was least at very high altitude. I did not anticipate the extremely high wind velocities above thirty thousand feet and they came as a very disagreeable surprise."

Hansell intended to lower the bombing altitudes as far as possible to improve accuracy, and the Akashi mission had been flown at around twenty-five thousand feet. He did not contemplate bombing below twenty thousand feet, where enemy flak made them "at least apprehensive," and cloud cover was one problem that could not be solved by merely lowering the altitudes. Hansell did not feel that LeMay got the breaks, but with a steady inflow of more and better B-29s, and the imminent capture of Iwo Jima, the situation would improve automatically.

Service groups provided much of the maintenance for the B-29s, and an important element were the technical representatives from Boeing, Wright Aeronautical, Minneapolis-Honeywell, General Electric, and others. One Boeing tech. rep. with the 73rd Wing was Dick Morgan. He had worked on the design of the B-29 power plant and had argued at the time that the cowls were not properly designed, but had been "overruled." When he got to the Pacific he told everyone not to let the enlisted men know that the R. M. Morgan on the power-plant drawings was he.

The Akashi mission was "a source of great satisfaction" to Hansell, because "it proved a point — it *was* possible to destroy selected targets in Japan through selective precision bombing."

Had Akashi come earlier, perhaps at Musashino, Hansell feels that the doctrine might have survived a little longer, but does not think his commanding the 21st Bomber Command was "in the cards." There had been great pressure from the theater commanders to get the B-29s out of China, and LeMay was by then senior to Hansell and had a great deal more operational experience. Hansell was asked to stay on as vice commander but "would have been unhappy as a fifth wheel."

General Hansell confesses to a personal revulsion to area incendiary bombing, but his principal aversion to it stemmed from his unshakable belief that selective bombing of "vital industrial and social systems" was a much more effective approach.

Hansell may have stuck too rigidly to the book—the book he helped to write—but he did not have a lot of luck.

*   *   *

LeMay's early missions did not reveal any miraculous improvement. A strike against Nagoya's Mitsubishi engine factory on January 23 ran into clouds so dense that only twenty-eight B-29s bombed.

An attack on target No. 357 on January 27 was also ruined by weather, but developed into the most savage fighter-vs.-bomber battle of the B-29s' war. That day the 500th Group was directed to send out two weather planes, with a 73rd Wing command pilot, to broadcast target selection for the aircraft en route. Seven combat squadrons were to bomb either Musashino or Mitsubishi at Nagoya, depending on which was clear. If weather was similar at both, the attack would be on Musashino. Another innovation on this mission that lifted morale was the introduction of "Superdumbos," two 498th Group B-29s with extra radios and survival gear, which would assist B-29s in trouble.

January 27 was also the last day the 73rd Wing would go to Japan alone. For the next mission they would be joined by the 313th Wing from Tinian. The 73rd's experience would remain unique.

No aircraft bombed the primary, but 62 plowed through an estimated 900 fighter attacks over half of which were hurled at the 497th Bomb Group. It was estimated that 350 enemy planes attacked, and the B-29s claimed 60 as shot down. Actual Japanese losses were apparently about a quarter of that figure, but they claimed 28 B-29s destroyed, and only 5 were actually lost to enemy action. The statistics matter little.

The 497th, leading the wing, was first over Japan. The initial point was Kofu, about seventy miles west of Tokyo. Seventeen B-29s crossed the coast and turned to make their bomb run, led by Colonel Robert Morgan in *Dauntless Dotty*. Captain James Lampley was leading the 871st Squadron, with bombardier Ray Ebert in the nose, with his diary: "It gave me a sort of warm feeling to see the Padre out there at the end of the runway giving absolution as each plane went down the strip. . . . We are leading our formation with Peterson in the *Ghastly Goose* riding our right wing and Walker on our left in *Sweat 'er Out.* . . . At 1300 we passed over two Jap destroyers so I imagine our arrival will be no surprise. . . ."

The Japanese were waiting. Droves of fighters of all types were in the air. Not all of them waited for the B-29s to reach their target. Just as the first formation broke into sight of the coast five fighters came in and fired a few bursts, as if to raise the curtain on the two-hour battle. Then they pulled away, probably reporting the altitude, speed, and size of the bomber force.

The 497th was in a fight as it wheeled around Hamamatsu and headed for Kofu. Nearly two hundred Japanese Army and Navy fighters—Tojos, Tonys, Franks, Nicks, Oscars, Jacks, Irvings, Zekes—rose to meet the B-29s. It was a maximum defense effort.

Twenty-four-year-old Captain Teruhiko Kobayashi, commanding the 244th *Sentai,* would become the top Superfortress killer, with ten to his credit. On January 27 he was going for his sixth.

Kobayashi steered his red-tailed, mottled-green Tony toward the first formation as it was between Mount Fuji and Tokyo. Two B-29s had already gone down. He fired at the lead bomber, without result, then rammed the next B-29 in the formation. His Tony spun down, Kobayashi unconscious in the wrecked fighter. At about twelve thousand feet he came to and bailed out. Kobayashi's wingman was killed ramming another B-29, but three others survived, although one was seriously wounded.

The fighters hit the 497th in ones, twos, and threes, some from below, others diving vertically through the formation.

Flames licked the loaded bomb bay of *Haley's Comet,* which had taken both flak and fighter damage. She shuddered and lost speed. Lieutenant Walter McDonnell tried to urge the aircraft forward to gain the protection of the formation. It dropped back once more and was last seen veering to the north toward the protection of cloud banks.

The fighters pounced on Captain Elmer Hahn's *Werewolf,* which was straggling. The bomb bay was afire and the B-29 was ripped in two by a huge explosion. The front half of the plane, enveloped in flames, plunged quickly to earth, while the rear section seemed to float in the air. Then it too exploded.

As the others ground toward the target they were flying through a sky full of gunfire and the litter of battle. Fighters dashed themselves against streams of machine-gun fire. Some B-29 gunners burned out their barrels; in other planes ammunition was running out in some turrets, caus-

The 497th's Haley's Comet *went down on January 27. After the war, the only two 497th survivors found in prison camps were the radar operator and tail gunner from this airplane. (Prunuske)*

Shady Lady, Haley's Comet, Wheel'n' Deal, Texas Doll, *and* Peace on Earth *all carried paintings by the 497th's John Albright. (Prunuske)*

ing the pilots to maneuver their planes to bring working guns to bear on their target.

The formation rounded Kofu and bore down on Tokyo. Then Captain Raymond Dauth's *Shady Lady* was hit. She lurched, tried to swing back into formation, but instead plunged slowly out of place, her crew trying desperately to control a raging fire. She continued to hold formation for a while but was never seen or heard from again.

The 870th Squadron had entered the battle with four planes, and now only one survived, Colonel Robert "Pappy" Haynes' *Thumper*. "They were waiting for us," said bombardier Raleigh Phelps. "We figured out that more than one hundred passes were made at *Thumper*—I counted fifty-seven from the nose quarter alone. They barreled in without letup, usually alone, but sometimes in bunches. Some bored in to within four hundred yards and then turned off. But others really pressed the attack, clearing us by inches. They went down in droves, but the rest kept coming. We downed six and damaged at least a dozen."

Thumper was in trouble, with an engine out and alone. The blister gunners described one episode in the battle: "Four Tonys were playing tag just out of range. They wouldn't close but they were damned annoying. Finally Pappy got sore. 'Hang on, boys, we're going after those bastards.' We'd barely started banking to dive into 'em when we saw what the game was—about thirty more Tonys began boring in from the opposite side. God, it was a warm five minutes that followed."

Captain Lloyd Avery's *Irish Lassie* was rammed in quick succession by two fighters. A Zeke came rocketing down from directly above—the CFC gunner, Sergeant James McHugh, had six guns on it but it slammed into the left wing behind the No. 1 engine, tearing away eight feet of aileron, and mangling a gas tank so badly that fuel splashed out. The engine somehow kept working. The crew had four fighters to their credit as they held to their bomb run. More bullets ripped into *Irish Lassie,* wounding the radio operator.

Lieutenant Robert Watson, the flight engineer, said, "There was surprisingly little jolt when the Jap hit us, and our navigator didn't even know we'd been rammed . . . thought we'd lost an engine for sure. However, I glanced at my instruments and found that it was still in good running order. To keep it in operation, I immediately transferred enough fuel from the damaged gas tank into another tank so that the level of the fuel in the cell was below the point of the leak. Then I fed it back to keep the engine going."

Irish Lassie was about to unload her bombs when the tail gunner, Sergeant Charles Mulligan, called, "Jack at six o'clock again . . . this baby's really coming in!" Mulligan was shouting. "He's low. Coming in fast."

As Mulligan kept his thumbs on his triggers a bullet clipped his right hand, but he kept firing, ripping pieces from the enemy fighter. It seemed just inches away when he flung his arms over his face. The Jack crashed into the tail compartment and *Irish Lassie* lurched sickeningly. The whole left side of the tail compartment was torn away, the left stabilizer was gone, and all the control cables on Avery's side of the plane were cut.

As *Irish Lassie* lost height the fighters followed her. Copilot Leonard Fox tried the controls on his side of the plane and found he could pull her out, and slowly but surely brought *Irish Lassie* under control.

Past the target, *Thumper*'s worst half hour was just beginning, a silent, frightening duel that nearly finished her. Breaking out of the fight, Haynes headed for home, and shook off all the fighters except one. But that one clung on with grim determination. *Thumper*'s aft turrets were empty and the fighter was apparently also out of ammunition. Yet he stayed with the B-29, making slow, delicate passes, trying to clip the B-29's great tail with his propeller. The quiet contest lasted for a hundred miles, pilot against pilot. Haynes' tail and blister gunners stayed at their posts, sometimes almost whispering as they reported the Tony's movements over the interphone. Up front Haynes waited and at the precise moment the Tony edged in he would shear *Thumper* away, right or left, up or down, keeping the B-29's graceful tail away from the whirling scythe of the Tony's prop. Finally the Japanese fighter gave up and turned back.

The fighters had followed *Irish Lassie* until she was sixty miles out to sea. Back in the shattered tail, Mulligan had managed to slap on an oxygen mask before he passed out. The hole in the plane was large enough for him to have fallen through, but jagged metal had caught his clothes and was holding him in.

The battered 497th had been hit hardest, but the other groups had not escaped a mauling. Leading the 500th Group formation of eleven planes was Major Robert J. Fitzgerald, with the group commander, Colonel Jack Dougherty, aboard. The formation was not good on the bomb run and the fighter attacks were increasing in fury. Lieutenant Frank "Chico" Carrico was flying *Pride of the Yankees* and just at the time of bombs away a Tony came straight in from above the B-29's left wing, riddling the No. 2 engine. Copilot Lieutenant Morris Robinson was flying the plane because they were on the left side of the formation, and Carrico told him to stay at the controls and hold tight. Carrico said, "At the time I'm trying to feather the damn thing, and naturally it won't feather. It's burning good by this time and I yelled to my flight engineer to cut it off and pull the extinguisher, but the whole gear came out of his panel. I thought our goose was cooked but just about that time the prop ran away and blew the fire completely out of the No. 2 nacelle. . . . We had another attack on the nose, which shot out two large plastic glass panels and put a bullet through the side, which came under my instrument panel and went between my feet. . . . My bombardier was wounded, leaving our nose unprotected in the level position and the fighters must have realized, because after we dropped out of formation we received nine concentrated attacks on the nose. We had a wind blowing through the nose compartment that I thought would surely freeze us. We had on jackets, gloves, and boots, but our legs were freezing to death. So we gathered flak suits, maps, paper, and anything else we could find to wrap around our legs. . . . One man would fly a few minutes and start shivering so much he couldn't stay at the controls, so we kept switching."

Captain Horace Hatch's plane was also in trouble, at about the same time. After ducking an attempted ramming by inches, his plane took a hit from an explosive bullet, and fragments dug into the pilot's left foot and started a cockpit fire. Major Robert Fitzgerald's plane dropped down out of formation and swung back to protect the 500th's two cripples. Slipping between them and the fighters, he drew the fire from them.

About an hour from the mainland Fitzgerald left them, and Hatch, with his own troubles under control, told Carrico he would see *Pride of the Yankees* home. Carrico continued, "I told my copilot to fly until the prop

Pride of the Yankees *was taken overseas by Captain Cecil Tackett and his crew. The artwork was painted by the 882nd Squadron draftsman, Corporal Henry Johnson, who signed himself as "The Drowsy Swede." (Tackett)*

Pride of the Yankees, *the way Carrico brought her back. She was the proud holder of a unique record: Carrico got her home to Saipan on two engines on January 27, then*

Tackett *brought her back from another mission with both outboard engines out. She was the only B-29 on Saipan to make the trip home twice on two engines. (Tackett)*

came off so I could watch and see where it went. . . . I had all the men out of the navigator's compartment and in their ditching positions. . . . The prop came off but the metal in the nose section had melted on the inboard side and the prop peeled off the inboard side in a flat position. It held there an instant and then went hurtling into the No. 1 engine. It damaged the mount braces, and all four blades on No. 1 prop bent almost double. It would not feather and the vibration was terrific. The left wing was vibrating through an arc of about twenty feet and I had the crew ready to bail out again, and was just pressing the mike switch when the damn thing feathered.

"We didn't have enough gas to make it and all we had to navigate with were a map and a pencil. An hour and fifteen minutes out of base we were picking up islands north of Saipan . . . we were short ten minutes of gas. I called Captain Hatch and told him we couldn't make it and got the crew to their ditching positions. Then my engineer called up and said he had found seventy-five more gallons of gas in the center wing section tank. We screwed up our hopes again and came on in." They made it.

The mission cost the 498th Group two B-29s: Captain Pierce Kilgo left the formation shortly after bombs away with two engines out and a pack of fighters tearing at his plane; Lieutenant William Beyhan's B-29 also had two engines out, his electrical system was wrecked, and he could not transfer fuel. Six men in rafts were sighted where Beyhan ditched, one hundred miles north of Iwo, but they were never found.

By the time the 499th Group had climbed to bombing altitude, three of their twelve B-29s had aborted. Lieutenant Prentiss Burkett was flying *Tokyo Twister* in "coffin corner" and remembers, "Things went well until we turned on our run over the initial point . . . the Japanese fighters were many and very aggressive. It seemed that at least one of our turrets was firing for the entire run. As we neared the target the fighters broke off and the flak started . . . thick and more accurate than I had ever seen it over Japan before.

"After we dropped our bombs we felt the aircraft lurch and the right gunner called to report a flak hit on the right wing behind the No. 3 engine. He reported that a large piece of metal came loose from the wing . . . the whole nacelle behind No. 3 engine was gone but no grave damage done to the aircraft."

One of the other 499th aircraft was hit over the target and lost speed and altitude as both outboard engines began to smoke . . . a swarm of fighters followed her all the way down. The B-29 seemed to be attempting to ditch in a large lake.

In *Tokyo Twister* Burkett had reached the coast "in fairly good shape," but his gunners were either low on ammunition, or completely out in some guns.

Burkett says, "As we turned to the right off the coast, a Japanese fighter was reported off our right wing. By the time our turn was completed the fighter was reported at two o'clock and a little high. When he was reported at one o'clock he started his run. All guns that could bear on him attempted to fire, but only one gun in the upper forward turret was firing. As the fighter passed we felt a decompression explosion and I smelled cordite. At the same time I had a sharp pain in my neck near the shoulder, and a burning sensation on my rear section. I saw the copilot, Rid Pace, slump forward on the wheel and called on interphone that Rid had been hit. The bombardier, Ed Kasun, looked back and stood up to push Rid off the controls. The next action came fast as the engineer reported that No. 3 was out, no manifold pressure, so I told him to feather it. It would not feather. We were losing power and had to leave the formation and head for ten thousand feet as we were depressurizing and thought we were on three engines. As we neared ten thousand the engineer reported the manifold pressure was coming up and soon we were back on four engines. The engine only had the turbosupercharger knocked out.

"At this time we were resting fairly easy. Rid had been laid out on the nosewheel door and had received a shot of morphine for the pain. He had lost quite a bit of blood and we thought he should have some blood plasma, but no one thought he could do the job right so we abandoned the idea.

"About five hundred miles off the coast of Japan, No. 1 quit and it was feathered. Now we had three engines and it was getting near sunset. We were not in very good shape with an injured copilot if we had to ditch, so we started trying to contact someone from the formation. We finally did contact another crew and gave them our position. After some time they thought they were near us and asked us to turn on our landing lights. They saw them and we joined in behind them.

"We set up for landing and the bombardier sat in the right seat to help as much as possible. The engineer reported the regular hydraulic system was inoperative but that the emergency system was pressurized. Also, when the wheels came down, the right gunner reported the outer tire on that side was flat, but the inner tire appeared good.

"We declared an emergency before landing and the runway should have been clear for us, but after touchdown, about the time the nose-

Lieutenant Prentiss Burkett, by the crumpled nosewheel of Tokyo Twister. *(Burkett)*

wheel was on the ground, I saw an aircraft taxiing across in front of us. I hit the emergency lever and slowed enough to let the aircraft pass. Then I found to my amazement the emergency system had one, and only one, shot in it and then it was gone; no brakes and still moving seventy to eighty miles per hour. I thought maybe we would go over the cliff at the end of the runway and into the drink. By kicking left rudder as hard as possible while we still had enough speed left, the rudder was effective and we finally got off the runway and into the rough between the runways. When we started hitting the boulders the nosewheel collapsed. I remember seeing Rid Pace being knocked to the overhead when the snap came and pitched into the nosewheel door where he was lying. We finally came to a stop."

In the 497th's *Irish Lassie*, copilot Fox, still in his heavy flak vest and other equipment because he had been unable to leave the controls, coaxed the B-29 in. Then she fell out of control, dropping below the level of the field, heading for a cliff on the approach to Isley. Fox dragged on the wheel but got nothing. He placed his feet on the instrument panel and gave a last desperate pull. Something snapped, and *Irish Lassie* came up quickly, cleared the embankment and banged down on the field. The

Lloyd Avery's Irish Lassie, *survivor of a double ramming on January 27, 1945. (Bob Watson)*

main gear held up but the nosewheel gave way, and came up under the fuselage and burst through inside the nose. She screeched along in a shower of sparks and screaming metal.

The No. 1 engine burst into flames; a wing caught an embankment on the edge of the strip and twisted the plane around violently. The blazing engine was ripped completely from the wing. Finally *Irish Lassie* came to a stop in two pieces, and they too had made it.

Irish Lassie *made it back to one of the most spectacular crash landings of the war. The tail gunner was wedged so tightly into the wreckage of his turret that it took an hour to release him and get him back where he could be given first aid. Approaching Saipan, his* *wounds had begun to bleed as the plane descended into warmer air, and his life was narrowly saved by the crew, who gave him morphine and plasma. Later his hands were amputated because they had been so badly frozen. (Watson)*

The gunners on Captain Carroll Horner's Jumbo II *were credited with destroying nine fighters over Japan on January 27, 1945. (Reineke)*

After bombs away, the remnants of the 497th had swung to the right and begun to head home. Many were damaged, some were crippled. Over the target Captain Dale Peterson's *Ghastly Goose* had been badly shot up, and was losing gasoline from bullet-punctured tanks. Captain Carroll Horner in *Jumbo II* provided cover for Peterson to land's end, and stayed with him until he was finally forced to ditch. Horner circled and accurately established the position, radioed the information to rescue operations, and dropped his own emergency equipment to the survivors before heading for Saipan.

That Saturday night on Saipan the wind and rain washed the blood from the wreck of *Irish Lassie*. The next day, at dawn, B-29s were already scouring the waters off Honshu for Peterson's crew. *Ghastly Goose* had made one of the most perfect ditchings: Crewmen had been seen standing on the wings as the bomber rocked in the water, and crawling into life rafts. Then for five days a storm tore along Japan's eastern coast, and no trace of the crew was ever found.

On Sunday morning there were also dour thoughts: The 498th Group War Diary noted that the men were getting "most skeptical" of target No. 357, after "one of the least successful attacks to date."

As January ended, morale was very low. The odds did not look good for survival—some 73rd Wing airmen kept morbid, detailed accounts of the thinning of their ranks. It had once been natural to talk about the future; now the crews had to come to terms with the fact that tomorrow the world and the war might well be going on without them.

New Blood

North Field on Tinian had been built by the 6th Naval Construction Brigade with relative speed, and aircraft and personnel of General John "Skippy" Davies' 313th Wing had started to arrive in December 1944. By the beginning of 1945 two groups, Colonel James Connally's 504th, less its 393rd Squadron (which had been selected for another job), and Colonel Robert Ping's 505th, were in place, but the 6th and 9th groups would not be there until late February. Hansell had felt that the 504th and 505th were so lacking in unit training that he started them on a four-to-five-week program. Early in February they looked ready to be sent to one of Japan's less violent targets.

On January 28 LeMay had himself suggested the command should hit some easier targets, and Norstad assured him he had "fullest latitude."

When the 313th Wing began moving into Tinian, the Seabees who built the bases quickly adopted them. Along with the more usual form of artwork, the B-29s sported the insignia of the construction outfits: spitting *black cats, machine-gunning bees, and so on. This Seabee is guarding one of "their" B-29s: the 504th's* Indian Maid. *(Ed Hering)*

LeMay had thought of bombing Tamashima, but Norstad thought an incendiary attack on Kobe would be more useful; so LeMay's first February mission would be against the port and city area of Kobe, the sixth-largest city in Japan and her most important port.

On February 4 both the 73rd and 313th wings were up, but only sixty-nine planes made it to the target, where the fighters made Kobe anything but an easy target. The 497th had a good bomb run, but plain bad luck ruined it. About two minutes before bombs away the third-element leader was attacked by a fighter, and the bombardier, holding his toggle switch in his left hand and the mike button in his right, intended to call the left blister gunner. He pressed the wrong button, and the bombs tumbled into the ocean. All the 497th's planes except the leader followed suit. The next day Colonel Wright was at the bombardier's interrogation, and his language was colorful. He threatened to have a formation of the

Fighter attacks over Kobe on February 4 finished off Devil's Darlin' *after the bomb-bay doors jammed open and a dangling bomb-bay tank forced her to fall behind the rest of the formation. The pilot, Lieutenant Maurice Malone, was killed instantly by a cannon shell, and the radar operator was badly wounded by another. One engine was hit and would not feather, and all the instruments for the right engines were shot out. The left flap ran partway down, and the tail section was shot up. The copilot, Lieutenant Robert Burton, took over the controls in the bloody cockpit and managed to dive the crippled plane into clouds to escape from the fighters. Another B-29 came down to help and drove the fighters away. Once clear, the navigator helped Burton remove Malone's body and took over a set of controls. The propeller spun off the damaged engine and whirled clear of the plane, and Burton used the automatic pilot to keep the airplane level and on course. Then he con-tacted the pilot of the other B-29, and when he set his No. 1 prop at 2,200 rpm, the flight engineer on* Devil's Darlin' *was able to synchronize his No. 4 prop through its shadow and the shadow of the prop on the other B-29. By this method the engineer was able to work out how much fuel they were using. They finally had to feather the No. 4 engine, and* Devil's Darlin' *struggled along on two. They were sixty miles out from Saipan with fifteen minutes' fuel and fifty feet above the water. The crew prepared for a crash landing. It was nearly midnight, and then both engines died, still fifteen minutes from Saipan. It was so sudden that Burton was still flying the plane by automatic pilot, and the plane settled onto the water before he could take over the controls or the crew could take their ditching positions. Although four men were injured, it was a good ditching: Everybody got out before Malone and* Devil's Darlin' *disappeared beneath the waves. (Francis Ryan)*

bombardiers walking around the base dropping rocks on the leader and yelling "Bombs away!"

However, the overall results of the mission were much better than the Nagoya incendiary "test," and production at Kobe was hurt.

The next target was the Nakajima plant at Ota, with high priority because it was manufacturing the Ki-84 fighter, a very dangerous aircraft, known as "Frank" to the Allies.

The weather at Ota on February 10 was better than expected, but the accuracy was not good. Even so, eleven buildings and seventy-four Franks were destroyed, most of this damage caused by just seven incendiaries. Losses were grim—a dozen B-29s—and the 505th Group suffered a disastrous second Empire mission. It began when "*Jook*" *Girl* crashed on takeoff. Eighteen of their aircraft reached Japan, and they ran into their first opposition near landfall. From the initial point to the target they were victims of concentrated fighter attacks from out of the sun. The first squadron bore the brunt of the onslaught, which continued through meager, inaccurate flak. Some attacks came in pairs, and after bombs away one succeeded in dislodging *Sassy Lassy* from the formation. A fighter roared in from eleven o'clock high as if intending to ram, but it pulled up short and curved above the B-29. To avoid a collision *Sassy Lassy* pulled slightly out of formation, just enough to allow fighters to fly between her and the rest of the B-29s. They finally wedged *Sassy Lassy* completely away, where she was easy prey. The last the 505th saw of her she was under attack by about ten fighters.

About two miles east of the target a white burst or puff of smoke erupted below *Slick's Chick's;* then she collided with another B-29. Both went down, one with no tail, the other missing its nose.

On the way home three more 505th planes were lost, forced to ditch. Lieutenant John Halloran's *The Deacon's Delight* was damaged in both inboard engines after tangling with fighters just past the target. About thirty miles off the coast they had to feather No. 3; then a few minutes later the oil pressure dropped on No. 2, but it would not feather. They jettisoned everything they could, including their shot-up radar set. They made contact with a Superdumbo three hours later, lost it, then regained it. Somewhere down below, in the blackness, there was a rescue ship, and then the crew saw a beam of light shoot into the sky a couple of miles away. It was a searchlight from the rescue ship *Bering Sea*. Halloran had a parachute flare fired, then circled the ship twice with his landing lights on. The ship's searchlights were turned onto the sea, and *The Deacon's Delight* hit the water at over ninety miles an hour, about one thousand

Sometimes the paintings hardly had time to dry. The 505th's "Jook" Girl crashed taking off for Ota on February 10, the group's second Empire mission. (Leonard Carpi)

The 505th's Slick's Chicks was another casualty of the disastrous Ota mission. (Carpi)

The crew of The Deacon's Delight were lucky: They were picked up minutes after ditching. (Carpi)

yards ahead of the ship, parallel to its course. Water rushed into the B-29, filling the cabin to within a foot of the ceiling and the rear section to knee depth, but *The Deacon's Delight* did not sink. It was nearing midnight by the time Halloran and his crew were safe aboard *Bering Sea*, which then riddled the B-29's hulk with cannon fire to sink her. She refused to go down, and the rescue ship finally had to ram her twice before she disappeared beneath the swells.

Bering Sea picked up another entire 505th crew, but four men were lost in the other ditching; that B-29 struck a swell and broke up, the fuselage parted in two places, and the left wing was ripped away.

Two other 505th survivors ran out of gas on the runway when they got back and had to be towed clear, and *Country Gentleman* was damaged when her brakes failed completely as she taxied after landing.

Iwo Jima: Volcanic Godsend

Neither Arnold nor LeMay were keen to use B-29s to provide tactical support for ground or sea operations, but the Iwo Jima campaign was unique in that attacks against Japanese homeland targets could be called indirect support for the amphibious landing there.

Iwo Jima had risen from the sea within living memory, and it was important in several ways. Lying about halfway along the route from the Marianas to Honshu, Iwo played an inordinate role in the operations of the B-29s. In American hands it would protect the Marianas from sneak attack, allow formations of B-29s to proceed directly to Japan without sidestepping Iwo, give them navigational aids, provide a base for friendly fighters, it could be used for staging longer B-29 missions, it could be a base for rescue units, and, most importantly, it would provide an emergency landing field for B-29s in trouble.

The Japanese had built two operational fields on Iwo and were working on a third. While the danger to the B-29 bases was truly minimal, Iwo had been pounded relentlessly as soon as the Liberators had moved up to the Marianas in August 1944. The ugly little island was under attack through October, and as the B-29s began moving to Saipan it had become even more important.

Although the Japanese were able to launch nuisance raids from Iwo, they were in no position to mount a serious offensive. The last large attack on Saipan was on Christmas night in 1944; minor raids had continued during the next week, and enemy planes were seen on Iwo up to early February. The Japanese effort against the B-29 bases amounted to about eighty sorties, and nearly half of these had been lost. Eleven B-29s had been destroyed and others damaged. The Japanese had been fairly effective, killing forty-five men and wounding more than two hundred, and the ledger on the Japanese side was not looking bad. It was a pretty costly nuisance.

Like any commander, General Arnold was "touchy" about seeing planes destroyed while they sat on the ground, the black days of December 1941 etched in his memory. Air-raid precautions were quickly tightened, and Hansell had sent the B-29s to help pound Iwo, with Arnold's wholehearted agreement. The job was then given back to the Liberators, but it became obvious that it was not possible to completely neutralize the island.

The nuisance raids were still not enough to justify an invasion of Iwo Jima—that decision was made a month before the raids began, and the island was invaded seven weeks after they had ended. The decision to take Iwo was based on its potential value rather than its potential danger. For instance, there was no fighter that could fly with the B-29s from Saipan to the Japanese Empire, and the possibility of heavy B-29 losses to new and excellent fighters like the Nakajima Frank had worried Arnold during the early stages of planning for the 21st Bomber Command's operations.

When Nimitz turned against the idea of invading Formosa, he was receptive to an operation aimed at capturing Iwo Jima, and then Okinawa in the Ryukyus. Admiral King of the joint chiefs accepted his view.

On February 15, 1945, as the fast carriers moved in to strike Tokyo and the invasion forces were heading for Iwo Jima, LeMay sent the B-29s on their first indirect-support strike. They went back to Nagoya's Mitsubishi engine works, but hit an unexpected cold front, which completely upset the fairly close formation. Only thirty-three planes ended up bombing the primary, but they were able to inflict a good deal of superficial damage.

The first Marine assault wave hit Iwo northeast of Mount Suribachi on the morning of February 19, and under a barrage of covering fire they were able to gain a strong foothold. By the end of the day thirty thousand Marines were ashore; the 5th Division had driven almost across the island at its narrowest point, but the 4th had been stopped near the edge of Motoyama Airfield No. 1.

On the day of the landings the B-29s were sent to Musashino, in an effort to discourage any reinforcement of Iwo, but cloud cloaked the target

The 6th Group flew its first mission to Japan   flown before markings were fully applied to
on February 19. Often early missions were   the aircraft. (Harry George)

completely. Yet another precision mission cost six B-29s for no worth-
while return. A black Nick rammed Lieutenant Martin Nicholson's 499th
Group aircraft, tearing off a wing, and another broke a 500th Group B-
29 in two over the target. One aircraft ditched on the return trip, another
simply disappeared. Over the target the B-29 piloted by Captain James
Pearson and Lieutenant Ed Porada of the 500th Group was hit by cannon
fire in the right inboard engine. Porada recalls, "We immediately lost all
pressure in this engine's system and could not feather it. The prop
started to windmill and ran completely away. The hub got red-hot, and
soon the prop spun off, falling back and hitting our plane just in front of
the engineer's seat, cutting a gaping hole in that side of the plane. All
controls on the starboard side of the plane were cut. We now had to fly
with one engine completely useless and one at about half power. We had
two good engines on the port side. We flew back to Saipan at approximately five hundred feet above the Pacific crabbing along and hoping
that the fuel would hold out and that the plane would hold together."

They finally made it to Saipan, and made a straight-in approach.

Porada continues, "The plane mushed and wallowed, groaned and strained on the approach, and we got the landing gear down. When the wheels hit the landing strip, we lost all hydraulic pressure and we had no brakes. We went down the runway out of control, and all we could do was cut the port engines. The plane veered off the runway to the left since the one engine on the starboard side was still running at about half power."

The wrecked B-29 slammed into the 497th's *Sky-Scrapper II* on her hardstand, "slicing right through it like it was made of hot butter." They next hit a cletrak with their nosewheel and lost control entirely. "We slid grinding and crunching along, nose on the ground and tail in the air," Porada said. They finally hit a small knoll, which stopped them, and at the same time the plane broke into two pieces where the propeller had sliced it. The crew suffered shock but all survived.

On Iwo Jima the Marines were faced with the job of digging the Japanese out. A Marine intelligence officer noted that the intricate Japanese defense system was probably the result of the tremendous bombardment the island had suffered over the previous six months. It was March 16 before Iwo was secure, and hundreds more Japanese would be killed in last-ditch battles long after that.

A lucky crew from the 500th. Ed Porada, standing third from the left, by the wrecked nose of the "big, beautiful, wonderful" B-29. (Porada)

The rapid development of airfields began immediately. Along the central plateau the Japanese had three strips laid out, all named Motoyama after the neighboring village. They were more simply known as South, Central, and North fields. South had two strips and was developed for fighters and other types; Central had two runways in the form of an X and was developed primarily for staging Superforts en route from the Marianas to Japan.

Three Seabee units went ashore with the Marines to begin work as soon as the fields were taken, but the dogged resistance ruined the schedule. As soon as the fields were captured they were patched up for local fighter use, and on March 4 Iwo paid its first dividend when the 9th Group's Lieutenant Raymond Malo landed his B-29 there.

The island was found to be capable of supporting a larger air establishment than had been anticipated, and a new plan to convert Central Field into a huge airdrome with two B-29 strips, two fighter strips, and a com-

Iwo paid its first dividend quickly. The fighting almost stopped on March 4 as Lieutenant Ray Malo's 9th Group B-29 circled the field. The bomb-bay doors had jammed open over the target and the drag had caused high fuel consumption, and they were unable to use fuel in the reserve tanks. Malo circled three times, then put her down. As the wheels touched the soft, newly rolled strip, they sank, but not enough to throw the B-29's tail over, and in fact acted like additional brakes. Malo stopped her after using only about three thousand feet of runway, and he flew out of the embattled island about two hours later. It was only a lease on life: He and most of his crew were lost on April 16.

bat service center was formed. Airfield construction on the volcanic rock was extraordinarily difficult, and the work went slowly until the commander of the 9th Naval Construction Brigade, in charge of the task, put his Seabees on a schedule of two ten-hour shifts daily.

The Mustangs moved up from Saipan on March 6, and South Field was in continuous use as the construction work went on. More B-29s arrived, some unable to continue on to the Marianas again. LeMay sent a repair team of twelve enlisted men with Major Leonard Sherman in charge, and they began working on the crippled B-29s on South Field, dodging sniper fire, living on cold rations, and sleeping under the wings of planes.

Soon more men were sent up, and Central Field was operational on March 16. That day Colonel William Robinson, LeMay's staff engineer, came to Iwo to look it over with a view to developing it as a B-29 base. He was sure that North and Central fields could be made to serve as many as 150 B-29s. LeMay approved his plans immediately, which involved combining North and Central fields into one massive base covering half the island, with two B-29 runways.

Building airfields on Iwo was complicated; the island was still a semiactive volcano, and sulphurous steam oozed from crevices. Parts of the ground were honeycombed with steam pockets, which meant that they had to be avoided when runways or underground gasoline lines were planned. Although Iwo's volcanic ash was easier to work than coral, it eroded easily when it was wet, and asphalt could only be laid on the base when it was dried out. The heavy rains of spring 1945 held back construction when the surfaces remained wet for up to a week at a time.

*   *   *

Washington was still not ready to turn the B-29s to area incendiary attacks, due to the limited size of the B-29 force, but they were eager for more tests. A week earlier Norstad had reminded LeMay that the two test incendiary missions had been inconclusive and asked for another major incendiary attack.

Norstad liked Nagoya as a target, and a new directive on February 19 moved test fire missions to a higher priority than aircraft assembly plants. LeMay had a maximum strike lined up in support of the Iwo Jima operation on the fourth or fifth day after the landing, with the target either Tokyo or Nagoya, but weather prospects looked good for neither. He decided to send a maximum-effort fire-bomb mission to Tokyo on February 25. This attack, with more than 230 B-29s airborne, was the

Construction of North Field on Guam got under way in November 1944, but amid a constant battle over priorities. After bulldozers had knocked down a tangle of palms, banyans, and cedar trees, and peeled off a three-foot layer of mud, the engineers blasted a huge vein of coral, using a couple of tons of dynamite a day. The first Guam runway was completed on February 2, but two weeks later the area around the hardstands had still not been cleared, so this had to be done by bulldozers before any steps could be taken to provide even the bare necessities for maintenance. These early, unmarked 29th Group aircraft are preparing for their first missions while the clearing work goes on.

largest yet flown, and included aircraft from General Thomas Power's 314th Bomb Wing from Guam. With less than a third of its aircraft, and only part of its shakedown missions completed, it was a gamble, but LeMay was sure the crews would be able to handle the Tokyo mission.

Over the target 172 B-29s unloaded their bombs and burned out nearly a square mile of urban Tokyo, results like nothing accomplished

The 9th Group's Ready Teddy, *at North Field, Tinian. Beside her are five-hundred- pound incendiaries, with their tail fins on the right. (John Swihart)*

before. This was the conclusive incendiary test, but one more precision strike, at Musashino on March 4, was scheduled, and this underlined the possibilities of a change in strategy: Target No. 357, hit seven times by the B-29s, was still essentially intact. And on March 4 heavy cloud forced the Superfortresses to bomb other targets.

The great hopes of the B-29 and daylight precision bombing from high altitudes had been dashed. Of the nine top-priority targets, not one had been destroyed. Again, it was probably the indirect effects of the B-29 raids that were most significant. They had proved that the Japanese homeland was wide open to massive bombing, and industrialists were beginning to lose faith in immunity from air attacks. They started to look for underground and other cover, and a government directive to disperse in mid-January only sped up what was already being done.

Perhaps half the B-29s sent out had bombed their primary targets, and losses had been high. Although the Japanese had expended much of their fighter force in other areas, they were particularly effective because the pattern of the B-29 missions allowed them to concentrate their fighters in the target areas.

The long trip over water took its toll of B-29s, and the losses since the heady days of November 1944 showed that fighters had claimed twenty-nine Superforts, flak only one, flak and fighters nine, operational causes twenty-one, and fifteen were missing without any known cause.

The devotion to the doctrines of strategic bombing had to be part of the reason for the failure, but there were other factors, which were far beyond human control. Installations in the Marianas had been inadequate from the beginning. During the seven months prior to his death in February 1945, General Harmon had worked diligently to get the B-29s into the theater, and get them there as quickly as possible. He found Nimitz sympathetic to his cause, but there were many other demands, and, with King's backing, Nimitz fell back on the original joint chiefs directive, which provided for only four B-29 groups in the Marianas. While these had enjoyed the highest priority, the subsequent increase to twelve groups left the priority for the other eight to be determined by Nimitz. Although he was as co-operative a theater commander as could be hoped for, he would provide for these only as circumstances permitted.

It was difficult for the XXI Bomber Command to carry out its mission to the best of its ability without certain prerogatives of command over the procurement of bombs, aviation gasoline, and other essential services. There was some concern over the fact that while the B-29s were undertaking the only continuous combat operations against the Japanese from the Marianas, their assigned priority was often low. A base for the 314th Wing on Guam was item No. 91, the 315th Wing's base was No. 95, and a headquarters area for the bomber command itself was No. 110. These

The 500th's Draggin' Lady *was on a test flight when sudden loss of power in two engines on the same side caused it to roll over and crash into the sea just off the shore. Although everybody waded or swam to the* wreck to try to get the crew out, three men were trapped in the nose and died. Later the B-29 was hauled ashore. February 27, 1945.

The 498th Group's Tanaka Termite *flew a total of sixty missions before she was sent home as war weary in August 1945.*

Joltin' Josie *(below left), the airplane which brought General Hansell to Saipan. Her luck ran out on April 1, 1945. She was being flown by Captain Wilson Currier and his crew and a small explosion was seen shortly after takeoff; the B-29 burst into flames and plunged into Magicienne Bay.*

The 497th's Texas Doll *(below right) saw two crews through their missions. She was brought to Saipan on October 29, 1944, by Captain James Arnold, and passed on to Lieutenant Edward Cutler.*

Lucky 'Leven *proved to be an accurate name. Lieutenant Barton Yount and his crew took her on the first Tokyo mission and she flew her sixtieth on August 14, 1945.*

Milt Caniff's Miss Lace *was always a popular airplane name. This 498th Group B-29 flew forty-nine consecutive missions without an abort.*

Lieutenant John Bauman's Geisha Gertie *was ditched after the January 14 Nagoya mission. The entire crew was lost.*

Forbidden Fruit *of the 498th Group was the queen of the B-29s. She flew sixty-five missions and survived the war.*

The 498th inherited **Heavenly Body** *from the 505th Group in January 1945. She was so badly shot up during the April 1 mission to Target #357 that she was sent to the Guam Air Depot and lost to the group.*

Destiny's Tots *of the 497th Bomb Group.*

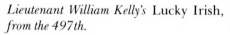

Lieutenant William Kelly's Lucky Irish, *from the 497th.*

(All photos by Edward T. Donnelly)

were all well down the list after the construction of roads and numerous naval installations. LeMay obtained a copy of this priority list and forwarded it to Arnold, professing pained disbelief. LeMay acidly commented, "They had built tennis courts for the island commander; they had built fleet recreation centers, Marine rehabilitation centers, dockage facilities for interisland surface craft, and every other damn thing in the world except subscribing to the original purpose in the occupation of these islands."

While the B-29 people were living in tents, the Navy appeared to be living extra well, an opinion LeMay formed after dining with Nimitz and then the island commander, and finding it impossible to return their hospitality in a similar fashion. He doesn't recall what they were building at that particular time: "maybe a roller-skating rink."

From the crowded bases it was a strain for the newer crews just to get airborne, to keep a worried eye on their instruments and hold to a tight takeoff schedule without overheating the engines by too much ground idling. The congestion made formation assembly complex, because of the excessive time between the first and last takeoffs it caused. The climb to altitude gulped fuel and cut back bomb loads, which were actually around three tons, falling far short of the theoretical loads. Fuel was always a worry, and a navigational error or headwinds could absorb the normally slender reserve. General Hansell recalls cruise control as the "most critical" problem: "It took us a long time to find out how to get the theoretical range out of the airplane . . . the first operations out of Saipan were very marginal indeed." For a B-29 that had used increased power settings to get out of trouble over a target, the long, downhill slide home, sustaining a descent of fifty to one hundred feet per minute, was a nerve-wracking experience. Bill Duffield from the 497th remembers his "greatest worry during all of combat was thinking of the possibility of ditching in that dreary ocean . . . those long hours returning from the target area on the deck *hoping* a crippled aircraft will make it home are the most haunting of all my memories."

There was a dual payoff if rescue could be made more effective: Morale would improve, and combat performance of the B-29 would increase. To get bombs to Japan, fuel loadings were kept to a minimum in the B-29s, which led to damaged aircraft, or aircraft with mechanical problems, being in a truly critical position. Far too many B-29s simply disappeared from the face of the earth.

Air-sea rescue followed the same learning curve as other B-29 operations, and there was a grim period when things were really bad. The beginning, though, was auspicious: On November 8, when a 498th Group crew ditched on the way back from an Iwo mission, part of the crew was saved, and on the first Tokyo mission the entire crew of the sole ditched aircraft was picked up by a destroyer. Then things tapered off. On November 27 a ditched 500th Group plane was lost with the entire crew. There were sixteen ditchings in December, fifteen in January, and fourteen in February. There were twenty missions to Japan in that period, and planes hit the water on all but three. On February 10, Ota, the ditchings had peaked: eight B-29s.

These figures caused concern to both Hansell and Arnold. Shortly before replacing Hansell, Arnold wrote him that he understood "some of these airplanes must naturally be ditched," but that three or four B-29s going down each mission, particularly without any known cause, was not acceptable, and something had to be done.

Hansell was nearing the end of his command, but he had begun measures to cut these losses, and his work was carried on by LeMay.

There were two aspects to the ditching problem: First, reduce the number itself; second, get more of the crews out of the water.

Hansell had begun to emphasize the training of flight engineers in the critical art of cruise control. Another device that worked was first tried by Pappy Haynes and his crew in the 497th's *Thumper*, with Hansell's encouragement. Major C. C. Gibson was an engineer who could prove on paper that the way they were loading B-29s was wrong, and Haynes volunteered to try his ideas. They took a bomb-bay gas tank out of *Thumper*, removed the 20mm cannon and some of the armor out of the tail, and so on. The total weight reduction amounted to about three tons, mostly resulting from the fact that the gas tank weighed over two tons when full. The other pilots were not convinced this would work, and Haynes himself admitted he found it impossible to eat prior to the first mission in the lightened aircraft. However, *Thumper* got back, with more gas to spare than the other normally loaded aircraft. The reduction in the weight carried not only decreased fuel consumption, but also lessened wear on the engines. On the first mission after the modifications had been duplicated throughout the 73rd Wing there were no ditchings — that was Hansell's "too late" mission of January 19 — and on January 23 only one aircraft was forced to ditch.

To snatch more men from the sea required better equipment, more equipment, and better planning. The crews were lectured and given practice in air-sea rescue procedures, including swimming lessons when necessary, and information on the rescue setup was an integral part of

Peace on Earth was ditched on March 4; although the water landing was good, two of the crew were lost. (Prunuske)

each briefing. Inspections showed that equipment was being treated casually . . . the flashlights from Mae Wests were being forgotten in tents when they should have been on airplanes. And even the "best" ditchings could go wrong: The 497th's *Peace on Earth* went into the sea with Lieutenant Norman Westervelt and his crew on the way back from Tokyo on March 4, and nine men were rapidly rescued by a Dumbo amphibian. One man was not seen after the ditching, and Westervelt was washed off the wing as he tried to reach safety and was never seen again.

On December 19 the submarine *Spearfish* picked up seven 500th Group crewmen but it was not until the end of March that another submarine rescue was achieved. Sometimes survivors broadcast their positions in the clear, which made the submariners edgy about going to them. Other survivors, especially those near the enemy coast, would not use either radio or flares for fear of being captured.

Despite this, submarine rescues became more frequent during the late spring of 1945.

A lot of the organization of the rescue system was done by four B-29 crewmen who had survived ditchings themselves: Lieutenant Alton Ayers and Captain Francis Murray of the 498th had gone down on the December 3 Musashino mission and floated around for eleven days until a destroyer picked them up; Lieutenant Robert Pope had ditched his crippled B-29 alongside a destroyer and was rescued within minutes; and Lieutenant Harold Bodley had ditched in the English Channel while flying with the Royal Air Force.

Air search and its effectiveness was the key to the problem. Men in rafts who were lucky enough to survive sometimes reported formations of B-29s going overheard but not seeing their signal mirrors—the crews were constantly reminded to keep a lookout for survivors. At the end of February there was a feeling in LeMay's headquarters that "Navy effort per

ditched B-29 seems ridiculously low," but it was only the B-29 itself that could fly patrols for long hours off the Honshu coast, where the cripples were likely to go down.

From the beginning the B-29s used the "buddy" system, where a B-29 would stay with a cripple for as long as possible when it went down, and the wings were given permission to conduct their own searches with combat aircraft.

About the time LeMay arrived, the shortage of B-29s was easing, and from late January a couple of them were on station for every mission.

Not all the 73rd Wing B-29s were unlucky or doomed to short lives. Some of the early planes established outstanding combat records. The 497th's Thumper *flew forty missions before being sent home;* Forbidden Fruit *of the 498th completed sixty-five. The 500th's* Slick Dick *survived to return to the States, and their* Fever from the South *flew fifty missions. The* Big Stick *of the 499th survived the war with a grand total of forty-four missions. (Morgan, Prunuske, Ryan, Bill Sikes)*

The Superdumbo was developed for this special work, and it carried a crew of twelve. There was an extra navigator and radio operator replacing the bombardier, extra radio equipment, and a range of droppable equipment including rafts, rations, survival kits, and radios. The Superdumbos worked closely and effectively with Navy vessels or submarines, and it became standard procedure to have two Superdumbos orbiting the northernmost submarines by day and one at night, with four more on alert at Iwo Jima.

If there was one crucial factor affecting the success of the B-29s it was weather. The frontal conditions often encountered by the bombers drained fuel, broke up formations, and complicated navigation. Cloud conditions were incredible. Southeasterly trade winds, warm and moist, surged up against the opposing cold winds from Asia along the shores of Japan. The clouds formed in layers and decks all the way up, moving at different speeds and in different directions, confusing bombardiers. A leading formation might find a target clear and bomb visually; a few minutes later it could be socked in.

The tremendous jet winds encountered six miles above Japan were new and strange problems. Sometimes these winds reached velocities above two hundred miles an hour, and drift was difficult to correct. Bombing Japan directly upwind or downwind caused its own unique problems: An upwind attack against a heavily defended target into such a gale was unthinkable, but attacking downwind under similar conditions meant that the B-29s raced over the target at ground speeds greater than five hundred miles an hour, impeding the effectiveness of bomb sights and bombardiers. The winds also made second runs over targets nearly impossible.

LeMay had no magical powers to achieve what Hansell had not, but he was more flexible. When a Wright Aeronautical technical representative told him that the short life of engines was due to the climb to twenty thousand feet with heavy loads, LeMay told him that they weren't there to save engines, and sent him home. When General Echols and a party including Wellwood Beall of Boeing arrived late in January, Beall suggested that the B-29s should fly at low altitude, taking in "ground effect" before the term was really known, until the fuel in the center wing tank was burned, which improved wing bending, and then climb to altitude for the bomb run. The plan was a success, although LeMay was skeptical at first—engine life more than trebled. LeMay had inherited the problems that had bedeviled Hansell, but by early March LeMay was about to circumvent them.

IV

LeMay's Inferno

During that first week of March 1945 General LeMay caustically appraised the 21st Bomber Command: "This outfit has been getting a lot of publicity without having really accomplished a hell of a lot in bombing results."

There were several sound reasons for a change in tactics: The B-29s were suffering steady losses, precision bombing was not precise, and the Japanese cities would apparently burn readily. An earlier intelligence study indicated that, unlike European cities, the Japanese were far more vulnerable to "sweeping conflagrations." These fires would engulf "shadow" industries, home factories, and small organizations. As the most important major industries were gathered in a few large cities, there was an added appeal to the estimate that the twenty most important cities in Japan could be reduced to ashes with less than a couple of thousand tons of M-69 incendiary bombs.

There was also a longer view: The punishment that Japan would suffer after the capture of the Philippines and the imminent victory at Iwo Jima needed to be emphasized to the Japanese people. Massive fire raids against the cities would achieve this; precision strikes against factories would not.

Whether these factors appealed to Arnold, or whether he had simply decided that precision attacks were not getting anywhere, is unknown. Either way, Arnold and Norstad had shown more and more interest in area fire bombing.

That March found LeMay in a position to achieve a great deal in a

The 500th Group's Su Su Baby *ditched due to lack of fuel returning from a weather strike mission on March 7, 1945. The aircraft, piloted by Captain Theodore*   *Holmes, was carrying a crew of twelve; eight were rescued, but two of them died later. (Robert E. Sebring)*

short time. He had three wings of B-29s, but there had not been good weather for visual bombing since the Akashi mission on January 19, and spring promised worse and less predictable conditions. This suggested radar bombing on a large scale, and with the men and equipment available, precision radar bombing was not a realistic solution.

The way to burn the cities down was subjected to intensive study by LeMay and his staff on Guam. The results at Tokyo at the end of February were good, but that had been a high-altitude mission, like all the previous fire-bombing experiments, and the high winds and poor ballistics of the fire-bomb cluster led to a high degree of inaccuracy. If the B-29s went in at lower levels, accuracy would be improved, they could carry a much larger bomb load, and the engines would suffer less strain. On the other hand, losses might increase dramatically.

LeMay, the "operator," summed it up this way: "The weather situation the way it was, at the end of six weeks, I took a look at what I had done, and I had not done very much. . . . The B-29 had got to pay its way. We had to show them. . . . One of the things I wanted to do was see if we couldn't do something with radar at night and get to fly more missions. . . .

I looked at all the reconnaissance pictures they had, and I could not find the low-altitude flak the Germans had in their defenses, and it looked to me like it would work."

There were other considerations: Radar operators were considered to be poorly trained before they arrived in the Marianas, but a large target with good land and water contrast was not a difficult one. The enemy would certainly not be expecting a radical change in the B-29s' tactics, and surprise would be at least an initial factor, so the missions would have to be run over a short period of time. LeMay talked to "very few" people and largely kept his own counsel as the plan began taking shape.

If pathfinder planes could mark the target with a ten-mile flaming cross, the less experienced crews would have little trouble setting up their bomb runs . . . if guns and ammunition were removed from the planes there would be even less strain on the engines—the bomb bays would be crammed full anyway—and nervy gunners would not shoot up other bombers in the darkness. Anyway, LeMay believed that Japanese night fighters were ineffective. No matter how he looked at his plan he felt it would work.

Some of his staff mentioned the word "murder," but LeMay had decided. Some, including General Tom Power of the 314th Wing, agreed with his theory.

General Hap Arnold had suffered a major heart seizure on January 15, and was recuperating at the Hotel Biltmore in Coral Gables, Florida. General Norstad was in the Marianas, and LeMay, who did not know Arnold very well, tried to "feel out" what Norstad thought Arnold's reaction would be to "something unorthodox." Was Arnold a gambler? LeMay found little comfort in quizzing Norstad. "He wasn't much help," said LeMay. "It was my neck, not his."

During the first week of March the 314th Wing began flying a new mission, gathering radarscope photographs of the Japanese cities. The first of these was flown on the night of March 4, when eight 29th Group B-29s went to Nagoya, and while seven of them climbed to twenty-six thousand feet to bomb, Colonel Carl Storrie bombed from seven thousand feet and remained in the area for over fifty minutes, obtaining thirty excellent photos of the landfall, initial point, and target for future missions, as well as preparing a report on the effectiveness of Japanese defenses.

The following night a similar mission was flown by the 19th Group: Colonel John Roberts, the group commander, volunteered to secure radarscope photos of Kobe. Nearing the target, eight B-29s climbed to twenty-five thousand feet, while Roberts, in Captain John Hancock's

Lieutenant Charles Lucas' Slick Chick, *of the 19th Bomb Group. (Roy Fagan)*

plane, went in at five thousand. They flew over the city for two hours, reporting on the Japanese antiaircraft fire and searchlights. The 19th's Major Robert Irwin commanded a similar mission to Tokyo.

With the first really solid information available, some of LeMay's advisers still believed it was suicidal to hit a city like Tokyo from five thousand or six thousand feet, but LeMay was convinced, and the planning went ahead. The lead squadron would drop M-47s, napalm bombs to start fires that would bring out motorized fire-fighting equipment. The rest of the B-29s would carry maximum loads of M-69s. The intervalometers would be set at one hundred feet in the pathfinders, fifty feet in the main force, which would mean perhaps twenty-five tons of incendiaries for every square mile of Tokyo. The planning was completed in unusual secrecy. Norstad was briefed on Guam on March 8, and Arnold learned of the plans that afternoon. Norstad told the Twentieth Air Force public-relations staff to be ready for "what may be an outstanding strike." The decision had been late, and the field orders were not cut until March 8, perhaps accounting for variations from the plan within individual groups.

Originally Salt-Peter Resistor, *this 19th Bomb Group airplane was commanded by Captain Fred Blakeley, kneeling on the right. With Major Robert Irwin, standing second from the left, as acting command pilot and technical observer, this B-29 brought back the low-altitude radar photos of Tokyo. (Stan Fisher)*

The Night Tokyo Died

The 29th Group's briefing hut was overflowing onto the white coral path outside, and the assembly heard the words, "You will come over the target at an altitude of five thousand feet." There was much more, but that was enough. Everybody had plenty to do, but Colonel Carl Storrie gathered the crews together for a talk. He had flown thirty missions from England in Martin Marauders, and the thirty-nine-year-old, pipe-smoking Texan spoke with quiet assurance. He paid particular attention to crews who would be flying their first mission, trying to pass on the tricks of the trade. There would be about three hundred planes over the target, and everything had to be precise. Otherwise there would be collisions, or planes hit by others' bombs. The crews were to wear amber glasses to avoid being blinded by searchlights.

On Saipan and Tinian crews were also listening to briefings for the mission in silence. Their reaction was always surprise: Leonard Carpi recalls that in the 9th Group the crews were "about ready to go over the hill," and Bill Duffield in the 497th remembers some thinking that LeMay must be "crazy" . . . Colonel Glen Martin of the 504th recalls a "roar of surprise and enthusiasm" as details of the mission were given.

Frantic activity followed as the preparations were completed. While the ground crews labored, the air crews slept, or tried to sleep, late the next day, and a late breakfast was arranged.

Each 73rd Wing group had supplied its three most experienced crews to take off first and act as pathfinders. They and the 313th also supplied "homing" aircraft with no bombs, extra fuel, an added radio, and the best radio operators. These aircraft were fully armed and would begin transmitting homing signals twenty minutes prior to the arrival of the main force. The 29th Group's *Snatch Blatch*, piloted by Major Tony Simeral, carried no bombs but was fully armed; it was the observation plane and would carry the 314th Wing commander, General Tom Power.

The decision had been so late that while none of the main force carried any ammunition, only the 497th and 505th had removed the machine guns from the turrets, and a few crew members recall some people putting them back in before takeoff. Crews of each plane varied, from some groups with only eight, to eleven or twelve.

A total of 334 B-29s loaded with over 2,000 tons of bombs began taking off in the late afternoon of March 9; the 314th Wing's 19th and 29th groups left North Field on Guam 40 minutes before the 73rd and 313th wings started roaring off the runways at Saipan and Tinian. In less than three hours the whole force was airborne.

The air was vibrating with the constant drone of the B-29s as they streamed toward Tokyo. The commanders were flying with their groups: Colonel Jack Dougherty was leading the 500th in *The Cannuck*, the 9th Group's new commander, Colonel Henry Huglin, was in *Tokyo-ko*, and so on through the huge armada.

The B-29s proceeded individually to the target at three thousand to thirty-five hundred feet. In the yellow-and-black pattern of the radar-scopes the coast of Japan appeared as they made landfall at the southern tip of Chiba Peninsula, then proceeded to the bomb-run turning point,

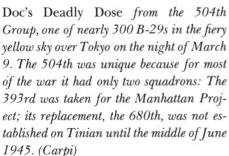

Doc's Deadly Dose *from the 504th Group, one of nearly 300 B-29s in the fiery yellow sky over Tokyo on the night of March 9. The 504th was unique because for most of the war it had only two squadrons: The 393rd was taken for the Manhattan Project; its replacement, the 680th, was not established on Tinian until the middle of June 1945. (Carpi)*

The fighter opposition over Tokyo was weak, but an Irving did score a few inconsequential hits on the intriguingly named 504th airplane "Doc" Said All I Needed Was — Affection. (Carpi)

up the eastern coastline of the peninsula, then to the initial point just north of the town of Goi.

Two hundred and eighty-two B-29s got over the target. The pathfinders performed perfectly, and there appeared in the blackness an oblong of yellow flame. In a moment it was crossed by another: The target was clearly marked in fire.

The 73rd Wing went in first, bombing from around seven thousand feet. It was a few minutes after midnight and the weather was better than usual. There was a little light cloud and visibility was about ten miles as the parade over the target began; each B-29 dropped its five-hundred-pound clusters of M-69s, little six-pound devices resembling a piece of steel pipe. When detonated, they spewed burning liquid jelly, which clung tenaciously to any surface and burned for ten minutes. Each little bomb created a puddle of flame a yard wide.

The darkness over Tokyo was cut by the searchlights, reaching up and down, trying to find the altitude of the planes. Flak began to explode in yellow, red, and white bursts, and soon the thin clouds were tinged with a pinkish glow as the fires took hold and more were started.

Fires spread through the modern district east of the Imperial Palace, as the early arrivals bombed on the pathfinders' mark. Later planes just headed for the glowing clouds and the columns of oily smoke. They ranged wide in search of cool spots, the bombardiers simply aiming for black patches among the glowing fires.

The glare from the searchlights was blinding, and the B-29s were being bounced around crazily in updrafts from the flames below. As the bomb bays opened there was a faint smell of burning wood in the aircraft.

On Guam, LeMay and his staff had waited up for the report of bombs away. Above the inferno *Snatch Blatch* was cruising, observing, and Gen-

Lieutenant Gordon Savage of the 19th Group headed for an area of Tokyo three or four miles inland that was not burning, then about thirty seconds before bombs away his B-29 was coned by searchlights. His No. 1 engine caught fire and was feathered; then No. 4 lost all oil pressure and it too had to be feathered. The B-29 was taking hits all the time, and the right blister gunner was wounded. The fuel-transfer system had been hit and gasoline had sprayed all over the bomb bay, the left tire and wheel of the left landing gear were damaged, and the flux-gate compass was inoperative. Savage struggled back to Iwo, but when he lost speed the rudder was not effective, and with the damaged landing gear and a crosswind from the left the B-29 "weather-vaned" to the left. The No. 4 propeller hit a truck, the left flap hit a Jeep, and the plane finally stopped when it hit a slope. (USA)

eral Power was sending cryptic radio reports and filling his map with red pencil crosses, each indicating a fire.

The 314th Wing, last over the target, had the roughest time. The 19th Group lost three planes, and the 29th lost *Cherry the Horizontal Cat* and three others, while a fifth ditched. Returning airmen reported seeing only one parachute over Tokyo that night. Lieutenant Charles Shaffer, in *Oily Boid*, was caught in lights on the bomb run, and trapped for fifteen minutes. Intense and accurate flak hit his right-wing fuel tanks, setting them afire. He continued his long bomb run, despite the danger of an explosion; after bombs away *Oily Boid* was caught in the turbulence from the fires and went into a dive. The pilots managed to pull her out about 1,000 feet from the ground, and the tremendous speed of the dive and the self-sealing tanks enabled the fire to be extinguished. Shaffer got *Oily Boid* home, riddled by flak hits. Captain Chuck Hawks and his crew reported that the bright glare in the sky over Tokyo could be seen 125 miles away.

One of the last planes over the target was the 505th's *Dangerous Lady*, piloted by Lieutenant Thomas Cox; they had taken off about half an hour late after overcoming last-minute mechanical difficulties. Arriving over the target all alone, they were caught by searchlights on the bomb run and bracketed by flak. Just before bombs away a tremendous thermal

The morning after: Captain Dean Fling, operations officer of the 1st Bomb Squadron, brings his B-29 back from Tokyo on March 10.

Lieutenant Ed Cox's Dangerous Lady, *framed by Japanese wreckage on Tinian.*

Dangerous Lady *of the 505th Group was one of at least sixteen 313th Wing B-29s with a Seabee motif on one side of the nose,* and typical art on the other. (Ed Hering, Carpi)

caused by an explosion below tossed the aircraft up five thousand feet.

Captain Thomas Hanley and his 497th Group crew returned with the strangest story of the mission. On the way to the target his crew were listening to Tokyo radio to pass the time. As usual, the Japanese were playing some well-known American records, and after a few minutes the melody of "Smoke Gets in Your Eyes" came through the receiver and the crew smiled.

* * *

Down below, Hell had come to Tokyo. Just before the first bombs hit, a high wind had gusted through the city, and this fanned the first flames and spread them quickly. The fires were jumping fire breaks and canals easily.

An unshaven General Tom Power reports to Generals Norstad and LeMay after the first fire-blitz mission.

The residents, accustomed to B-29 raids, had become almost nonchalant about them, dubbing them the "mail run." Although the entire civilian population had been mobilized through neighborhood associations as a part of air-raid defense, there was too much exhortation and too little real effort. Each association learned and passed on instruction in fire fighting and "disposal" of incendiary bombs, how to construct air-raid shelters, and procedures for evacuation. While women and children were allowed to take shelter during an incendiary raid, it was the duty of the men to remain in their houses or nearby. The fire-fighting equipment they had was primitive: Each home supposedly had a grappling hook, a shovel, a sand bucket, and a water barrel. There was a shortage of some articles, but most homes had a barrel of water.

Air-raid-shelter construction, particularly in the lower area of Tokyo, was complicated because they could not be more than a few feet deep without encountering ground water. Most dwellings had some kind of shelter, but usually about like a foxhole, and useless in a raging fire storm. People suffocated as they lay there, or were roasted alive.

Tokyo's Fire Department was hopelessly inadequate to cope with a massive incendiary raid. The water supply was already partially destroyed, and the eight thousand trained firemen were caught by surprise on the night of March 9. Many of their more than seven hundred pieces of motorized equipment were destroyed, and the situation in Tokyo was uncontrollable within a half hour.

That cold, clear night came alive with the noise of sirens as the people headed for shelter or stood their ground by their supplies of sand and water. Houses flared like torches and became part of the rolling, roaring fires. Frantically, people began to try to escape as the walls of fire, whipped by the winds, raced through the city, over canals, streets, and firebreaks. People tried to reach the bay, or vacant lots and parks—any open areas. As the flames gained momentum, other B-29s were starting new fires. Showers of incendiaries landed with a sharp crackle, engulfing the city in flames.

In the streets it was as bright as day and the crowds of people were choking and gasping on the hot, burning air. Relentlessly pursued by one fire, they would find escape blocked by another, as the streets of Tokyo became a deadly, confused maze. The wind kept shifting, and people were trampled underfoot in the panic.

The fires fed the wind and whole blocks of houses simply disappeared. People running to reach bridges found them gone, and crowds piled up at the approaches. Others jumped into rivers and canals to escape, but some

Lieutenant John Cather took his 3rd Photo Squadron F-13 over Tokyo on March 10. Large areas were still ablaze, and smoke was rising from nine individual fires. (Reineke)

of the smaller canals were boiling. The people looked up at the B-29s with a mixture of awe, hatred, horror . . . and despair. Glowing hunks of timber and white-hot iron roofing showered down on them. Some of the luckier ones survived the night knee deep in the icy waters of Tokyo Bay.

Clouds built up and were lit from below by a pink light. The sky was red. The flickering light of the fires was reflected on the silvery wings of the B-29s above until finally, after an eternity, no more came.

As the B-29s returned to their bases there was only the roar of the four engines as the tired crews passed the rest of the long night. Then the clouds began to turn gray with the early dawn, and a brilliant white as the morning sun touched them.

In Tokyo, dawn was a ghostly bluish haze, as the glow of the sun was met by the glow of the raging fires. Everything was being gobbled up by them — automobiles, buses, bicycles, food, clothing. By the middle of the morning they had almost burned themselves out, stopped only by wide breaks like the river.

The Japanese fighters had not accounted for any B-29s, but flak damaged more than forty and inflicted the total loss of fourteen B-29s on the mission. Five of the crews were picked up by air-sea rescue.

Official Japanese casualty estimates, probably well short of the true total, established that 78,660 people died that night. The area burned out was 15.8 square miles. It was nearly a month before all the bodies had been removed from the ruins, and no other air attack in history had ever been so terrifyingly effective.

*   *   *

Two days later, in the evening of March 11, over 300 B-29s, again bloated with fire bombs, took off for Nagoya to burn the heart out of that city. This time the planes carried a couple of hundred rounds for each tail gun — some group commanders thought the gunners might be able to hit some of the searchlights.

The B-29s that made it to Nagoya dumped nearly 1,800 tons of incendiaries, 125 more tons than Tokyo had received. The 314th Wing was on target, but the other two dropped short. Hundreds of fires were started, some spreading until they were stopped at firebreaks, and a submarine lurking 150 miles off Japan reported that visibility the next morning was limited to a mile by a haze of wood smoke. Yet there was no raging inferno like that which had partially razed Tokyo, partly due to the fact that there was no wind to spread the initial fires, and because Nagoya had an adequate water supply, good fire breaks, and an efficient fire department. Also, the planning of the mission had an important weakness: The tremendous results on the night of March 9 had created a wrong impression. The crews' reports indicated that a lot of bombs had been wasted by dropping them so close together, so for Nagoya the intervalometer setting used was 100 feet rather than 50, and the incendiaries were spread too thinly.

The Cultured Vulture, *on Iwo for refueling after the Tokyo raid.*

However, the only B-29 lost was one that ditched shortly after takeoff, and it was clear that LeMay had judged the Japanese capacity to defend their cities against these attacks most accurately.

For the third fire blitz mission, Osaka was chosen. On Osaka Bay, this was Japan's second city in both size and industry. It had suffered many natural disasters, and accordingly had a network of fire breaks in congested areas, and natural protection from many canals and modern buildings. The crowded dwelling districts were still perfect incendiary targets and, trying for another Tokyo, the intervalometer setting was taken back to fifty feet and the crews were briefed to get a higher concentration in the target area.

The ordnance and maintenance crews again worked mightily, and for the third time, three hundred B-29s were in the air, on the evening of March 13. The bomb load was the same — six tons of incendiaries in each plane — but this time the low wing was carrying ammunition in the lower gun turrets as well as the tail.

Osaka was well covered by cloud, but this proved advantageous. The need to bomb by radar rather than sighting on pathfinder fires meant a controlled run, which led to a denser and more regular pattern than had been achieved at Nagoya. In about three hours just over eight square

*Decorating airplanes was a creative busi-
ness. In the 497th Group there was a minor
trend to break away from the normal bomb
stencils for missions completed.* Thumper
had the Disney rabbit, Destiny's Tots *had
diapers,* Lucky Irish *had shamrocks,* Star
Duster *had stars, and* Marianna Ram
had small white goats. (Watson)

miles of Osaka were burning. The turbulence over the city was tremendous, and the center of Osaka was a "solid sheet of flame," according to
General Tom Power. In the 9th Group's *Thunderin' Loretta*, Lieutenant
Stanley Black and his crew reported, "We had just finished the bomb run
over Osaka and turned away from the target. A blast from the ground
slammed us up in the air and tilted us at such an angle that we lost most
of our flight instruments. We no sooner pulled out of that than we were
hit by another and much more terrific blast. This one flipped the ship
over on her back . . . before we came out of it we lost air speed and about
six thousand feet of altitude. I was afraid to pull up too fast because the
strain on the airplane was terrific. The ship actually was out of control for
about seven minutes, but we were upside down for only a few seconds. As
soon as we were righted the copilot made a quick trip through the plane.
All kinds of small articles, from candy bars to oxygen bottles, were hanging from the ceiling. So was the bombardier. The navigator's chute flew
from the front of the plane all the way to the rear, and the CFC gunner
banged down through the floor in the rear of the plane and broke the
plywood. It looked like a mess, but no one was injured, and the only damage to the plane was that the wings were slightly wrinkled." So wrinkled
that both outer wing panels had to be changed when *Thunderin' Loretta*
got back to Tinian.

Osaka cost two B-29s. On the night of March 16 it was the turn of
Kobe, Japan's principal overseas port and across the bay from gutted

Osaka. Again some details were refined. This time the field orders called
for a controlled radar run over the city before making visual corrections
to the specific aiming points. Kobe was a fine radar target, with a long, irregular waterfront, and the crews were told not to try to spread their
bombs by visual means. To get a greater concentration, and easier merging of fires, the flight schedules were tightened to bring the B-29s over
the target for a shorter period, and the aiming points were brought closer
together. It was also necessary to alter the bomb load, because the supply
of incendiaries was running low. The change in B-29 tactics had been too
sudden for the supply pipeline to handle, and while high-explosive
bombs were lying idle in the stockpiles the incendiaries were getting
scarce.

So for Kobe LeMay had to resort to the M17A1, a cluster of four-
pound magnesium thermite bombs. These were designed for industrial
targets, and were not as effective against urban areas as the devilish M-
69s.

By another herculean effort, the command was able to launch more B-
29s than ever before for this fourth attack. Three hundred seven
dropped their fire bombs in just over two hours, and the attack was
highly concentrated. The Japanese responded more strongly than before
—over three hundred sightings of enemy planes were reported, and
more than ninety attacks. However, they were still not a serious problem,
and none of the three B-29s lost were victims of the fighters.

Flak Alley Sally *was one of a half dozen* *foreground; Iwo was a real problem, as*
6th Group aircraft that were low on fuel *runways were constantly buckling from*
and headed for Iwo after the Kobe mission. *poor drainage and pressure from un-*
Steam rises from bulldozed earth in the *derground steam. (USMC)*

The situation in Kobe was promising: The fires were quickly out of control, and many individual targets were destroyed or heavily damaged, but there was a little disappointment that only about a fifth of the city area had been burned out.

A return trip to Nagoya rounded out the blitz. On the night of March 19 every third plane was loaded with a couple of five-hundred-pound high-explosive bombs to interfere with the fire fighters. The bomb bays were filled with whatever incendiaries were available—the 314th Wing carried M-69s, the 313th had M-47s, and the 73rd a mixture of M-47s and M-76s. Two hundred ninety B-29s got to Nagoya and burned out about three square miles, a 50 per cent better result than on the previous mission. The fires destroyed some important targets, such as the Nagoya arsenal, but the Mitsubishi plants received only minor damage. The only loss was the 505th's *Jackpot*, flown by Lieutenant Warren Shipp and his crew. They had two engines shot out, limped away from the target, and nursed the airplane along for about one hundred fifty miles after crossing the coast. Then *Jackpot* hit the water and for two days and nights the whole crew drifted within easy range of Honshu. Finally a Superdumbo spotted them and the destroyer *Gatling* came around and picked them up.

The blitz was over. LeMay had sent out five maximum efforts in ten days, and put nearly sixteen hundred sorties over the four cities. The B-29s had unloaded three times the weight of bombs dropped during all the early, frustrating missions prior to the March fire raids.

The statistics are too cold to adequately describe what had been achieved: The B-29s had put the torch to thirty-two square miles in four of Japan's greatest cities. It had worked, as LeMay believed it would. As he said later, "*My* decision and *my* order . . . there has to be a commander."

Morale soared after the Tokyo mission, and it stayed high. The crews, both air and ground, had withstood the tremendous strain well.

To the men over the burning cities it had been unbelievable: the glow ahead as they approached the target, the searchlights, the creeping heat of the fires, which could be felt in the aircraft as they passed over the target area, the soot on the glass, the tremendous smoke clouds. Coming out of the smoke into the brilliant light of the fires, and seeing nothing but a sea of flames . . . inside the B-29s they could read charts by the glare. Some crews did not like the fire raids—the blinding lights; the sight of B-29 shadows on the pinkish clouds above them; the fear of the turbulence or of ramming another B-29. To one bombardier, flying into the "blackest blackness" of the smoke and the indescribable turbulence that blew B-29s like leaves in the wind was "the most terrifying thing I've ever known." Captain Robert Zeller's 498th crew were looking for a "cool spot" over Tokyo when thermal waves rocked their B-29 and ripped off the right bomb bay door. It swung out, hit No. 3 engine's propeller, bending it, then slapped back against the right wing. It hung, fluttering in the prop wash, all the way back to Saipan.

Experience over the target varied widely, group to group, plane to plane. At Kobe the flak was generally moderate and inaccurate, but the 504th's *Satan's Lady* was caught in a torrent of accurate ground fire, which punched about two hundred holes in the plane.

The searing heat created thunderheads over the cities, which added to the dangers. Several planes were struck by lightning, and Lieutenant Robert Borgos and his crew in *Bedroom Eyes* were temporarily blinded by it—they thought that they had been hit by flak.

When artwork appeared on both sides of an airplane's nose, there were usually subtle differences, as was the case with the 498th's Bedroom Eyes. *(Reineke, Prunuske)*

Following the first mission the groups had all wanted higher altitudes, particularly for later arrivals, and after the lively March 16 mission, more ammunition for the tail and some ammunition for every other turret, arguing that some of the fighter attacks might have been countered successfully had the turrets been loaded.

Many things were tried: For the second Nagoya raid the 504th Group loaded two of the four guns in the upper forward turret, and also the lower aft and tail turrets, while the 9th Group loaded all turrets except the lower forward.

After every mission the 499th Group recommended altitudes of ten thousand feet for aircraft entering the target area after the fires were started. Their intelligence officer, Major Manila Shaver, also made the point that the "crews do not appreciate being threatened with low-altitude bombing in the daytime if they do not hit the target at night." His report to the group commander also recommended that "advice such as a 360-degree turn over the target and a second run being made not be given at briefings as it merely brings a laugh."

Sergeant Harold Tucker, right blister gunner on the 497th's *Thunderhead*, recalls, "Some crews, such as the one I was on, flew at very low altitude during these fire missions. We flew at two and three thousand feet above the target area with a reduced bomb load but with all gunners and a full ammo load. Our mission, which was timed over the target area so we were clear of other aircraft, was to shoot out searchlights. Some fun! When I returned from those missions, the gunners were painting silhouettes of searchlights beside their blisters."

After the stunning success of the first mission to Tokyo, Arnold had wired LeMay: CONGRATULATIONS. THIS MISSION SHOWS YOUR CREWS HAVE GOT THE GUTS FOR ANYTHING.

A few days later, Norstad praised LeMay "for solving an acute operational problem by using high-altitude Superfortresses at low level to achieve the unloading of a large tonnage of bombs in a short time."

The results of the five fire blitz missions were clear: Morale had skyrocketed, the B-29s had really performed well, bomb tonnages had risen dramatically, and engine performance was quite satisfactory. Radar, adequate for the new tactics, had foiled Japan's protective weather. The losses, a total of twenty-one B-29s, were proof that Japanese night defenses—flak and particularly fighters—were limited. The Japanese put up literally sheets of smaller-caliber fire, but this was more spectacular than effective.

Some of the best nose artwork in the 313th Wing was painted by a Marine named Scott. Among his works were the 504th's Satan's Lady, Dina Might, Island Queen, and Good Deal, and this unnamed 505th Group aircraft. Then around the end of February there came an order to remove all the artwork. The directive came from Washington and was the result of some war-weary B-29s taking their artwork back to the States. Apparently several women's religious groups protested violently to Arnold about the lewdness of the paintings. The reaction in the field was usually unhappy: The 499th requested on behalf of the crews that they be allowed to modify the paintings "to meet the approval of the Ladies' Aid Society," feeling that "combat crews have a deep feeling toward their aircraft and combat and are not machines." The 73rd Wing appointed a board, composed of six people from the groups, to recommend "proper limitations" for airplane insignia. Brief, the theater magazine, commented, "The war, it would seem, is being cleaned up, just like burlesque.... It marks the end of a great tradition and means the loss of one of the last personal touches in an already impersonal war.... Most of the bomber crews we know named their plane at first only because it was expected of them, but after a couple of rugged missions, the plane became as close to them as any one man in the crew and they would rather have parted with their wings than with their insigne...." (Carpi)

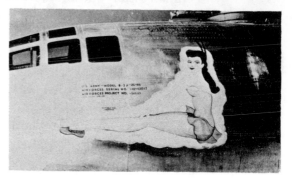

The Twentieth Air Force was anxious to capitalize on the situation, and the joint target group picked out thirty-three urban areas as targets significant enough to be included in an overall incendiary attack.

Additionally, they selected several important industrial targets: Japanese Army and Navy arsenals at Osaka, Kure, Hiro, Kokura, and Sasebo, and the chemical works at Koriyama.

By drawing up targets for both area and precision bombing, a trend was begun that would continue throughout the rest of the war. After the blitz LeMay came to believe that air power alone could force a surrender, and some of Arnold's staff in Washington had the same feeling. Arnold was hopeful but unsure.

During the blitz the B-29s had flown eighty hours a month average, and LeMay was more short of crews than aircraft. However, it was believed that the maximum continuous strain a crew could bear was sixty hours a month. Yet if they could stand to fly eighty per month for six months the crew shortage would never become critical. The wing commanders and flight surgeons felt that the airmen would be burned out, but again LeMay decided to gamble on his judgment. His crews would be asked to fly eighty hours per month in the hope that this effort would bring the war to a quicker end. He advised Norstad that here was "the opportunity of proving the power of the strategic air arm." But before he could begin methodically destroying Japan, LeMay had commitments to the Okinawa invasion, which would begin with the landing there on April 1, and a very specialized job for the B-29s.

Operation Starvation

When the war began, neither the Navy nor the Air Force had shown much interest in the use of mines as offensive strategic weapons. This attitude slowly changed, partly through the missionary zeal of enthusiasts in the Navy's Mine Warfare Section.

Japan's island position, with her reliance on sea transportation both for essential imports and to supply her military forces overseas, made the enemy unusually vulnerable to mining operations. The Allied blockade had already forced the Japanese to channel most of their shipping through the Inland Sea, and the "spout of the funnel," the Shimonoseki Strait, could be plugged with aerial mines. Most of the initiative came from the Navy, which saw the superiority of a heavy land-based bomber like the B-29 for a sustained mining campaign, and which lacked similar

The use of black-and-yellow fuselage bands to identify lead airplanes was a 504th Group idea that was adopted throughout the 313th Wing. There were many devices to aid assembly in the target area: the new, higher-visibility tail markings, and proce- dures such as the lead plane lowering its nose wheel, the second-element leader rais- ing his upper forward guns, and the third-element leader raising upper and lower forward guns, among others. (Carpi)

aircraft. Navy agencies in Washington had tried for the use of B-29s for mining early in 1944, and Nimitz was even more insistent.

Arnold's staff was not receptive. To take a considerable part of the B-29 effort and devote it to mining would interfere with the primary mission, so any kind of mining on a major scale had to await the buildup of forces in the Marianas. Within Norstad's office the Navy view was considered "another hope for a relatively painless method of winning the war," a slow process that might take a couple of years. A major mining campaign should not, they felt, be begun until the aircraft industry had been knocked out and then only if a complete blockade seemed possible and looked more rewarding than any other target system.

Nimitz, however, continued to urge the early commitment of B-29s, asking Arnold to assign at least 150 sorties to mining from January 1945 and a heavier effort after March. Arnold hedged in November, promising aid when his forces were larger and the weather was not as suitable for daylight missions. If not really keen about mining, Arnold was determined to give it a try. Hansell had objected in vain.

The 73rd Bomb Wing had its hands full and was taking heavy losses, so to have begun mining early in 1945 would have further interfered with a bombing campaign that was in trouble anyway. In holding off, Arnold and Hansell were hardly being unreasonable.

So the Air Force was being cornered into a mining program, a Navy task, because they had the best aircraft for the job. The air planners had no idea just how fantastically successful this new campaign for the B-29s would be.

There was some hope that the job could be done by just one group, maybe even a beefed-up squadron. LeMay soon found that a larger force would be needed to give the plan a fair chance, and his scheme, submitted late in January, suggested that fifteen hundred mines be laid in April, with an entire wing being used for the operation, though not exclusively. He nominated the 313th Wing, then settling in on Tinian at North Field.

Training, which involved teaching the crews the theory of aerial mining, followed by a series of practice flights with five radar approaches each and a couple of actual drops at the end, was begun in February. The tactics were molded by the same factors that had effected bombing operations and by the experience of the 58th Wing. Daylight missions at high altitude were unsuitable, particularly because parachuted mines were not accurate. The best way was for the B-29s to make individual, night approaches and release by radar. This would be safer, more accurate, allow a greater load of mines, and be less at the mercy of weather.

The Navy provided technical assistance and logistical support, but Norstad clearly stated that the operation was experimental and should not upset established bombardment plans, as some feared would happen. In spite of doubts in Twentieth Air Force headquarters, LeMay continued to prepare, and on March 11 ordered the 313th to fly its first two mining missions, coded appropriately Starvation I and II. The target was the Shimonoseki Strait, always an important sea route but by the end of March the most important in Japan. The Japanese had been closing convoy routes at the end of 1943, and by September 1944 they had lost regular contact with the South and Southwest Pacific and other areas. The Philippines campaign had resulted in a crisis, and the loss of Iwo Jima and the imminent assault on Okinawa completed the strangling of regular traffic southward. The harbors in Tokyo and Ise bays lay idle more often and convoy routes from Kyushu to Formosa and Singapore

A 9th Group B-29 during a practice mining mission. On mining flights the navigator was the bombardier.

were given up. By March 1945 Japanese shipping was restricted to the Yellow Sea, the Tsushima Strait, and the Sea of Japan. The situation increased the importance of ports on the Asian side of Honshu and Kyushu and in the Inland Sea, the natural canal that was the vital link in the enemy's transportation system. The great bulk of shipping was passing through Shimonoseki Strait.

Also, at that time, Shimonoseki was assuming a particular tactical importance. With the invasion of Okinawa set for April 1, the mining of the strait would hamper the flow of supplies and reinforcements and hinder the movements of what was left of the Japanese battle fleet.

General "Skippy" Davies, commanding the 313th, set up the first attack for the night of March 27 with three formations totaling over one hundred B-29s. They were to go in singly, with only enough time between formations to prevent confusion. With the release altitudes varying from five thousand to eight thousand feet, most of the B-29s could carry six tons of acoustic and magnetic mines. They got off as scheduled, and ninety-two dropped their mines in the primary areas. Japanese air opposition was light, but there was a lot of flak at the low altitudes, some of it from ships, and three Superforts were lost. The western approach to Shimonoseki Strait was laid about as planned, though slightly to the south of the main shipping lane; in the eastern approach a heavy concentration sank into the main channel, but the field thinned out on either side, and a bomb-rack failure in a B-29 left a gap of three miles.

The second mission, flown the night of March 30, completed the plugging of the eastern approach and blocked the approach to Sasebo and the southern approach to Kure and Hiroshima. The northern approach, where the attack was marred due to four planes aborting, was not closed entirely but was certainly dangerous to shipping.

On April 1 six aircraft dropped mines from altitudes above twenty-five thousand feet to avoid flak from the enemy fleet anchored at Kure, and the results were excellent.

The Japanese quickly stepped up their minesweeping activities, and to keep the fields full LeMay instructed the 313th to sow at least two thousand mines in April. Several hundred were laid in a series of small missions, but far short of LeMay's demand.

The 313th, like the other wings, was involved in support of the Okinawa battle and strategic strikes, so fell behind schedule in mining, and LeMay decided on two maximum efforts to lay fifteen hundred mines, but the other commitments continued to impede the effort, and limited the mine tonnage for April to under three hundred.

General John H. "Skippy" Davies, commander of the 313th Bomb Wing.

LeMay's directive of April 18 included repeat missions to Shimonoseki, the total blockade of the approaches to Kobe and Osaka, and attrition fields at Tokyo, Yokohama, and Nagoya harbors. Kobe and Osaka, at the eastern end of the Inland Sea, were second in importance only to Shimonoseki. However, these missions simply could not be fitted into the schedule until early May.

During April three F-13s were loaned to the Thirteenth Air Force for a series of special missions, mapping areas around Java. They operated from Morotai, where artwork like Double Exposure's *made them a major drawing card. (Australian War Memorial)*

In spite of the occasional faulty drops, and the April lag, the mining campaign had begun very well. The first Japanese reaction had been to hold shipping in harbors while channels were cleared after an attack; by sweeping, bombing the shallower fields, or using small suicide vessels they were able to open some channels, but the countermeasures were never really adequate, and were complicated because the B-29s varied their tactics and types of mines and increased the number of targets. Food shortages, aggravated by the fire blitz, which had destroyed a quarter of the emergency rice stocks, were so serious that ships simply had to keep moving. It became normal to let ship captains decide whether or not they would attempt to run a freshly mined channel. LeMay's people estimated that by the end of April more than thirty ships had gone down or been damaged at Shimonoseki. Postwar investigation cut this back to eighteen ships sunk or permanently crippled, but the true figure is relatively unimportant, because the fact remains that much of

The 3rd Photo F-13 Yokohama Yo-Yo *was eventually returned to the States to take part in a war-bonds drive. One problem confronting the 3rd was that it was stationed at Depot Field, Guam, from January 1945, which was not long enough to permit full-load takeoffs, so photo planes going out on long missions had to be flown from Depot Field to North Field or Saipan before missions. Another thorn in their sides was that higher command insisted on poststrike* *photos so soon after missions that the pictures were unsuitable for assessment purposes, and another mission would have to be run when the area was clear of fire and smoke. However, the 3rd's loss rate was lighter than expected, and they had an overflow of F-13s; these were farmed out to other groups, where they were used for weather or radar scope missions. (John Mitchell)*

Japan's shipping was tied up after each attack. The aim of the campaign was blockade, not attrition. The tactical results were also pleasing: No major warship had passed through Shimonoseki after March 27. Some destroyers made it through during the Okinawa campaign, but the Japanese acknowledged that at least four were sunk in the attempt. When the task force headed by the mammoth battleship *Yamato* sortied from the Inland Sea on April 16 it was forced to use the Bungo Strait between Kyushu and Shikoku, and was soon spotted by Captain Frank Scheible in the 3rd Photo's *Yokohama Yo-Yo,* and subsequently destroyed.

On May 5 nearly one hundred B-29s mined Tokyo Bay, Ise Bay, and the Inland Sea. Special radar countermeasure precautions were taken for the small force going to Tokyo Bay. Five minutes before the arrival of the first of the four mining aircraft, two Superdumbos came in on a different course dropping "rope"—four-hundred-foot lengths of thin, half-inch aluminum tape. The four mining B-29s entered the bay area, also dropping "rope" and attempting to barrage-jam the enemy radar. Led by Colonel Howard Hugos, the 504th Group's deputy commander, the four airplanes' assigned mine field was far up the bay, deep in the Tokyo defense area. Hugos reached the objective at eight thousand feet as the beams of myriad searchlights focused on his plane. At the release point the mines in the front bomb bay dropped successfully, but some of the mines in the rear would not release due to faulty shackles. Hugos decided on a second run. Banking the plane around and passing over more than a dozen heavy flak batteries at Kawasaki and Haneda Airfield, he tried again. Again the release failed. Hugos made a third run, but still the mines hung there. After an hour's work in the bomb bay they were finally jettisoned.

For two weeks from May 13, the 313th sent out over two hundred B-29s in eight mining missions, most to Shimonoseki, the rest to ports on the Sea of Japan. During May the Japanese improved their sweeping methods but, as they later admitted, the weight, variety, and spread of the 313th Wing's attacks were too much to cope with. The small western ports, lacking minesweepers, were closed for three to five days after an attack, and traffic was dangerous long after that. Even at Shimonoseki they were only able to clear a narrow channel, and that imperfectly. The strait was completely closed for four days in May and partly closed on other days. Even with these precautions about a third of the ships trying to get through were crippled. During May 1945 aerial mines took a heavier toll than submarines, for the first time.

Crisis at Okinawa

It was realized during the planning for the Okinawa invasion that the landing would be exposed to attack from all types of Japanese aircraft based on Kyushu, just over three hundred miles away. Also, the distance of Okinawa from the nearest American base would prevent American land-based fighters covering the invasion area. An agreement had been roughed out that the Superfortresses would provide reconnaissance and

The mines could be touchy and dangerous. On May 20, 1945, the 9th Group's Thunderin' Loretta was taking off when it exploded, obliterating Thunderin' Loretta *and destroying two 504th Group B-29s. Lieutenant William Caldwell and his crew were killed, except for the tail gunner, who miraculously survived. (Swihart)*

raid the airfields in Kyushu and on Formosa that were within radius of the landings. Such diversion of B-29 missions worried both LeMay and Arnold. While the joint chiefs and the other commanders accepted this scheme with some modifications, Arnold withheld his final approval until he was certain that the B-29s would not be wasted. Airfields were not "appropriate" B-29 targets under normal circumstances.

LeMay's first part in the Okinawa operation was to provide photo reconnaissance of the island. The weather was bad, and numerous missions were flown to get the required coverage until finally, on February 28, Lieutenant J. D. Litton found a bright, clear day and covered the island from end to end in a single F-13 mission.

During the first week of March 1945 LeMay had met with Nimitz and others to thrash out the final part the B-29s would play. Included in the comprehensive plan were maximum efforts against Honshu targets, reconnaissance, the mining of Shimonoseki Strait to close it for a month, and strikes against the Kyushu airfields. Five days before the landing, LeMay would revert to full-scale strikes against Honshu. LeMay was unhappy with the program, and wanted to limit the airfield strikes to just one attack. Arnold agreed at first, then held back judgment until the specific Kyushu targets were nominated. In order of priority they were airfields and installations at Kanoya, Miyasaki, Tachiarai, Nittagahara, Kagoshima, Omura, Oita, and Saeki. Arnold went along, but conditionally: The B-29s were to attack installations, not bothering with airstrips unless they were crammed with planes. Norstad advised LeMay that the main concern was to save time and casualties at Okinawa, and to advise Nimitz that the B-29s were available to him whenever they could be used effectively, under emergency conditions or not. Nimitz, in reality, gained control of the B-29s for the next five weeks.

The B-29s flew their first Okinawa support mission to Kyushu on March 27, hitting Tachiarai, Oita, and the Omura aircraft factory. While the 73rd and 314th wings hit the Kyushu targets, the 313th was mining the Shimonoseki Strait. The missions were part of an extensive campaign to fulfill both a strategic and an immediate tactical role. On the night of March 30 a dozen 314th Wing B-29s struck the Nagoya Mitsubishi engine works, and the following day the B-29s returned to Tachiarai and Omura.

The landings on Okinawa began on Easter morning 1945, and the Marines and Army infantrymen quickly got a foothold. Four days later they were in control of a large piece of the island, containing two vitally important airfields: Yontan and Kadena.

Then on April 6 the Okinawa situation changed dramatically. The Japanese struck the forces on and around the island with a massive air attack, including over three hundred kamikazes. The crisis would have caused Nimitz to exercise his emergency option for B-29 support even without the unusual powers he had been given for the Okinawa campaign. On April 8 LeMay sent the B-29s to airfields at Kanoya, where the enemy suicide planes seemed to be coming from, but with these targets blanketed by clouds, the B-29s were forced to bomb Kagoshima city. Nimitz asked for an attack the next day, and the B-29s were sent to bomb six Kyushu airfields. It was not possible to accurately gauge results, but Nimitz felt that the multiple strikes kept some of the heat off Okinawa for most of the next day.

The Japanese threw everything at the island, coming back again and again. The B-29s had to help as much as they could, and for over three weeks most of LeMay's efforts were expended in direct support during the Okinawa bloodbath. The Superfortresses flew more than two thousand sorties against seventeen airfields on Kyushu and Shikoku. Opposition at the targets varied: sometimes none at all, sometimes fairly stiff. On April 18, Lieutenant Ed Cutler, pilot of *Texas Doll*, had expected a "piece of cake." But Tachiarai airfield was empty, the Japanese fighters all in the air waiting for the B-29s in "two swarming balls," one on each side of the 497th's flight path. In the nose, *Texas Doll*'s bombardier, Jack Bisanz, remembers three things happening virtually at once: *Coral Queen*, on their right, was hit heavily in the left wing and tail; *Texas Doll* was hit, and depressurized; *Gonna Mak'er* was rammed. To Cutler, it all seemed to happen so very slowly. He saw "bullets just stitch a line of holes through *Coral Queen*'s No. 1 and No. 2 engines, along the wing section from front

The B-29s could absorb heavy damage. Lieutenant Holly Anderson of the 29th Group stares into the gaping hole left by a burst of heavy flak that hit the unpressurized aft section, severing the rudder-control cables and knocking the aircraft out of formation. To add to his troubles, enemy fighters then singled him out, but Anderson was able to make it to Iwo. May 3, 1945. (Reineke)

to rear, and then through the tail . . . then fuel began to pour out—not leak—pour! We all knew he was going to blow up any second . . . right in front of us."

Incredibly the B-29 did not explode, but kept flying. As this was happening, another fighter was shooting holes through *Texas Doll* and Cutler remembers it as "the only time we ever heard the roar of battle, screaming, pounding fighter engines, guns and cannon, theirs and ours, all going at the same time . . . one after another they flew right through our formation from all directions. Then one flew right into *Gonna Mak'er*. I watched, spellbound, as the tail and right wing (almost all 123 feet of it) came off, and the No. 4 engine broke loose and climbed majestically straight up—all by itself, still running!"

Gonna Mak'er flipped over and spun down in flames. The fighters seemed to be focusing their attention on *Texas Doll,* and there was a whoosh of air as the B-29 suffered explosive decompression. Cutler remembers talking to his embattled airplane and "making all kinds of phony promises to God." *Texas Doll* managed to struggle home, riddled with about 350 holes, large and small, but no injuries to the crew. She was flying again less than three weeks later. The damaged *Coral Queen* ran out of luck, ditching just 35 miles short of Iwo; only three survived.

That same day, on the way to Izumi Airfield, a 500th Group B-29 commanded by Captain Robert Cordray lost two engines and became the first B-29 to make an emergency landing on Okinawa.

Lifeguard

The Kyushu airfield missions led to one of the most dramatic rescue stories of the war. It began, in a way, with a letter from General Hap Arnold that accompanied a replacement B-29, which found its way to the 314th Wing on Guam. This letter advised that the B-29 should be named *General Andrews*, in memory of General Frank Andrews, who had been killed in a B-24 crash. It went on, "Because General Andrews was one of the first to foresee the power of very-long-range bombardment—the purpose of the B-29—I direct that the first mission in which this aircraft participates shall be officially designated as the 'General Andrews' mission and to be so enrolled in the history of the squadron to which this plane is assigned."

Assigned to Lieutenant Ben Powell and his crew, the *General Andrews* was not to complete even one mission. On April 27 she went with the 39th Group to bomb Kushira Airfield. Over the target a flak burst damaged her and a phosphorous bomb set fire to an engine. The aircraft began

The first control tower at Iwo was Spartan —and dangerous. Whenever a plane was coming in to land it was the signal for every Japanese gun still left on the northern end of the island to open fire. The men manning the tower considered themselves the un-disputed winners of the "All-island, All-service Foxhole-diving Championship," with expertise in the jackknife, the double flip, and the swan dive. They learned to get a plane down and then "run like hell." (Reineke)

going down, struggling to reach the coast for a ditching. The fire devoured the wing and it began to crumple back. The *General Andrews* went into a sickening spin and crashed into the sea about twenty-five miles offshore. Three of the crew had succeeded in bailing out and they were picked up by a Lifeguard submarine, the *Gato*, commanded by Captain Richard Holden.

The next day, during a strike on Miyazaki Airfield, the 499th Group's *Salvo Sally*, with Captain William Canada and his crew, was seen to take a direct flak hit over the target, which blew a large hole in the radio compartment. There was little definite information after that. Two 499th aircraft reported seeing a B-29 with two engines out and smoking, and one of these added that this B-29 made what looked like a good water landing; the nose and tail broke off when the plane hit the water, but the center section floated a few minutes before sinking. One B-29 dropped a five-man life raft, and two chutes had been seen, but these were more

Alvin Bowers' Ready Teddy *with two sets of markings, old and new. It took time to change the tail insignia: On the April 27, 1945, mission, only two of the four 9th Group lead aircraft had full markings; one just had a large black circle, the other had no tail markings at all. (Swihart)*

than a mile apart, and the waves were large. Another B-29 circled the wreckage for ninety minutes but no survivors were spotted. The *Gato* had been seen to surface, but the B-29 could not make contact with the sub, although it appeared to be heading for the ditching area anyway.

The CFC gunner on *Salvo Sally* that day was Sergeant Jack Cannon, and he believed the flak burst that hit the front section must have killed or wounded the copilot, navigator, and bombardier, although apparently the pilot was not hurt. Another flak burst had hit the rear section, and a third hit between the right engines. No. 3 caught fire and began wind-milling; No. 4 was feathered.

Salvo Sally started down "like an anvil" but Canada regained control. Cannon reported, "He sounded calm on the interphone. We asked if we should bail and he said, 'Hell, no, everything's going to be all right. Ride her down and prepare to ditch.' He headed her for the coast. I sat tight until the flames swept back and my blister started to melt. Then I went to the waist. One of the men was hanging out the hatch by his hands, plead-ing for permission to jump. We pulled him back in, and again asked the pilot whether we should bail. He said to stick with the ship, so I went back to get some rations and water and other gear stowed back there. When I got back the men were bailing; the pilot gave them the O.K. when he started to lose control. I hung on for a couple of minutes while we went lower and lower, and I could see fleets of sampans flashing past under-neath as we cleared the coast. Then I went out, the last one to jump. . . . I pulled the ripcord and nothing happened. The tail of the plane passed overhead and I pulled again and this time it opened. Almost at the same second, it seemed, I hit the water."

Cannon lost his gun, signal mirrors, and the water and rations he had jammed in his pockets. All he had was his Mae West and dinghy. It was late morning when he hit the water, and he passed the afternoon trying to dry out in the sun. With dusk he began to doze fitfully, and at dawn the next day he saw the mountains of Japan. He was gradually floating ashore, and began to paddle furiously, but barely held his own against the current. Then about nine o'clock he saw a Superdumbo overhead, which dropped him food, marker dye, and signal mirrors.

The Superdumbo was from the 498th Group, piloted by Lieutenant Alfred Stendahl, one of two preceding a force striking Miyakanojo on April 29. After dropping the gear to Cannon, Stendahl contacted the Lifeguard submarine, *Gato*. Then the B-29 crew spotted eight sailing ves-sels heading for where they had made the telltale drop. Stendahl zoomed down and made a mast-height attack, his turrets chewing away at four of the vessels until they sank, and the other four headed for safety from the strafing B-29. Then Stendahl began searching for the crew of his own group's *Little Jo,* which had just been reported going down in the same vicinity. They found them, but had to leave because their Superdumbo was running low on fuel.

Little Jo *was hit over the target on April 29, and the crew bailed out as soon as they had crossed the Japanese coast. Eleven parachutes were seen, but only six men were picked up. (Watson)*

Meanwhile, the other Superdumbo, piloted by Lieutenant John Buck of the 497th Group, was covering the *Gato* as it moved perilously close to the Japanese shoreline. Behind the B-29, invisible in the sun, came four Japanese Pauls. One of them flashed across the deck of the sub and dropped two bombs. Captain Holden radioed, "Take care of that bastard for us, will you?"

As the float-plane fighter dashed by, the B-29's guns ripped into him. Buck wheeled into a turn and set after the fighter, which was in trouble. Streams of fire blossomed, and the enemy plane skipped across the wave-tops then slid under. Buck chased off another by blocking the path to the sub with his B-29, and as the fighter passed overhead a burst from one of the top turrets damaged it and it changed course abruptly. Buck then chased the other two out of the area. He dropped a seven-man life raft to Cannon and then he too was forced to head for home, low on fuel.

Cannon clambered into the big raft, hoisted the sail, and headed away from shore. When he first sighted the submarine he thought it was Japanese and tried to hide under a blue blanket, nearly managing not to be rescued. As soon as he realized they were Americans he jumped up and was hauled aboard the *Gato* like a sack of mail as it went by. A sailor with a Thompson machine gun fired a burst into the raft, sinking it.

The *Gato* headed away until dark, then turned around and came back again. Shortly after dawn on April 30, several miles north, the sub's lookout saw a flash from the water. It was Lieutenant Earl Fisher and his radioman from *Little Jo,* sharing a one-man life raft that was riding almost under water. In the next hour *Gato* picked up four other members of the crew.

The survivors of *Little Jo, Salvo Sally,* and the *General Andrews* gathered in the cramped haven of the submarine, which had managed to save ten men in three hectic days. *Gato* then resumed her regular job of hunting shipping, and the B-29 crewmen had several weeks to see another side of the war before she put into port.

*　　*　　*

Overall, losses during the Kyushu raids were light, and although it was hard to assess what the B-29s accomplished, the effort could not have been withheld under the circumstances.

Nimitz sent a message of thanks and surrendered control of the bombers, and by then airfields on Okinawa and Ie Shima were able to handle defending fighters. With their "unprofitable" job over, the B-29s were ready to return to their main task: the destruction of Japan.

The 505th Group ran into stiff opposition at Oita Airfield on May 7. Fifty to sixty fighters hit them, and they lost two B-29s. Honorable TNT Wagon's *gunners claimed three fighters: a Jack, a Tojo, and an Irving. (Carpi)*

The concentration on urban incendiary attacks, mining, and meeting the demands of the Okinawa campaign had not meant that precision strikes against priority targets had been totally abandoned. After the March fire blitz had proved so successful, LeMay had tried to create a method for night attacks against individual targets, particularly during the periods of bad weather expected.

The summer monsoon would lead to more cloudy conditions than the winter monsoon, and LeMay's weather section had estimated that the main target areas in Honshu could be attacked visually on about three days each in April and May, and only one day in June. A night precision method was never perfected, but the B-29s did beat Honshu's clouds by a variety of attacks that were tremendously successful.

The main factor was fairly simple: On clear days multiple forces hit various targets visually; on cloudy days urban areas were bombed by radar.

An earlier experiment in night precision attacks was suggested by Arnold, who had hoped that the devastating effects of the fire blitz could be directed more specifically. The first trial was a major effort, a strike of 250 B-29s on Mitsubishi at Nagoya, flown on March 24. Operational plans were similar to the British Pathfinder technique: Ten B-29s would light up the target with flares, then 10 more would start marker fires, and 5 minutes later the main force would hit the area with high explosives. On March 24 the timing was fine, but the clouds so obscured the target that the attack was doomed to failure. The clouds and the smoke from the incendiaries dimmed the light from the flares, and although this was the heaviest attack ever sent to a single aircraft-industry target, there was little in the way of results.

Effectively lighting the target was the key, and LeMay decided to let Power and O'Donnell run their own missions, with their own techniques. The 314th Wing strike was purely experimental, utilizing but 14 B-29s. Three were flare ships, 7 carried high explosives, and the other 4 carried a mixed load of bombs and flares. Despite the abundance of flares, the 12 planes that reached Nagoya missed the Mitsubishi plant.

O'Donnell's 73rd Wing attempt was much larger but little more successful: On April 1 he sent 121 B-29s to Nakajima's Musashino plant, each plane's load including 4 flares. Of over, 1,000 tons of bombs dropped, only 4 tons hit the area.

As a last attempt, LeMay ordered the three wings to attack three separate targets, each using its own method of lighting, but again there was no tangible success, and LeMay abandoned the experiment.

The 498th Group lines up for a night take-off on April 1, 1945, bound for target No. 357. The plane taxiing through the dark- *ness is the second Fay, and she will never be heard of again after this mission.*

Taking advantage of the first break in the Okinawa missions, on April 7 LeMay split his forces between his two top-listed targets. The 313th and 314th Wings drew the Mitsubishi engine works at Nagoya. Bombing from 20,500 feet in nearly perfect conditions, the B-29s showed that the job really could be done. This attack destroyed 90 per cent of the plant's facilities.

The 73rd Wing went to target No. 357 and bombed from even lower altitude, and also had the first friendly fighter escort experienced by the B-29s: 97 P-51s from Iwo Jima. The results at Musashino could not be assessed individually for this mission, but the combined results with a mission flown five days later amounted to the destruction of nearly half the total roof area.

To protect the bombers on these two missions a combined technique of barrage radar jamming and "rope" was used, but the results were not conclusive. Flak damaged nearly two thirds of the planes over Musashino

The B-29s provided navigation for the P-51s. The 498th Group's Joltin' Josie *is leading Mustangs of the 15th Fighter Group.*

and more than half of those over Nagoya, the highest damage rates ever, but conditions were perfect and the Japanese preferred visual-sighting methods.

In the clear, bright sky over Nagoya, Captain Charles Crowe of the 29th Group experienced a fuel-system malfunction about twenty minutes from the target that caused all four engines to backfire and smoke violently. Crowe held formation, then fifteen minutes before bombs away the formation was attacked by fifty fighters, who singled out Crowe's aircraft with its beckoning streamers of smoke. The gunners held them off, and the bomb run was made successfully through intense, accurate flak. After bombs away the crippled aircraft, which had taken a dozen flak and bullet holes, successfully escaped.

The 29th also lost a B-29 to flak thirty seconds before bombs away: A burst ripped off six feet of the left wingtip, and the plane soared up out of control, then went down in a flat spin engulfed in flames. One chute was seen. Then Captain Frank Crowcroft's plane was rammed: The left wing of a Nick hit the No. 1 engine. The B-29 burst into flames, turned over on its back, and went down as the fighter disintegrated.

The 313th Wing had their problems too. Over the target Captain Frederick Sheaffer's 9th Group aircraft took a direct hit in the No. 4 engine, and smoke streamed from it. The engine could not be feathered and it looked like a ditching was coming.

Captain William Weinert, in *Destiny's Tot*, buddied up with Sheaffer's crippled aircraft. As they lost altitude, Sheaffer's crew fired all their ammunition, and threw out the bomb sight and anything else that might fly about the plane during a ditching. Some of the flak suits got caught in the bomb-bay doors, jamming them open. At about one thousand feet the No. 1 engine started to cut out. The flak burst that had damaged the No. 4 engine had also knocked out the supercharger on No. 3, meaning they were flying on less than two engines. One of the crew was hanging by his hands in the open bomb bay, kicking loose the obstructions. He succeeded and they closed the bomb-bay doors.

Everyone was in ditching position; then about ten feet off the water the fire in No. 4 went out and the No. 3 engine was performing satisfactorily at the lower altitude. The pilots, Sheaffer and Lieutenant Leonard Carpi, decided to try for Iwo Jima. They flew all the way at ditching altitude, because if No. 1 quit altogether the other two engines could not keep them going with No. 4 propeller windmilling, and after landing safely they counted several hundred flak holes in their B-29. It was so completely wrecked that it was junked.

So at last, on April 7, the 73rd Wing had hurt target No. 357. Tokyo's weather had been as nearly perfect as Nagoya's, and the one hundred

The Ancient Mariner, *from the 500th Bomb Group. (Ray Clinkscales)*

planes had carried newly arrived two-thousand-pound bombs. They caused heavy damage in the machine shops and destroyed about 10 per cent of the plant's buildings. Captain Ray Clinkscales, flying the 500th Bomb Group's *The Ancient Mariner*, had been over the target when he left the formation to protect another B-29 that had an engine shot out and was on fire. Clinkscales escorted and protected the damaged Superfort for over an hour, warding off around seventy fighter attacks. His gunners claimed five fighters destroyed and one damaged. When they ran out of ammunition, Clinkscales drove off the last fighter by turning *The Ancient Mariner* into its line of flight, forcing it to roll away from the damaged B-29. Throughout the fight, three tons of bombs were hung up in *The Ancient Mariner*'s forward bomb bay, handicapping maneuverability and draining precious fuel, but Clinkscales got her home.

The 73rd Wing went back to Musashino on April 12 to finish it off, but because of haze they had to make a radar bomb run. They missed the Tama section, which had escaped damage five days earlier, but got sixty-four tons of bombs in the eastern section of the plant, resulting in heavy structural damage.

Musashino, after eleven missions, was finally just about destroyed. The top priority target had been bombed on seven missions, and only the last two were really successful, but officials at the plant had abandoned repair efforts long before, concentrating on dispersal. Production stopped altogether after the April attacks.

On April 12 LeMay had sent the 313th and 314th wings to Koriyama, north of Tokyo, in an effort to split the Tokyo defenses. The planes heavily damaged two chemical plants, Hodogaya and Koriyama, and an aluminum plant. The primary targets were selected because they produced tetraethyl lead for aviation fuel, but the oil shortage in Japan was so bad that the production of these plants was actually not needed, and the good mission was of little strategic importance. It also failed as a diversion—the fighters stayed over Tokyo. Koriyama, however, remains a hallmark mission in the B-29 story: It was the day Sergeant Henry Erwin of the 29th Group performed a superhuman feat of courage.

Major Tony Simeral's B-29, *Snatch Blatch*, named for a character from Rabelais and decorated with a witch riding a broom, was the lead plane of the 52nd Bomb Squadron. Simeral had his regular crew and an observer, Colonel Eugene Strouse, the squadron commander. Sergeant "Red" Erwin was flying his eleventh mission as a radio operator.

As squadron lead, *Snatch Blatch* would head a tighter formation at the initial point, and it was Erwin's job to drop flares and a smoke bomb to in-

The 29th Group area on Guam. Snatch Blatch, *Simeral's B-29, is the airplane with the* lead-crew stripe *and numbered 37.*

dicate the assembly point. He removed his earphones and got ready.

The phosphorous smoke pot was a thick canister weighing about twenty pounds, with a six-second delayed-action fuse to allow it to fall about three hundred feet before detonating. The bomb was dropped through a circular release pipe near the bomb bay.

By now they were crossing the Japanese coast, and Erwin prepared to drop the signals as the first flak came up to meet them. *Snatch Blatch* shuddered and Erwin fell to the floor. He got to his feet, gathered up the flares and the phosphorous bomb, and stood by the release pipe, awaiting the drop signal from Simeral.

The pilot raised his hand and looked back from his seat at Erwin. The sergeant dropped the parachute flares through the pipe. As they exploded, the pilots of the other B-29s watched the lead ship, waiting for the phosphorous signal. Erwin set the fuse, held the bomb over the pipe, and let it slip through his fingers. The bomb clattered through the pipe, but did not fall through the release gate at the bottom. The flap must have jammed after the last flare. The phosphorous bomb bounced momentarily, then exploded. A stream of white fire shot from the tube into Erwin's face. The bomb shot back up the tube, a deadly fireball burning at 1300 degrees, spitting phosphorous particles all over Erwin.

Snatch Blatch was loaded with three tons of incendiaries, and with the smoke pot detonated inside the plane she became a giant flying fire bomb.

The blinding fireball zipped through the B-29 like a big, lazy incendiary bullet. It hit the roof and bounced back, its white heat engulfing Erwin. His nose was burned off, most of his right ear was gone, and the whole top half of his body was charred. He fell backward, his scorched arms flailing, his mind a sea of confusion and unbearable pain. The bomb finally came to rest on the floor of the aircraft, burning and sputtering, just feet from the bomb bay and the incendiaries. One of the gunners thought maybe he could smother it with parachute packs and let it burn its way through the floor, but the bombs were too close, and the thick white smoke was choking everyone in the B-29. Erwin somehow managed to stagger from the floor, his mind numbed and hazy. Almost blind, his eyes a mass of blisters, he lurched toward the glowing bomb. He was nearly there when the nose of the B-29 dipped, throwing him sideways into his radio compartment. Up front Simeral and his copilot were choking from the white smoke filling the cabin. *Snatch Blatch* was out of control, falling at a sixty-degree angle. Colonel Strouse, who had been looking over Simeral's shoulder for most of the flight, was thrown into the tip of the nose with the bombardier. Now only perhaps seven hundred feet from the ground, Simeral could not risk jettisoning the bombs because of the blast. He fought to regain control of the airplane. As he struggled

*Koriyama on April 12 was the first Japan   manded by Colonel Elbert Reynolds, who
mission for the 330th Bomb Group, com-   led the mission. (Jonas Carpenter)*

with the controls, Erwin was locating the bomb with his fingers. The
clothing on the upper half of his body was almost gone, and the skin was
burning as he lifted the bomb in his hands. Slowly, laboriously, he edged
toward the nose of the plane, away from the bomb bay. He felt his way
around the top turret well, but the navigator's table blocked him. He
cradled the bomb between his arm and his body, freeing one hand to
unlatch the spring lock that held the table. Crying and coughing, he held
the phosphorous bomb in his hand as his wrist burned to the bone.

Simeral screamed, "Get it out the window!"

The trudging, burning figure made his way toward them. His trousers,
shoes, whole body were on fire. "Open the window," he cried, bumping
into the copilot, who was already pointing to the window. He reached for
the bomb himself, but somehow Erwin found the opening and heaved
the bomb through it. Then he collapsed, fifteen seconds of unbelievable
effort over. *Snatch Blatch* was down to three hundred feet and Simeral, all
thoughts of target, mission, and enemy far from his mind, leveled off,

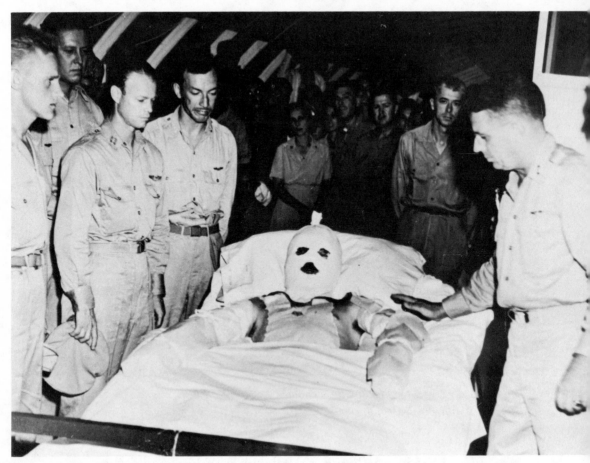

Red Erwin receives his Medal of Honor from General Hale as Simeral and Strouse, *third and fourth from the left, look on. (Simeral)*

gained altitude, and turned the aircraft around. The incendiaries were salvoed and the dash to Iwo began. Strouse radioed the rest of the planes to proceed to the target.

The crew knew that Erwin must die, but they had to try to help him. His body was sprayed with foam until they were sure all the fires were out, and Lieutenant William Loesch, the bombardier, administered morphine. Erwin just lay there, croaking incomprehensibly, then screaming as consciousness washed over him. One of the crew got his radio equipment working and sent a Mayday signal to Iwo. Erwin was the only member of the crew with any emergency medical training, and while they knew he needed blood plasma, nobody knew exactly how it was administered. Then Erwin stopped shrieking, as his tortured mind somehow grasped consciousness. He could just manage to speak, very slowly. Lying there, he instructed the crew how to give him the plasma, followed by more morphine. Then he lay there listening to the crew's efforts to convince him that he would live. For the next couple of hours he was not once granted the relief of unconsciousness. He just stared at the ceiling above him.

When *Snatch Blatch* reached Iwo, Simeral raced straight in, slammed the B-29 down, and braked to a shuddering halt. Stretcher bearers carried Erwin out and raced him to hospital.

For four days Erwin was given transfusions, injections, and internal surgery. Then he was flown to the larger hospital on Guam, and his miraculous recovery began.

The twenty-three-year-old sergeant, encased in bandages, was presented with the Medal of Honor by General Willis H. Hale.

*   *   *

On April 24, with weather looking bad for Kyushu but good for Tokyo, LeMay ran a mission to the Tachikawa plant of the Hitachi Aircraft Corporation. The target was completely wrecked. No effort was made to repair it, and production stopped. Going in unescorted and at unusually low altitude, the Superforts ran into stiff opposition from flak and fighters, and four B-29s were lost.

On May 5, on a mission to the Hiro Naval Aircraft Factory at Kure, the 73rd Wing was joined by the 58th, flying its first Honshu strike from the Marianas. Attacking from 20,000 feet, the B-29s bombed well enough to cut production at the target almost in half.

Six days later a moderate force of Superforts went to the Konan plant of the Kawanishi Aircraft Company, and the mission was again highly successful: The company quickly removed almost all of the machine tools from the wrecked factory.

With the two most important engine factories finally knocked out, LeMay decided to concentrate on the great cities; except for an abortive mission against the Tachikawa Aircraft Company on May 19, no precision attacks were scheduled until the second week of June.

LeMay had been able to send two major fire missions to the Tokyo Bay area. One, on April 13, had burned out more than eleven square miles of the arsenal district of Tokyo northwest of the Imperial Palace. Two nights later over three hundred B-29s incinerated another six square miles as well as a few square miles of Kawasaki.

The pilots of this 504th Group aircraft made nine attempts to land on Iwo, all unsuccessful. Damaged during the April 24 Hitachi strike, the B-29 plowed through the P-51 flight line, destroying four fighters. The crew escaped.

That night, while the 73rd Wing took care of Tokyo, the larger force, composed of the 313th and 314th wings, had gone to Kawasaki. Captain Earl Russell of the 29th Group was flying as a pathfinder, and five minutes from the target was attacked by fighters. The enemy planes tried desperately to force the B-29 from its bomb run. They set fire to one of the engines, and the blaze was spreading fast, but Russell held rigidly on course and dropped his bombs. The fighters had stayed with the damaged B-29 but as Russell turned the aircraft away and tried to make the coast the fire was being brought under control. Then the fighters attacked again, and the B-29 began going down fast. When last seen it was crashing into the sea with its turrets still exchanging fire with the fighters.

Victory in Europe led to plans to force a quick end to the Pacific War, and May would become a month of massive fire-bomb missions, involving all four wings of B-29s at LeMay's disposal.

The curtain-raiser for the new series of strikes was the northern area of

Deacon's Disciples *of the 444th Group at* *West Field, Tinian. The 58th Wing soon* *learned that the Seabees on the island were* *a reasonable bunch, and that liquor was* *held in high regard. One enterprising* *officer and his tentmates were soon moving* *to live in an imposing "four bottle" struc-* *ture, but the authorities quickly called a halt* *to such unauthorized construction.*

The 19th Group's Maximum Load *is prepared for the April 13 Tokyo strike;* crewmen are fixing shackles to M-47 incendiaries.

The 19th Group lumbers out for "Perdition No. 1," the April 13 mission to the Tokyo arsenal area.

An enemy fighter shot up two of Ramblin' Roscoe's *engines during the April 15 Tokyo raid, as well as damaging the main-gear tires. The B-29 made a night landing on Iwo and ran into a truck, killed a Seabee, and injured two men sleeping in a tent before this embankment stopped her.*

When the advance echelon of the 58th Wing reached the Marianas, they were promptly put to work. The 444th's Shanghai Lil Rides Again flew the April 13 Tokyo mission with the 6th Group. The 676th Squadron insignia, Disney's Reluctant Dragon, appeared on the noses of most of their airplanes. (Carpi)

Nagoya, around Nagoya Castle, which included the top priority target, the Mitsubishi aircraft-engine works. The mission was flown on May 14, in daylight. Colonel Patrick McCarthy, the "Mad Mapper," took off from Guam in a 3rd Photo Squadron F-13 to take movies of this largest-ever bombing raid against the Empire. More than 500 B-29s left the runways of Saipan, Tinian, and Guam, their exhaust stacks and superchargers glowing cherry red as they roared through the darkness. At Nagoya they dumped 2,500 tons of incendiaries from altitudes between 12,000 and 20,500 feet. Colonel McCarthy in his photo plane made four runs from the initial point to the target at 20,000 feet as the waves of bombers went in; then the smoke became so thick that additional photography seemed pointless. The mission cost 10 B-29s to aggressive but uncoordinated resistance.

LeMay sent the Superfortresses back to Nagoya on the night of May

During May the 9th Group provided B-29s *of the flight leader was taken from* Ready
to navigate for the 318th Fighter Group's Teddy. *(Swihart)*
P-47s as they moved to Ie Shima. This photo

16, in what would be the last great attack on the city. This time the dock
and industrial areas in the southern part were singled out for destruction. The mission underlined the difference between night and day attacks. While fifteen fewer B-29s reached the target, the low-altitude, individual approach meant a heavier bomb load, and a thousand more tons
of fire rained down on Nagoya. Smoke and thermals forced the later B-
29s to drop from levels much higher than those briefed, diminishing their
accuracy. There were still good targets left in Nagoya, but not for area incendiary missions. The B-29s would go back six more times, but for
precision strikes.

Tokyo's turn came next. Four raids had already destroyed more than
thirty-four square miles of the city, and the next two attacks were
planned to obliterate it. The target for the night of May 23 was the district stretching south from the Imperial Palace along the west side of

Over Tokyo on May 24 the 498th Group lost four airplanes, including Captain Everett Zweifel in Danny Mite, *which lost* *two engines over the target and was last seen struggling to reach the coast.*

Tokyo Harbor, a residential and industrial area. The massive attack, well over five hundred planes strong, had been planned to skirt the heaviest ground defenses, but even so, the intense flak led to the loss of seventeen B-29s. The weather was poor, and the bombardiers were troubled by the smoke and searchlights. Another five square miles of Tokyo were burned to ashes. That night the Japanese *Bakas*, manned, rocket-powered suicide planes with over a ton of high explosives in their noses, literally flying bombs, were up, and their psychological effect was probably greater than their own effectiveness, making gunners trigger-happy: Three 462nd Group crew members reported that a B-29, with an engine afire, was shot at by another B-29. The burning bomber exploded, broke in two pieces, and fell in Tokyo Bay.

The B-29s went back to Tokyo two nights later, again over five hundred strong, to strike the area just north of the previous target. This included some of the financial, commercial, and government districts. There were light clouds, and combined with the smoke they forced most B-29s to drop by radar. The opposition was again tough, crews describing the flak as the heaviest of the campaign, and the losses from all causes were twenty-six B-29s, with another one hundred damaged. The pathfinders ran into a hot reception. Captain John Harvey of the 39th Group was one of the first over Tokyo, and their entire journey from the initial point to the target was made through searchlights and a withering concentration of heavy-caliber flak and fire bombs suspended from parachutes. Immediately after bombs away they were attacked by a fighter and five *Bakas*. They shot down the fighter, and almost simultaneously the CFC gunner exploded a *Baka*. They shook off the remaining *Bakas* by violent evasive action.

Another Tokyo casualty was Captain Claude Hensinger's Jo, *"sideswiped" by another B-29 over the target.* Jo *got to Iwo with no brakes, and no injuries to the crew. They found a piece of the tail of the other B-29 in one of her engines. (Reineke)*

Ready Teddy *on Okinawa. Copilot John Swihart recalls the events following a Shimonoseki Strait mining mission on the night of May 25: "We did not have enough fuel to reach Iwo Jima. We made the decision to go to Yontan and we flew around Okinawa on the east side and came up to Yontan on the west side. . . . Arriving very early in the morning at Yontan, we found many fires burning in C-46s, C-54s, and B-24s, and what appeared to be the remains of a Japanese bomber lying in the middle of the runway. We circled out over the fleet (which, by the way, was bombarding Naha, and every salvo of sixteen-inchers from those BBs sounded like a direct hit on 'Teddy') and attempted to raise the tower at Yontan. . . . After what seemed to be an interminable length of time, someone called and directed us to go to Kadena, a 'mud' fighter strip for Marine Corsairs. The wind was blowing at ninety degrees to the runway at* about thirty knots. As we came down the approach and touched down, a road grader started out on the fighter strip about three thousand feet down the field. During the heavy braking to avoid the grader, we blew one tire and took at least twenty of the twenty-two plys off the other on the right landing gear." Ready Teddy *was taxied back and maneuvered into a revetment by a Cletrac, and the crew went by truck to Yontan to pick up a couple of wheels and tires. There was no further damage or injury to plane or crew, but the airmen spent most of the day underground. Most of the fires they had seen at Yontan had been caused by the Marines on flak towers depressing their cannon to shoot at Japanese suicide commandos, who had tried to land five Sallys on the strip. Only one made it, in a wheels-up crash landing. After a couple of hours the commandos were all dead.*

Lieutenant Robert Moulton ditched this 6th Group B-29 offshore when Iwo was fogged in on May 26, 1945. The plane was towed ashore and parked on a reef, but broke up four days later in a bad storm.

The 444th Group lost one of its best crews that night. Captain Jack Siler was flying as a pathfinder to light up the Ginza district. Coming in upwind, all that was reported by one of the other pathfinders was a flash and glow in the sky, which appeared to be an aircraft exploding. It was probably Siler, claimed after thirty-two missions. Siler's wife's name was Eileen, and he was flying the *Princess Eileen IV*. His plane had been featured in newsreels, comic strips, bond drives, and recruiting posters.

Twenty of the losses that day were to "unknown causes," and the plight of the cripples was desperate, because Iwo Jima was fogged in. Lieutenant Robert Moulton of the 6th Group had been shot up after leaving the target and had an engine feathered; another was malfunctioning, but Moulton managed to reach Iwo despite the fact that his air speed was dangerously low. The undercast made landing impossible, and he had no hope of reaching Tinian. After circling Iwo for three hours in the hope that the weather might clear, he decided to ditch off the western shore.

Three of his crew suffered minor injuries but were picked up safely after Moulton put the B-29 down near to anchored shipping.

Another 6th Group B-29 was in trouble in the murk. Piloted by Captain Arthur Clay and Lieutenant Harry George, it had been caught by searchlights and held. Harry George recalls, "The plane shuddered several times as we caught pieces from flak bursts in the wings. . . . As I looked at a B-29 just a quarter mile to the right of us, I saw the tail gunner firing furiously at a target above and behind him. This was a 'ball of fire,' which seemed to be following down the tracks of the incendiary bullets. It kept coming and rammed the B-29 just in front of its tail section, exploding with such terrific force that we rocked from it. Parts of both planes rained down . . . we saw no parachutes.

"As our plane reached the release point, a barrage of flak opened up all around it. The bombardier punched the bomb toggle button, releasing the bombs in train, then turned his gunsight to fire six forward guns at a fighter strafing the plane from above. Just as he shouted, 'I got him!' the

Three 6th Group crew members who bailed out over Iwo on May 26: from the left, Lieutenant Lester Moellen, Captain Arthur Clay, and Lieutenant Harry George. (George)

plane lurched, rocked, and started to dive. It had caught a direct flak burst. Clay instinctively pulled back on the control column, but it flopped useless in his lap. I grasped my controls and they responded. Someone called, 'I'm hit,' and then the interphone went dead. I called for a crew check on emergency interphone. The engineer, navigator, and radio operator answered immediately, and after a long pause the tail gunner answered, 'O.K.' No word or sound came from the four men in the waist compartment.

"Clay took my controls and I went back through the plane to check the damage. Two engines were out, gasoline was streaming from holes in the fuel tanks, several fires were burning inside the plane, and in the waist compartment the left gunner's face was a mass of blood and protruding bone. The right gunner's leg was bleeding from pieces of flak that had gone through. The CFC gunner was just staring with unseeing eyes. He was in complete shock. I immediately told the radar operator to get on interphone and then administered blood plasma, morphine, and other

The 19th Group's City of Burlington *was returning from a training mission on May* *27 when she crashed on Guam. Two enlisted men were killed. (Jim McWethy)*

medical aid. About one minute later the right gunner announced in a shaky voice, 'There is a ball of fire just five hundred feet behind us and keeping right on our tail.' We felt that this was it. . . . This time, luckily, the tail gunner did not fire, and the suicide pilot must have been confused at seeing the exhaust of only two engines. Four minutes later his rocket sputtered out and he dropped into the sea.

"For the next five hours the plane somehow stayed in the air. . . . There were five or six holes as large as basketballs in the body and about seventy-five smaller ones. There was one in the tail you could put a bushel basket through. The whole tail section was twisted about fifteen degrees out of line and just peppered with smaller holes. The front bomb-bay doors were hanging open, and control wires were flapping out. We were flying on two engines at an air speed just above a stall. The engineer had little idea of how much gas we had lost over the target and his gauges were not dependable. We encountered five or six thunderstorms in which we had lightning, hail, and turbulence to contend with. Our navigation instruments were only half accurate and it was doubtful if we would be able to find Iwo . . . . All we could do was sit, swear, and sweat. It was an indescribable feeling."

The wrecked B-29 staggered through the air, and about dawn they spotted Chichi Jima, just north of Iwo, and their hopes rose. But where Iwo should have been there was just a bank of clouds, with the ugly peak of Mount Suribachi poking through them.

George continues, "We managed to make radio contact with Iwo and learned it was impossible to attempt a landing there. We were advised to bail out but no member of the crew wanted to leave the left-blister gunner, who was bordering between life and death. It would have been a miracle for him to survive a bail-out, and certain death if he missed the small island and went into the water.

"For two hours we circled, until the engineer estimated we had just fifteen minutes of gas remaining, and it was decided to attempt a radar-controlled landing. We lowered the gear and let down through the soup — searching, feeling, and straining for the ground. . . . We broke out over a cemetery with rows and rows of white crosses. Our altitude was just twenty-five feet. The runway was nowhere in sight.

"Up we went again, our two engines churning madly, and around for another attempt. This was not much more successful: We broke out at fifty feet but still no runway in sight. We stayed at fifty feet until we were right out over the water and then had to make a dangerously low right turn that must have been close to the water. The right-blister gunner, still

This 505th Group airplane was circling Iwo with a battle-damaged propeller running wild. Before the plane could get down, the prop flew off, knocking out No. 4 engine and ripping open the radio compartment. With only two engines, and one of the others burning, Captain Edward Fitch made a good landing but lost control at the end and the plane crashed into a damaged 497th Group airplane. The only injury in the entire incident was a sprained ankle when the bombardier jumped out after the collision.

at his position, cried out over the interphone, 'Your wing is going to hit the water!' But we made it around for another attempt at landing. I believe I saw the top of the control tower way off to my left this time, but it was too far off to make a landing pass, and we started up again.

"We were just breaking through the top of the cloud layer at about fifteen hundred feet when No. 2 engine sputtered. No. 4 was also sputtering. There was only one thing to do: Level out and bail out.

"We managed to get the plane headed over the longest part of the island and out we went. They dumped the left gunner out the back and the rest of us poured out all exits. The last I saw of the plane it was headed north out to sea."

All of the crew except Clay landed on the island, three of them in the

The smoke boils up over Yokohama as more B-29s go in to feed the fires. (McWethy)

grounds of the hospital. Clay hit the water several miles north and was picked up by a boat.

Five minutes later the crew of the 498th's *Lady Eve* bailed out over the island, and the next day a Dumbo found *Lady Eve* out about ninety miles from Iwo, where she had ditched perfectly by herself. The 444th's Lieutenant Donald MacRae and the crew of *Shanghai Lil Rides Again* bailed out over the water, and all except one of the crew was found.

The Tokyo strike was costly but effective. This time the fires had gutted nearly seventeen square miles, the biggest result from any one mission. More than half the entire city of Tokyo no longer existed.

Next on the schedule was Yokohama, sprawling on the west side of Tokyo Bay. It had felt the heat of incendiaries that had spilled over, and awoken to find the ashes of Tokyo everywhere . . . but it had never been singled out. LeMay sent a daylight mission there on May 29. The losses in the last two Tokyo missions were serious enough to cause concern, so a

A 468th Group B-29, dwarfed by the huge smoke cloud at Yokohama, which reached well over the bombing altitude of around twenty thousand feet. (McWethy)

new variation was tried. It was a high-altitude formation attack with the groups crossing the Honshu coast at four-minute intervals. The aiming points were assigned to the wings according to a schedule calculated to give the B-29s, bombing downwind, at least one drop in the target area before smoke blotted it out. Expecting enemy fighters, LeMay brought in his P-51s, and over one hundred Mustangs joined the bomber stream at Mount Fujiyama. The Japanese fighters came up but were no match for the P-51s. It was still a tough mission, with five B-29s going down and many more damaged. The earlier formations were able to bomb visually, but the massive smoke cloud forced the rest to bomb by radar. A third of Yokohama was destroyed, and the main urban areas around Tokyo Bay were now ashes.

The Japanese reacted stoically. Families had buried all their clothing, bedding, and family treasures because they knew their homes would probably be burned. When a B-29 crashed in a residential area the peo-

Yokohama, May 29, about 20 minutes be-   *burned out in this single massive incendiary*
fore the last of more than 450 B-29s passed   *attack. (Reineke)*
over. Nearly 7 square miles of the city were

ple, in an act of utter futility, beat the dead bodies of the crew with sticks. Children would watch with a strange fascination as the incendiary clusters dropped and broke apart as they fell earthward. Friends would simply disappear, with their houses, as if they had never existed. There was little food and constant hunger. Every Japanese knew the name Boeing B-29. It meant horror and destruction, and the sight and sound of the bombers filled them with terror.

Although the latest missions were devastatingly effective, morale in the Marianas was not high at the end of May. LeMay's statement that the crews might have to fly more than thirty-five missions, and the fact that some of the 73rd Wing "pioneer" crews were going home after thirty, did

The 497th's Thumper *went home and toured the Boeing plants after her forty missions were completed. (Boeing)*

not please the other wings. In the 58th it was felt that Fate was dealing harshly with the older crews—in the 462nd Group all but one of their losses since arriving on Tinian had been crews with twenty-five or more missions. The 40th Group historical officer noted, "The majority of the men in the 40th seem to have lost sight of the reason for their being here. . . . There is the subconscious feeling among them that they are working for a boss for a certain length of time (the shorter the better) or for a certain number of missions, at the end of which they will be permitted to go home." Morale improved when it was announced that men with thirty-five missions did not have to fly more combat.

Rescue, the most frustrating, most rewarding kind of work, was also

Celestial Princess *was declared war weary after twenty-five missions and sent back home in June 1945. The coming of the 58th Wing to West Field inspired many expedi-* *tions to view and photograph the girls painted on the noses of their aircraft. (Swihart)*

paying off. With the low rates of bad months like January, and the exceptional months like May, when four out of five downed crewmen were picked up, the overall figure was 50 per cent. Yet that 50–50 chance of survival underlined the fact that possibly luck was the deciding factor. On June 2, 1945, Lieutenant Robert Laack of the 39th Group took off in the *City of Toledo* to look for survivors of a B-29 ditched north of Iwo. It seemed an impossible task, as solid cloud rose from sea level to five thousand feet. Laack and his crew decided to give it a try and, flying blind, they picked up a radio signal and homed on it by radio compass. The signals were intermittent, so *City of Toledo* circled in the clouds when they stopped, then resumed course when they started again. They contacted a Lifeguard submarine and directed a three-hour rescue operation without once sighting the downed crewmen or the submarine.

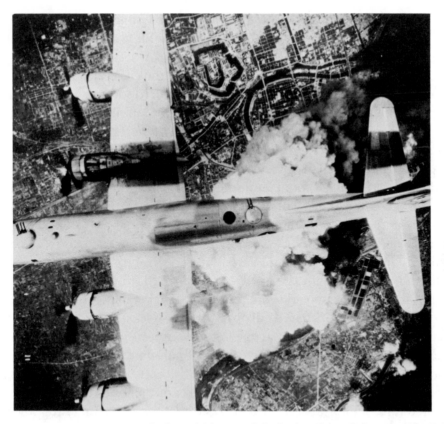

Lieutenant Floyd Calvert of the 504th Group was hit by both flak and fighters over Osaka on June 1. The fighter fire knocked out the pilot's controls, perforated the throttle column, and severed the cord of Calvert's headset. Flak punched sixty holes in the airplane, set No. 3 engine on fire, and damaged the brake system. Calvert put the B-29 into a dive to try to get the fire out, and it worked. The prop would not feather, and finally spun off, knocking a foot from the tip of one blade on the No. 4 propeller, which had to be feathered. With a "buddy" navigating for him, Calvert made it to Iwo.

With the Tokyo Bay targets ruined, LeMay turned West, to Osaka Bay. In Osaka there were important targets that had escaped the March fires, but since the center of the city had been obliterated, these were scattered and unsuited to the usual night missions. On June 1 a daylight mission was flown to Osaka, with bomb loads varied from wing to wing to suit their specific targets. The Mustangs were to provide cover, but suffered a catastrophe. Running into a solid weather front, which rose from sea level to twenty-three thousand feet, they acted on information from a weather plane that led them to think they would be through it quickly. The fighters bored into the front, and a severe thunderhead. They tried

to turn back, but in the turbulence and poor visibility there were collisions, and when it was over twenty-seven fighters had been lost, and
twenty-four pilots.

Osaka was rugged. A 330th Group plane took direct flak hits, which
jammed the elevator controls and bomb-bay doors. A shell crashed
through the nose and exploded in the cockpit, killing the airplane commander and severely wounding the pilot. The explosion closed the
bomb-bay doors, preventing release of the bombs; sheared off the
airplane commander's control column; and knocked out the interphone
and all electric navigational equipment as well as most of the engineer's
instrument panel. The shattered airplane plunged from twenty thousand
to eleven thousand feet. The bombardier, Lieutenant John Locerot,
helped the wounded pilot to lower the nose gear so the survivors could
bail out, and then by placing his weight and strength against the control
column he helped right the airplane and bring it under control. For the
rest of the flight he stayed there, in the mangled cabin. They were heading for Iwo Jima and had to drop to twenty-five-hundred feet to pene-
trate a weather front, then struggled back up to seven thousand. When
they reached Iwo the elevators were still jammed and Locerot and the
pilot maneuvered the plane so the rest of the crew could jump. The pilot
was so badly wounded that he could not get out without help, so Locerot
assisted him, then grabbed the controls to get the plane in a safe position
so he could bail out himself.

Captain William Orr's 39th Group aircraft already had an engine malfunctioning, and was hit by flak in a second engine just after bombs away
over Osaka. About an hour away from the target, the propeller from one
of the damaged engines tore loose and whirled into the fuselage, cutting
the plane almost entirely in half. With only two engines, on the same side,
and one of them damaged, Orr battled through the overcast with his
right wing drooping. He had to tack the aircraft back and forth across his
course, slowly losing altitude all the time. In spite of the wandering
course the navigator, Lieutenant William Costa, kept track. When they finally got through the overcast they saw a small, uninhabited island, and
Orr told them to jump. Flight Officer James Frodsham, the copilot,
knowing the engineer could not swim, parachuted with him on his back.
In the fall the engineer was dragged from his back by the force of the
wind, and next day all but the unlucky engineer were picked up by a
naval vessel.

In all, ten B-29s were lost on the Osaka mission, but over three square
miles of the target were destroyed.

A shower of bombs heads for Kobe, already well alight, on June 5. (Reineke)

On June 5 the B-29s crossed Osaka Bay to strike Kobe. Going in very low for a daylight mission, they bombed from altitudes up to eighteen thousand feet. The fighters came up to tangle with the unescorted B-29s, and eleven were lost to fighters and flak, but there would be no need to return to Kobe. Ivan Potts, flying the mission with the 40th Group, recalls the mission: "The antiaircraft over Kobe was very spectacular. There were ships in the harbor and these just had fabulous accuracy. But the thing I remember most of all was this George fighter. . . . As we were coming in on the target we were flying lead plane and in the right-hand flight of the lead flight and we could see this George circling around down below us and all at once he decided to make his move. He pulled up and he circled around in front of us and you could almost tell that he had picked us. As he came in level against us he rolled that baby over with that

Major Tony Simeral was leading a formation over Kobe. Two minutes before bombs away his plane received a direct hit in No. 4 engine; eight hundred gallons of gasoline gushed out of a three-foot hole in the outer wing panel and burst into flame. The deputy leader had already been shot down, so Simeral decided to keep going, although the plane might explode at any minute. By keeping power on the burning engine, Simeral was able to maintain his air speed and altitude. Past the target the engine was feathered and Simeral dropped out of formation. As the crew battled the fire they were under sustained fighter attacks, and Simeral's gunners claimed three as destroyed. Near the coast the fire was out, but more fighters came in, and three turrets on the B-29 were out of ammunition. Two other B-29s dropped back to drive off the fighters, and Simeral made it to Iwo.

big round group of cylinders on this thing that reminded me of an old Gee Bee sportster like Colonel Roscoe Turner used to fly back in the thirties. This was a beautiful day, it was clear as could be, and he was out several hundred yards, and he headed right in our direction, closing on us at a tremendous rate of speed. He rolled that George over on its back and fired two 40mm cannons at us and headed straight down. All the time

Lieutenant Ivan Potts' crippled B-29, Rankless Wreck, *limps toward Iwo Jima after having an engine shot out near the* target. *The photo was taken from the "buddy" B-29 escorting him. (Potts)*

our new bombardier was pointing and saying 'Look at him come,' and as I remember I said, 'Look at him, hell — shoot, shoot!' but nothing ever happened. I don't think we got a shot at him from the nose.

"One of the cannon shells hit our left outboard engine. It was a monstrous shell and that engine went out immediately — we were able to feather it. The other shell hit us absolutely in the middle of the bomb bay. This was only about 15 or 20 seconds after the bombs had gone. Later on they told us that they counted 148 holes in the bomb bay of this airplane. And of course, we really figured we were in trouble at that time. We didn't know whether we were going down, whether we were gonna be able to keep that baby up there, or just what in the world was going to happen.

"All the electrical systems in the airplane went out and we ended up with the bombardier cranking the bomb-bay doors closed. The turbos

Evan Roberts' Forever Amber *of the 6th Group received a direct flak hit over Kobe that ripped a gaping hole in the left side and gouged out the rear bomb bay. Most of the controls were so badly damaged they were practically useless. The direct hit killed the radar operator, wounded two of the gunners, and blew the arm off the third; al-though the radio operator tried to save him with a direct blood transfusion from the pilot's arm, he died later. Reaching Iwo they found themselves in bad weather and among dozens of other aircraft circling and waiting to land. Against all the odds, they made a perfect landing, although* Forever Amber *never flew again.*

were all out and we suddenly found ourselves lost from the rest of the formation. Pretty soon we looked around and here was one of our 29 buddies who had seen our trouble and decided to stay with us. He flew with us out across Japan and we were under attack a couple of times by fighters but fortunately we fended them off without further damage. Of course, without our turbosuperchargers and with 3 engines about all we

Colonel Morris Lee, 499th Group commander, was flying in this airplane over Kobe on June 5 when a head-on fighter at- tack mangled the right horizontal stabilizer. (Lee)

could do was start a power glide from 16,000 feet and hope we could pull that thing as far as we could get it. We kept it airborne and we kept flying it, and as I recall the air speed was somewhere around 165 miles an hour . . . the props turning so slow you could almost see 'em turning around out there. We barely made it into Iwo and landed on the gravel fighter strip. We didn't have any brakes and when we ran out of fighter strip we were still doing around 95 miles an hour and we went out in this big ol' airplane across the shell holes and the pot holes and ended up turned sideways and everybody scrambling like crazy. It didn't burn, we all got out, and the amazing thing about it, none of us had a scratch."

Osaka was again the target on June 7, with the Osaka Army arsenal and other transportation and industrial targets singled out. Three wings used

The cost of Iwo Jima was heavy: Over 4,500 Americans died to win it. The value of Iwo as a fighter base lessened in proportion to Japanese fighter strength, and its use as a staging base was never great. But it was a haven. By war's end some 2,400 B-29s had made emergency landings there, the greatest number on the night of June 8, when 93 came out of the night skies, another 9 landed after providing navigation for fighters, and an F-13 came in, for a total of 103. The aircraft lined the field from one end to another in a double row. The assertion that lives saved "exceeded lives lost in the capture of the island itself" is a most accurate and just one. (Via Charles A. Mayer)

incendiaries, but the 58th carried high explosives to get the largest arsenal in Japan. There was heavy undercast, and the more than four hundred planes bombed by radar.

Osaka had a week's breathing space before LeMay sent his planes back to finish the job. What was left did not require a maximum effort, so the mission was flown with two mean points of impact in Osaka and three more in nearby Amagasaki. There were no losses, and only one B-29 was damaged.

(Via Charles A. Mayer)

The mission completed the first phase of the destruction of Japan's major urban areas. LeMay had deviated from the joint target group's list only by substituting Kobe for Yawata, concentrating his forces against the three main areas on Honshu. Japan's six most important industrial cities were charred ruins. Where precision bombardment had failed, the incendiary missions had succeeded. Huge factories were gaunt shells, smaller factories and household industries had disappeared. Millions were homeless, and the casualties were numbered in the hundreds of thousands.

The 19th Group heads out. (Roy Fagan)

On June 9 the 313th Wing hit two Empire targets. The 9th Group went to Aichi's Atsuta plant at Nagoya, and this B-29, flown by Captain Walter Tulloch, was hit by fighters. Oil from No. 4 engine has streamed back across the wing and along the fuselage, but the plane made it home safely. (Swihart)

V

An Airpower Victory

LeMay believed he was ending the war and that there would be no invasion. He was also aware of the existence of a new type of weapon, a special bomb that would possibly have more destructive power than anything the world had ever seen.

While the B-29s were burning Japan's great cities to the ground, LeMay's staff had been putting together a plan for the late spring and summer, when the weather would be dominated by clouds. Now the B-29s would never ease up, because when radar weather was predicted they would fly fire missions against secondary industrial cities; if visual bombing conditions were expected, precision daylight strikes would be sent against priority targets, mostly in the aircraft industry. The industrial targets and the urban areas were no longer large enough to require maximum efforts, so the policy became to nominate several targets for several separate forces.

These operations commenced on June 9, when good weather was expected. LeMay sent three small formations: Two groups bombed the Kawanishi Aircraft Company's plant at Narao, very successfully; another two groups heavily damaged Aichi's factory at Atsuta; and a single group went to the Kawasaki plant at Akashi. Forced by cloud to make a radar release, they hit a village instead of the factory.

The weather looked good for the next day too, so six targets were nominated in the Tokyo Bay area. Again on June 22 there were six targets, this time in southern Honshu: Kure naval arsenal was assigned to

255

six groups, and the other targets, all aircraft factories, drew forces ranging from one to four groups.

On June 26 LeMay sent out nine formations against southern Honshu
and Shikoku targets, but while good weather had been predicted, heavy
clouds over the area made assembly difficult, and a lot of the B-29s had to
bomb targets of opportunity, some alone, some in small flights.

Overall, the weather had been better than expected, but then nearly a
month passed before visual conditions again prevailed. On July 24 the
command put up over six hundred planes, bound for seven targets in the
Nagoya and Osaka areas, targets picked to give the several formations a
choice according to the local conditions.

While the precision attacks bent to the will of the weather, the B-29s
had been continuing their fiery work in the darkness. It had been obvious
that the tactics used against the larger cities could be used against the
smaller ones, and the effectiveness and low cost of the night missions, and
the weather predictions, were strong arguments. LeMay's intelligence officer, Colonel James Garcia, emphasizing the effect of raids run close together, suggested a systematic attack on the medium cities because there
was "a possibility of achieving a decisive effect with air power." He
selected a number of cities based on the key factors of congestion and
flammability, amount of war industry, transportation facilities, size, and
suitability for radar bombing. His list of twenty-five cities, with popula-
tions ranging from over three hundred thousand at Fukuoaka to sixty
thousand at Hachioji, was a tentative one but was a good guideline as the
operation began. Of the first fifteen targets, all but two were on Garcia's
list, and in the end all but five were hit. By the end of the war fifty-eight
smaller cities and towns had been fire-bombed.

On June 16, a day after the last attack on the major cities, LeMay informed his wing commanders that the new campaign would begin the
following night. The wings would each have a target: Omuta went to the
58th, the 73rd got Hamamatsu, the 313th Yokkaichi, and the 314th
Kagoshima. Except for the spread of targets the strike was fairly typical.
Japanese opposition, not expected to be heavy, was just about nonexistent. There was but one B-29 lost, to unknown causes.

The success of this mission, which destroyed six square miles of the
targets, got the campaign off to a flying start. From then on, whenever a
B-29 force was ready to go and radar conditions were likely, a night fire
mission was run.

Usually the B-29s attacked four cities, by wings, but sometimes the
targets were thought big enough to justify a larger force, so only three

Hel-Eter, *a P-51 from the 506th Fighter Group, off the coast of Japan with a 505th Group B-29. In the cramped cockpits of the fighters the pilots found the long missions difficult. . . . Back on Iwo they were given massages and took advantage of the island's underground sulphur springs to provide hot mineral baths.*

The red-ruddered Miss Judy, *from Colonel*
Alfred Kalberer's "Hellbirds." When the
58th Wing's markings were changed to an
outline triangle with a group letter, a per-
sonal letter from Kalberer to LeMay
requested that the 462nd be allowed to re-
tain their red rudders, and the request was
granted.

cities would be named. On the other hand, as the target list shrank and
the targets themselves were smaller, smaller forces were sent to more
towns.

While the Japanese reaction was pathetic, the hazards to the B-29s
caused by the fires themselves were considerable. A lot of the published
stories of the turbulence over the burning cities have a humorous twist,
but the danger and terror of the smoke clouds were real and constant.
Over blazing Shizuoka on the night of June 19 the 314th Wing lost two B-
29s to unknown causes; there were only four fighter attacks, and flak was
generally inaccurate and meager. One of the losses was a 29th Group

airplane, and others in that group, third over the target, had a torrid time. On the bomb run one of their aircraft was caught in a myriad of searchlight beams and exposed to heavy flak. They bombed successfully, but three incendiary clusters hung up. At the same moment a violent updraft caught the B-29 and tossed it up three thousand feet. A crew member called that one of the clusters had broken its shackle. The bombardier, Lieutenant Virgil Burton, knowing the bomb was armed to explode within a few seconds, had the bomb-bay doors opened, then threw off his parachute and scrambled back through the bomb bay. Hanging on by clamping his knees to the rack, he wrapped one arm around the loose end of the incendiary cluster to hold it intact, and with his other arm pressed the bomb-release lever. Just as the five-hundred-pound cluster cleared the doors some of the small bombs started to explode, throwing out fire that barely missed the aircraft. The fire attracted more searchlights, but in the blinding glare Burton was able to release the other two clusters, and the B-29 escaped into the night.

Captain Chuck Hawks, in *City of Arcadia* the same night, later wrote his wife about Shizuoka: "Ahead of us smoke was really rising when we arrived. We dropped our bombs where we were supposed to—then smack into a column of smoke—so turbulent and rough—I still don't see how our ship stayed together. When we first hit it we went up about a thousand feet and nearly on our back. Honest, we were tossed around like a piece of soot going up a chimney. Everything in the ship that could come loose did. Tore seats loose, ripped up floor boards in the rear. Broke a giant camera loose from its mounting and drove it out the bottom of the aeroplane. Life rafts popped open. My passenger and the bombardier, not belted down, divided their time between the ceiling and the floor. 'Twas funny in ways and somehow we never lost our sense of humor . . . the navigator has a beautiful black eye and small cuts . . . the radio operator tore the seat out of his pants and cut his butt, the tail gunner had two nasty cuts and bruises in his left shoulder, the CFC gunner had six stitches taken in his left shoulder, another suffered a nice two-inch gash in his leg . . . and other minor cuts and bruises. Bill Hagedorn the pilot and I fared the best—I bruised my lip trying to bite a piece out of the wheel once I guess. . . ."

The 29th's *City of Fort Gibson* was flipped almost on her back just after bombs away. The bombardier, Lieutenant Gerald Dunphy, said, "We hit the first thermal and went up four thousand feet before you could blink your eyes. The ship lurched and the pilot, Major Abbott, swung her in a violent bank to regain control. That meant we had to cut right back into

The 29th Group on Guam. Aircraft No. 20 is Chuck Hawks' City of Arcadia, which he recalls as "a B-29 with personality; when we took her over she was the most disliked ship on the line—slow, flew more like a steam engine than an airplane. We got her 'cause she was decorated with a lead-crew stripe, had an excellent bomb sight, and was the toughest to fly. For more than a week we worked very hard with her, both ground and air crew." Soon they could "boast the cleanest ship on the line for speed, and what's more important had the confidence that she'd get us there—and back. To the amazement of the other crews she made 'em go like hell to keep up—snorting and blowing in a climb that all could feel. What an airplane!"

the edge of the draft again and we were dumped two thousand feet before we had even recovered from the first shock."

The crew was being thrown around the plane when a package of dye marker burst, filling it with golden dust. Everyone in the B-29 was coated with the fine gold powder. *City of Fort Gibson* was also taking flak damage in the No. 2 engine. The thermal's force had ripped one bomb-bay door completely off and twisted the other three. Most of the radio and navigational equipment had been smashed. Three of the crew were seriously

*This 19th Group B-29, piloted by Captain   point on the June 26 Kagamigahara mis-
Ben Kordus, was rammed at the assembly   sion.*

wounded, including the radio operator, who had hurt his hip and back, and the left-blister gunner, who had a broken leg. *City of Fort Gibson* got to Iwo, where the three crewmen were hospitalized.

On July 9 a 499th Group B-29 piloted by Captain Sam Hanford was over Sakai, a suburb of Osaka. At several thousand feet, they noticed that the updraft and smoke were bad, but didn't think anything of it until daybreak, when the copilot looked out and saw something the size of a desktop clinging to the leading edge of their wing. Back at Saipan they discovered it was a badly burned tin roof. "It wasn't that we were flying low," said Hanford, "it was just that that damned roof was flying so high."

The 504th's Major Robert Langdale was over Wakayama the same night. "It was like being actually in the middle of one of those horror movies," said his bombardier, Lieutenant Richard Baskett. "We got in on the tail end of the run over Wakayama, an industrial city. It was already burning to hell and the thermal drafts were boiling up in scorching waves of air. Our first rough indication that something was wrong came with bombs away, when our armed incendiary clusters suddenly stopped falling, turned right around, and began climbing back into the plane, tearing away a bomb-bay door and some of them damaging the tail."

The navigator, Lieutenant Louis Avrami, continued: "Just then the plane flipped over on her back and headed straight back toward the target, flying belly up. I looked down through the bomb bay to see the fires, and instead there were the stars and the moon. Then I looked straight up and saw the fires. For a minute I thought I was dead."

*   *   *

On the night of July 1 the 58th Wing's target was Kure, and for the first time specially equipped B-29s were sent out with the single duty of jamming enemy searchlight and gun-laying radar. Four special aircraft

Special jamming aircraft for use on night strikes were informally named "porcupines," for obvious reasons. (Don Roberts)

orbited the target area for ninety minutes, and these "Angels" were apparently effective: Opposition was surprisingly light and the 58th Wing received no damage from enemy fire. However, the mission was unusual in another way: Ivan Potts of the 40th, in *Smilin' Jack*, noted, "The Japanese Fleet in the area apparently had some students firing practice ammo or were getting low on shells . . . flak was colored pink, orange, blue, and purple . . . a beautiful display of color."

Only one other target that month was considered heavily defended enough to employ the "Angels," and again no damage was done to the B-29s. The radar countermeasures aircraft carried sixteen to twenty preset jammers on platforms in the bomb bay for barrage jamming. Two operators were in the midsection, with intercept receivers and the rest of the jammers. They either "plugged holes" in the jamming barrage or set jammers on radars that were operating outside the predicted frequency band.

The Japanese never found an effective defense against the night incendiary attacks. They had no really good night fighter and no efficient way of putting their fighters on target in the darkness. Though the B-29 crews saw Japanese planes during the night missions the B-29s were never hit by a major force. The big cities had flak working with searchlights, but the smaller cities did not, and losses on those missions were startlingly light. Only one Superfort was definitely lost to enemy action in the whole campaign, and the other losses were due to operational or unknown reasons.

The weakness of the enemy caused LeMay to try another novel idea. To increase the psychological impact of the B-29 raids, he literally decided to "call his shots," by warning about a dozen cities in advance that they could be the next victims, then burning four of them. Although the crews were skeptical, the idea was less dangerous than it seemed. The warning was a display of supreme confidence, and also had a humanitarian aspect. Nimitz's psychological-warfare section went along with the plan, and preparations were made to drop leaflets prior to the incendiary mission of July 28.

The leaflets streamed from the printing presses on Saipan—six hundred sixty thousand of them. They were crammed into bomb cases, and on the night of July 27, six B-29s dumped them on eleven cities. The next night the B-29s struck the first six cities on the list. The idea was "not popular" with the crews, particularly the 462nd Group . . . they staged through Iwo to bomb Aomori, which was at the top of the list. The crews felt they should have been consulted, and only learned of the tactic when

This 500th Group B-29 fought two wars: she later flew in Korea with the 98th Group, *where she was named* September Song. *(Boeing)*

OPPOSITE:

On July 6 the 58th Wing set out to burn down Chiba, an industrial town on the eastern side of Tokyo Bay. The 468th's Captain Charles "Doc" Joyce was on his thirty-seventh mission, two over the quota, but he was flying his crew "out." Over the target he lost the oil in one engine and feathered it. Then there was an explosion in another engine and it lost all power. Joyce was too busy keeping Raidin' Maiden II *in the air to feather the second engine, and lost 10,000 feet of altitude in a few minutes.*

Soon he was crawling over Japan at 1,300 feet with an air speed of around 135 miles per hour. He could get no control over the aircraft and radioed that he might have to ditch. Everyone was at their stations when Joyce decided to give the feathered engine another try. The engine yielded enough power to allow Raidin' Maiden II *to laboriously climb to 6,000 feet and then slide down to Iwo. Joyce is standing on the left in the crew photo.*

Two 29th Group original airplanes with impressive records: Thunderbird *has thirty-four missions,* Oily Boid *twenty-four. Both survived the war. (via Charles A. Mayer)*

Incendiaries stream from the bomb bays of B-29s from Colonel George Mundy's 39th Bomb Group. (Orley Van Dyke)

listening to American radio broadcasts on their way to the target. They, like the others, were apprehensive, but although the enemy made a show of opposition, the forty or fifty fighters that came up did not manage to get any B-29s. They damaged half a dozen, and flak-holed five more.

LeMay used leaflets the same way twice during the first week of August, and radio broadcasts from Saipan issued similar warnings. The tactic came too late in the war to reach all the civilian population of Japan, but it was an additional pressure when every measure was important. The leaflets apparently had quite an effect, and completely destroyed any remaining credibility of the Japanese leaders.

The campaign to burn out the smaller cities had been extremely successful. The results averaged at over 40 per cent of the built-up areas destroyed, and in Toyama's case it was a stunning 99.5 per cent. The terror that had once been restricted to the big cities had reached all over Japan.

The Specialists

While LeMay's bombers ranged far and wide, day and night, a new wing, the 315th, became available. Its operations were partly independent of the other wings, and its B-29s were specially equipped.

The four groups in the 315th Wing had been told back in December 1944 that they were to be the pioneers in bombing Japan from very high altitude in stripped B-29s. A stripped Superfortress had been tested at Alamogordo and found to be capable of flying well above thirty thousand feet and faster than the Japanese fighters. In the early stages there was still some question as to the degree of stripping of the B-29s, but it was believed that the tail turret should remain. The crew was reduced to ten, two scanners replacing the three gunners. The 315th Wing's special B-29s would carry AN/APQ-7 "Eagle" radar, its antenna housed in an eighteen-foot-wide airfoil-shaped section under the fuselage. The antenna swept from side to side through approximately sixty degrees, the beam being formed in the forward path of the aircraft, in contrast to the revolving scanners, which swept through a full circle. A much higher frequency was used, giving a clearer presentation of ground images of the radarscopes.

On December 19, 1944, the groups were advised to begin stripping thirteen training aircraft each. The four fuselage turrets and all fire control and other equipment associated with the turrets were removed. The cannon was removed from the tail turret. All the armor except the glass

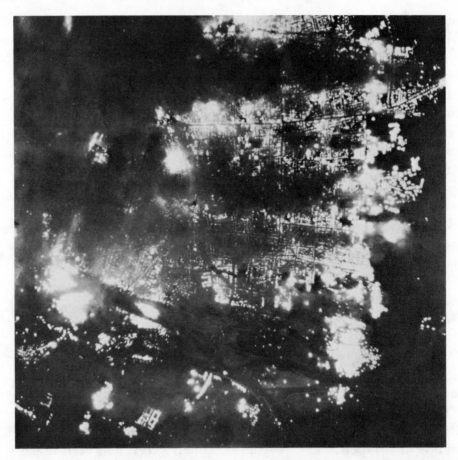

The entire 73rd Wing took part in the August 1 raid on Toyama, the most destructive fire raid of all. The photos confirmed the crews' opinion that the city had become one mass of flames. On one 497th Group B-29, the camera took ten pictures, although the shutter of the camera was normally activated by a photo flash bomb; while the B-29 carried one of these, the other nine pictures were apparently taken because of the brightness of the fires below. (Reineke)

forward of the pilots and the armor and glass to the rear of the tail gunner came out. To facilitate pressurization the turret wells were left in place and cover plates were installed, with smooth closures at the fuselage sighting stations. There were other modifications to electrical and radio equipment, the whole stripping process taking about four days.

During January 1945, 315th Wing B-29s were gradually equipped with a new radar tail turret, the APG-15, but no aircraft was yet fitted with Eagle.

Although the wing modified their own aircraft during training, the

Superfortresses that the 315th would eventually take overseas were Bell B-29Bs, a special variation from the Marietta production line. They delivered four Eagle-equipped aircraft in April 1945, and two of these, the 16th Group's *Ellie Barbara and Her Orphans*, commanded by Captain Ralph Howard, and the 501st's *Roadapple*, with Major Allen Titensor, headed overseas immediately, reaching Guam on April 26. As Northwest Field was not ready for operations, the crews and their special planes were temporarily attached to the 314th Wing at North Field. They were scheduled to fly a series of missions involving radarscope photography with the Eagle system. *Ellie Barbara and Her Orphans* flew her first mission on the night of May 5, over the Kawasaki Aircraft Plant, north of Nagoya. The only enemy opposition was a battery of searchlights centered on the plane as it left the shores of Japan. There was no flak, but an enemy aircraft trailed Howard for a distance of one hundred miles out to sea. Because of bad weather the crew never actually saw the plane, but picked it up on the tail-turret radar.

The 501st Group pioneer, *Roadapple*, was lost a couple of days later on a daylight mission over the Kawanishi plant at Kobe. Titensor and his crew took off from North Field in company with *Ellie Barbara* and simply disappeared. The crew of the other plane believed that the loss could have been due to icing, as they also experienced that trouble.

Ellie Barbara flew four more missions during May, covering targets at Osaka, Tokyo, Yokohama, and Tamoshina. The 16th Group's commander, Colonel Samuel Gurney, accompanied the crew on the May 31 flight to the Mitsubishi plant at Tamoshina. They managed to get radarscope photos ranging from good to excellent, and there was no opposition on any of these missions, which were flown at fifteen thousand feet, although sometimes flak felt for them.

Meanwhile, the new Bell aircraft were rolling off the production line and a stream of 315th Wing planes began arriving on Guam late in May. Bell had built a "special" B-29B for General Frank Armstrong, the wing commander, with the usual modifications plus fuel-injection engines and reversible-pitch propellers, and the aircraft was named *Fluffy Fuz III*. When she arrived on Guam, she used only half the landing strip.

The Eagle radar required a long bomb run, about seventy miles, but that was no great handicap in the present situation. The scheme had been to streamline the 315th's planes to bomb from extremely high altitudes, but General Armstrong was plain to say early that the Eagle radar was worthless above twenty thousand feet.

If the new radar was to be given a scientific test, it was believed that it

The 16th Bomb Group area at Northwest Field on Guam. The aircraft in the foreground is Loaded Dice.

should be used against a special group of targets, preferably large and located on the coast; Japan's oil industry filled this bill. The enemy depended on imports for petroleum, and the flow had been cut off entirely in April 1945. Intelligence believed that the situation was so bad that the destruction of remaining oil stores and facilities would have an immediate effect. So LeMay and General Barney Giles, who came to Guam as deputy commander of the Twentieth Air Force, decided that during its combat testing the 315th Wing should concentrate solely on oil targets.

When Colonel Boyd Hubbard of the 501st Group arrived, Armstrong told him to get an airplane and crew together because he was to lead the wing on its first five missions. As group commander Hubbard had no aircraft or crew of his own, so all the airplane numbers were put in a hat and Hubbard drew one out. He had picked the only "dog" in the group, but rather than draw again he and the 501st's engineering officer inspected the plane and its record. As a result, a rigging correction was made, an engine was changed, and other adjustments made. Hubbard's crew was selected from group and squadron staff.

The 501st's Fleet Admiral Nimitz, *spruced up for the presentation ceremony, with her namesake at the copilot's window.*

At a 315th Wing conference Armstrong announced that the 501st would be providing an aircraft to be dedicated to Admiral Nimitz, in recognition of the logistical support the Navy had given the B-29s. Hubbard proposed his finely tuned B-29B, and Armstrong agreed. Nimitz sent his own painter out to decorate the aircraft with his name and five-star flag.

On June 15, 1945, General Arnold made the presentation. After the official ceremony Nimitz and Arnold were shown the outstanding features of the aircraft. Before he left, Nimitz presented Hubbard with a five-star insignia to put in the upholstery, and a case of beer and a bottle of Haig and Haig for the crew to celebrate with later.

For its first mission, the 315th Wing briefing officers employed a new ultraviolet method of briefing, consisting of the use of fluorescent paint and special lighting. The crews thought that the briefing brought home information in a direct and dramatic form. However, the heat in the darkened room, caused by sealing up the Quonset hut, was so intense that they found it difficult to concentrate.

General Frank Armstrong has a last word with his men prior to the first 315th Wing mission to Japan. (Armstrong Papers, East Carolina University)

On June 26, with Colonel Hubbard leading in *Fleet Admiral Nimitz* and Colonel Gurney leading his 16th Group, the 315th Wing's gleaming, stripped B-29Bs were ready. The target was the Utsube oil refinery at Yokkaichi, No. 1 on the wing's priority list.

The weather over the target that night was almost solid cloud cover, and the B-29s bombed from between fifteen thousand and sixteen thousand feet. Although it was impossible to assess the damage because of the cloud, the Eagle radar penetrated the undercast easily, while the enemy defenses were blinded. Flak was meager, and although a few fighters were seen, they did not fire a shot. One, with its running lights on, made a pass at the B-29 flown by Gurney, but did not open fire. The B-29 gunners had naturally been instructed not to fire first and betray their positions.

The 315th Wing flew nine missions during July, beginning with

Fluffy Fuz III, *commanded by General Armstrong, prepares to take off on June 26; about an hour prior to the wing takeoff, Armstrong flew a radar photo mission and* bombed *an isolated target, then observed his wing at their target; Utsube. (Armstrong Papers)*

Loaded Dice *was the only aircraft damaged on the first Eagle mission—a small hole in the right rear bomb door. (AFM)*

Maruzen on July 2. Returning crews reported tremendous explosions, but photo reconnaissance indicated that only about one tenth of the target had been damaged, so four nights later they went back. This time crews reported flames so intense that they "burned a hole through the clouds" and the photos backed them up. The Maruzen oil refinery had been destroyed by radar pinpoint bombing that equaled any visual bombing performed in the theater. The crews had flown through a mixture of cloud and smoke and had been able to smell burning petroleum.

On the Kawasaki mission of July 12 the 16th Group lost two planes: One crew bailed out because of three runaway props on takeoff, and there were nine survivors. Lieutenant James Crim's crew disappeared without a trace. At Kawasaki on the night of July 25, the 502nd Group B-29B flown by Captain Henry Dillingham was coned by searchlights near the initial point. There were about twenty-five small, black bursts of flak before one hit. The Superfortress, in a steep left bank, burst into a sheet of flame and went down vertically.

During July the crews began painting the undersides of the aircraft black, a job that was not completed by the war's end, and the effectiveness of the paint was proved when individual searchlights only attempted to track unpainted B-29Bs.

Four planes of the 331st Group flew their first mission on July 9, and on July 15 four from the 502nd Group took part in their first Empire mission, and by the end of the month the 315th was usually putting up a force of around eighty airplanes.

On the July 28 mission to Shimotsu, the 16th Group reported that the reflection of the flames from the target flickered on the lower side of their wings. During August four missions were flown, and the 315th then received verbal instructions to prepare for attacks against nitrogen plants and bridges, as the refinery targets were running out.

Colonel Boyd Hubbard of the 501st Group described a typical wing mission this way: "A late-afternoon takeoff, a climb to eight thousand feet en route, with aircraft following at forty-five-second intervals and the second group climbing to ten thousand feet. With the same calibrated indicated air speed, this positioned the string of the second group at the target at nearly the same time so as to provide compressibility and reduce the defense fire power per aircraft to the minimum. Upon departing Guam, the ovens would be turned on and food trays would be served as we approached Iwo.

"Approaching Japan the climb to bombing altitude, fifteen thousand feet, would be made and then often a weather front would have to be

Bell B-29Bs from the 331st Bomb Group flew their first Empire mission on July 9, 1945. (Clyde Matteson)

My Naked—, *a stripped B-29B from the 501st Group, was flown by the 485th* Squadron commander, Colonel Franklin Cochran. *(Mike Goodwyn)*

penetrated with so much electrical activity that beautiful colors of St. Elmo's fire would flow in streams over the windshield and fiery balls could be seen at the ends of the winglike vane antenna of the Eagle radar. Soon rain would dissipate the charge and the radar navigator could 'see' again.

"The bomb run was also by individual aircraft with two-hundred-foot-altitude separation and on three converging tracks to the target from a ten-mile horizontal separation at the initial point.

"At times, weather permitting, other converging aircraft could be seen, and the radar-controlled searchlights would be probing the area for a target. As soon as one lit us up, rope would be dispensed . . . too late on the rope and the light would lock on . . . an aircraft lit up by searchlights was allowed to go to max power, and the acceleration was enough that the flak bursts were behind and biting at his tail. Everyone else in the immediate area got a free ride to the target.

"Because of the very strong wind shifts encountered quite often along the Japanese coast and the difficulty, if not impossibility, of applying the corrections on the bomb run, General Armstrong decided to send a wind-run aircraft to the targets a few minutes early and broadcast the drift encountered. Bombs could be carried and dropped. *Fleet Admiral Nimitz* took the mission.

"The bomb run: *Fleet Admiral Nimitz* was pressurized, on automatic pilot, and being established on track by my turning the aircraft to follow the pilot's direction indicator. The radar bombardier in the navigator's compartment was tracking the target on the radarscope cross hairs. Being electrically synchronized with the bomb sight in the nose, this sighting information set up the required track, to include drift, which was passed through to the PDI for course guidance by myself. The radar sighting also set up on the bomb sight the exact ground speed and time of bomb release. . . .

"Down in the nose the bomb-sight indicators come together, my red light comes on, bomb doors have snapped open, 'bombs away,' and the aircraft lifts. . . ."

The mission to the Ube Coal Liquefaction Company on August 5 was the wing's most spectacular. The refining units were totally destroyed or damaged, along with most of the stores and workshops, and half the nearby Ube Iron Works Company. The target was located at the water's edge, and when retaining walls were burst by bombs the majority of the plant was flooded.

By August 14 the 315th Wing had run fifteen missions against ten

Sergeant Ed Hering, an armament crew-chief in the 501st Group, with the three-gun APG-15 tail turret. The seven-pound scanning unit was designed by General Electric to enable a gunner to aim directly at an attacker irrespective of visibility; as the only feasible attack under such conditions was a stern chase, the B-29Bs could be protected by an essentially simple, short-range radar. However, the APG-15 saw little combat use and gave considerable trouble in operation. (Hering)

This 16th Group B-29B illustrates the cleanness of the stripped "Eagle" airplane. The radar vane did not materially effect the airplane's flight characteristics, although the drag caused by its supports exceeded that of a normal radome. (Bob Voyles)

targets, all petroleum refineries or synthetic plants. Very heavy bomb loads had been possible because the planes were stripped and attacked by night. With experience the crews were able to increase their bomb loads from around seven tons on the first mission to over ten.

The most difficult maintenance problem in the 315th Wing centered around the APG-15, which had worked well under laboratory conditions but not in the field. A perplexing problem was its tendency to calibrate perfectly on the ground but to require new calibration once it was airborne. Gunner after gunner returned from missions reporting it simply would not work—it might lock without searching, or search and refuse to lock on a target. "The occasional gunner who reported the APG-15 was operative was a curiosity," noted the 16th Bomb Group.

Difficulties with Eagle were less serious. An unexpected snag was the effect of the tropical climate on the leading edge of the radar "wing," which resulted in deterioration and excessive changes of the antenna.

Overall, the Eagle experiment was highly successful. The 315th Wing's formations had attacked their primary target on every mission, and the results were generally good. In some cases it had been necessary to go back to a target a second or even a third time, but by the end of the war their target system was virtually destroyed. The strategic effects were more apparent than real, as a lot of the storage tanks were already empty and refinery production was falling away before the campaign even began. With the end of the war the problems of the APG-15 were "dismissed as a bad job," but Eagle results were "beyond all expectation." There were plans to use it on the F-13s, and both APQ-7 and the APG-15 were being used on fully armed B-29s that were assembling on Okinawa with the new 316th Bomb Wing, the second Eagle unit.

*   *   *

The B-29s were hitting Japan with everything. LeMay's original plans had not been firm as far as mining went, and there was some hope around his headquarters that it might be reduced to a policing task. However, the success of the campaign was so encouraging that he was bound to continue it. In spite of all the other operations of the B-29s, mining was accelerated. The destruction of the Japanese homeland was still the first priority, even for the 313th Wing, but LeMay told Davies to use one group, when it was not required for other missions, to sow over four thousand mines in small increments. Davies assigned the task to Colonel Charles Eisenhart's 505th Group, which carried out fourteen missions

Although only the B-29Bs saw combat, Bell was producing fully armed aircraft with Eagle and APG-15 for the Eighth Air Force's new 316th Wing. The wing's first mission was canceled due to the Japanese "peace feeler" on August 10. (Boeing)

Artwork survived in the 315th Wing. "Jus' One Mo' Time" is a 501st Group B-29B. (LeRoy Henry)

Commemorating the capture of Iwo Jima, The Spearhead was dedicated to the 5th Marine Division. Previously Captain Dave Rogan's Man O'War II, *the airplane has symbols on the nose denoting ten bombing and nine mining missions. (Swihart)*

from June 7 to July 3. In around four hundred sorties they mined ten areas in the Sea of Japan and the Inland Sea; the mines were adjusted to sink ships of assorted sizes, and there was little hope of the enemy breaking the blockade. They made desperate attempts, but the onslaught was simply too much, and by July the situation was out of hand.

Captain Kyuzo Tamura, head of the Japanese mine-sweeping section, confirmed the success of the mining campaign: "About April 1, 1945, your mines changed from a nuisance to a problem. We increased the aircraft units and searchlight units attached to certain areas such as Niigata and Shimonoseki at the expense of the cities."

The Japanese made frantic efforts to counter the mining of Shimonoseki Strait—there was an intricate system of mine watchers stationed along the coast, on hills, and in fishing boats in the channels. Radar, searchlights, and underwater sound equipment were employed to assist in finding the mines. There was also an extensive research and countermeasures program.

During June Shimonoseki had been closed for five days; by the end of the month several anchorages were apparently completely abandoned. Ships were anchoring in small unmined harbors or in the swift current of the strait.

Throughout the final weeks of the war the 313th Wing continued to play its part in the onslaught on the disappearing Japanese merchant fleet. The Superforts continued their blockade of Shimonoseki and the northwestern Honshu ports, and extended their coverage to include Korea. Planes based on Okinawa could reach the south of Korea, so the 313th concentrated on ports farther up the peninsula. The missions to Rashin in Korea were the longest of the war—the initial points were just sixty miles south of Vladivostok, and they involved six hours of flight over the Japanese Empire. On the first, flown July 11, one B-29 flew the entire forty-one hundred miles from Tinian nonstop and returned to North Field after nineteen hours and forty minutes in the air. Because of the great distance, the B-29s going to Korea staged through Iwo Jima. The Korean targets lacked defenses against mining, so the 313th used magnetic and acoustic mines, against which the Japanese had developed a partial defense; the more deadly pressure mines were saved for Shimonoseki.

Crews about to take off on a long mining mission wait by their 6th Group aircraft. On missions longer than fourteen hours Benzedrine was issued to the pilots, navigator, and engineer. (Reineke)

On the night of July 15 Major John Layson of the 6th Group was Air Group Commander on a Rashin mining mission. After takeoff it was discovered that in order to complete the flight as planned, their plane, Look Homeward Angel, *would have to fly on extra power, cutting the fuel reserve. Layson decided to go on, and after the mining his problems were increased when an engine began to backfire violently and another cut out. Layson headed for Okinawa rather than the Soviet Union and internment, and was the first to land a B-29 on the Bolo fighter strip.*

Losses on the mining missions began to creep up a little—six B-29s in July, three of them on the night of July 27. The Japanese had moved searchlights and heavy flak guns to Shimonoseki, and the B-29s were sometimes forced to mine from altitudes as high as twelve thousand feet. Mines dropped from that altitude tended to drift over wide areas, but there were still plenty to keep the blockade tight. During July the 313th Wing dropped leaflets urging the Japanese to surrender or starve. It was not an idle threat.

Davies used the 6th and 504th groups in the last series of mining missions, and in fifteen attacks they laid mines in seventeen fields. About thirty planes went out on each mission, with several targets.

The 313th Wing had started late, mining for less than five months, and at a time when the Japanese merchant fleet was already reduced. However, during that time the B-29s' mines destroyed more shipping than any other weapon, accounting for roughly half the total tonnage destroyed.

LeMay was worried that the lack of recognition of this work might harm morale among the crews, who never saw the results of what they did. But eventually their achievement was recognized, and Admiral Nimitz acknowledged the "phenomenal results" of the B-29 mining campaign.

*   *   *

The Japanese situation was hopeless, and had been for some time. Only the stoicism of the people could account for the lingering agony they suffered. The expression *Shikata ga nai* (It cannot be helped) symbolized their fatalism. Even as their country was destroyed around them, they made plans for the last battle.

Back in April the Japanese Imperial General Headquarters had officially revealed *Ketsu-Go*, the plan to repel the invasion of the home islands. The Army and Navy Air Forces were to conserve as much fuel as they could, and as many planes and pilots, to launch an all-out kamikaze attack on the invasion fleet. It was to be suicide on an unbelievable scale. Normal air-defense operations continued, but more and more the pendulum swung toward preservation for the final, cataclysmic battle. The situation was so bad that regular air defense had only a limited future anyway.

Tokyo Radio apparently did not explain the situation to the people, instead placing emphasis on a claim that over six hundred American planes had been downed by flak in July. With such a record, there was little need to risk losing aircraft, the broadcasts said. Through most Japanese propaganda there ran a theme that "war weariness" and fear of "another Iwo Jima or Okinawa" were forcing America to a violent burst of activity designed to end the war before a landing became necessary.

Official enemy policy was to not even intercept smaller aircraft, and only retaliate against major B-29 attacks. With the losses at Okinawa, the lack of fuel, and the loss of aircraft production, plus the need to conserve forces for the final battle, even B-29 interceptions were cut back. So by the middle of 1945 the B-29s met little determined resistance. Then at the end of June Operation *Sei-Go* was begun, exclusively aimed at protecting the necessary forces for *Ketsu-Go* from the B-29s. Although this effort was to be directed only against the Superfortresses, the fighters often ran into P-51s and could not get to the bombers. *Sei-Go* was never

A 330th Group lead B-29, with black-and-yellow wing and fuselage bands. This airplane has the later APQ-13 radome; earlier versions caused unnecessary drag and the Denver Modification Center designed this streamlined, teardrop unit. (Jonas Carpenter)

The 40th Bomb Group flew their first mission from Tinian on May 5, 1945. (Gahagan)

The 314th Bomb Wing developed a uniform emblem for its airplanes, with B-29s in all four groups carrying this design on the right side of the nose. Quaker-City *was chosen by this crew because* City of Philadelphia *was already in use, and the airplane also bore the name* Sentimental Journey *on the left nose. She was flown by Lieutenant Lester Gilbert, standing on the right. After thirty-three wartime missions, the B-29 was put into storage, then later served with radar evaluation units until she was sent to Davis-Monthan in 1959. Ten years later she was loaned to the Pima Air Museum in Arizona, and is currently displayed there. (Jonas Carpenter)*

effective, and this late burst of Japanese activity in July never became a real threat.

A Strategic Air Force

Despite the punishment dealt to Japan, an invasion would still apparently be necessary and, with seven different air forces fighting the Pacific air war, there was an obvious need for a unified command. Many other units would be moving from Europe to the Pacific, and reorganiza-

As July ended, the 509th's B-29s had been marked with a variety of tail markings used by other wings. Strange Cargo *was one of four with 497th Group markings, four had 444th Group markings, four had 6th Group insignia, and three had 39th Group markings. (John Dulin)*

tion would be a necessity. It was belatedly decided to bring General Carl Spaatz to the Pacific, to command a United States Army Strategic Air Forces setup similar to what Spaatz had commanded in Europe. Spaatz, as commander, could operate more on parity and have "more influence" with Nimitz and MacArthur. Arnold believed that Spaatz was the only man "who has the chance to save for us a proper representation in the air war in the Pacific." The two strategic air forces under Spaatz's command

Strange Cargo *was Lieutenant Joseph Westover's aircraft. (Dulin)*

were planned to be identical in strength, each with five wings of B-29s. General Nathan Twining replaced LeMay as commander of the forces in the Marianas, the Twentieth Air Force, on August 2. General Jimmy Doolittle began setting up his Eighth Air Force at Okinawa on July 19, and was very near to flying combat missions when the Japanese surrendered. His 316th Wing had two of its groups, the 333rd and 346th, at Kadena, but many of their aircraft were destined to be parked on the airfields, slowly going out of commission.

Although the reorganization of USASTAF had not been fully completed before the end of the war, Spaatz had been making progress. Twentieth Air Force headquarters had been transferred from Washington to Guam on July 16, and Spaatz reached Guam on July 29. He organized his staff in a matter of days: General Barney Giles was deputy commander, General LeMay was chief of staff. Guam was now the center of American strategic air power.

All the elaborate plans would lead to little.

In August 1939 Dr. Albert Einstein had written to President Roosevelt about the possibility of constructing a bomb from uranium that would have unbelievable destructive force. He noted that the bomb might be too heavy to use with aircraft, but as the research proceeded that seemed not to be the case. A laboratory was set up at Los Alamos in New Mexico in spring 1943, and a staff headed by Dr. Robert Oppenheimer began producing the weapon. Though much of the early stage was based on theory, it was certain that the bomb would be large, a fact that naturally led to the involvement of the Boeing B-29. General Leslie Groves, director of the so-called Manhattan Engineer District, was in general charge of the bomb's development. He informed Arnold of the project and gave him the task of modifying the B-29s, carrying out ballistics tests on the bomb, and setting up a special combat unit to deliver the weapon.

In December 1943 a 58th Wing B-29 was flown to Wright Field, where changes were made to the bomb bay; two months later the aircraft was flown to Muroc in California, and ballistics tests began with models of possible atomic bombs. A couple of test drops were followed by more changes. The tests were resumed in the middle of 1944, followed by more modifications. It was late August before the aircraft was finally ready to be used as a basic guide for the modifications to the atomic bombers.

The task of organizing the special combat unit got moving in the summer of 1944. The man selected to command it was Colonel Paul Tibbets, who had flown B-17s with the 97th Bomb Group in Africa before going to General Doolittle's headquarters as a "bombardment expert." Tibbets was brought back to the United States at Arnold's request, to work on the B-29 program, but after the crash of the XB-29 in February 1943 Tibbets was sent to Orlando, Florida, with B-17s. When the B-29 was again a going concern, General Wolfe brought him to Marietta. Tibbets then went to Alamogordo, New Mexico, where he worked with Dr. E. J. Workman from the University of New Mexico. They were trying to find out how a B-29 could best defend itself against enemy fighters.

Tibbets was called to Washington, where he was briefed on the Manhattan Project, and then taken in to see Arnold. Tibbets later recalled, "He shakes hands with me, and wants to know what I think of the job, and I tell him I think it's a great challenge. He said, very matter of fact about it, you could almost say coldly indifferent, because he said, 'O.K. I've told them here to give you everything you want. If you have any trouble, let me know.' "

Tibbets' job was to organize, equip, and train a special unit to deliver the bomb; he would use normal channels for normal requests, but for anything else, the magic word "Silverplate" would open any door.

General Uzal Ent of the Second Air Force had selected a B-29 squadron as the nucleus of the new unit. The squadron he chose was the 393rd, training to go overseas with the 504th Bomb Group at Fairmont, Nebraska. It was a good squadron, already a going concern when it was picked for the most important mission of the war. The commander was Colonel Thomas Classen, who had flown B-17s in the South Pacific.

The core of Tibbets' unit was this normal B-29 squadron, but to give as much independence, and thereby secrecy, as possible, it was expanded to include supporting elements such as a troop-carrier squadron equipped with C-54s. The atomic-bomb unit was activated as the 509th Composite Group on December 17, 1944. Tibbets chose Wendover Field, Utah, as the training base for his unit in the interests of security. Security was paramount in the 509th, and it was rigidly enforced.

At that time Tibbets alone knew the real mission, although the others at least knew they were going to drop a special sort of bomb, and Tom Classen recalls, "Everybody knew about the bomb to some degree."

The 509th was naturally a most unusual group. Tibbets, with the greatest knowledge of the unit's role, was "gone about 90 per cent of the time," according to Classen. Tibbets seemed to be in a world apart, and would sit at a table for hours without saying a word to anyone. There was some friction when Tibbets began filling key positions with people from his old 97th Group: Major Thomas Ferebee as staff bombardier; Captain Theodore Van Kirk as staff navigator; Colonel Hazen Payette as head of group intelligence; and Captain Kermit Beahan as 393rd Squadron bombardier.

The 393rd Squadron's normal training was completed late in December 1944, and bombing runs were made at a nearby range to gauge the ballistics qualities of the bomb, with casings loaded only with an inert filler. In January 1945 ten of the 393rd Squadron B-29s went to Batista Field, Cuba, for further training, including visual and radar bombing from very high altitudes and long simulated missions over water, but not formation flights. In May the group was equipped with their modified B-29s, built by Martin at Omaha. These were stripped of all armament but the tail turret and had reversible-pitch electric propellers, fuel-injection engines, and a manifold fuel system. These were clean, fast airplanes: The reversible-pitch props alone gave a weight saving of four hundred pounds in the brake assemblies, and fuel injection gave better fuel distribution to the cylinders, prolonged exhaust valve life and resulted in lower temperatures and better acceleration.

By the end of May the squadron was ready to move out. Tibbets had given command of the 393rd to Major Charles Sweeney, and Classen had become deputy commander of the 509th. Command of the 393rd, the actual combat unit, was the job Classen wanted, and he felt he had been moved "out of the way" for the 509th's most important period.

The combat crews of the 509th began arriving at North Field, Tinian, on June 11, flying in in their own airplanes. After arriving in the Marianas the group shared some facilities with the 313th Wing, to which it was nominally assigned, although most orders came from the 21st Bomber Command, as LeMay was responsible for the training operation, planning, and execution of the missions. Later orders would come from Arnold or Spaatz. The command channels were highly irregular, and for the climactic missions the orders would have to come from the President.

The unusual command arrangements, the partial isolation of the group and its aircraft, the insignia of a black arrow in a circle, the rigid security, and the failure to take part in normal combat missions—all indicated that the 509th was a special unit. They became a curiosity, although there were plenty of solid rumors, and one of the most popular was that they were going to drop the big "grand slam" bombs that the British had used against Germany.

When they reached Tinian the 509th crews had participated in the usual seven-day 313th Wing indoctrination program, and on July 20 they began a series of combat strikes over Japan to familiarize the crews with target areas and tactics they would use on the final missions.

Each target was assigned to a single aircraft initially, then two. On July

Top Secret, *flown by Lieutenant Charles McKnight. (Dulin)*

20, ten aircraft were assigned to attack with the 313th Wing, and in all a dozen strikes were sent out over the next nine days, involving from two to six planes against each target. The missions were planned to simulate the final attack in all possible details: Navigational procedure, individual high-level approach (usually at about twenty-nine thousand feet), visual release, and radical breakaway after bombs away. The 509th was using a light-case five-ton bomb, which the group called "pumpkins" because of their bright orange color.

On July 24 ten B-29s struck ten targets: *Bockscar* had a direct hit, which resulted in a continuation of explosions throughout a large complex at the Sumitoma Aluminum Plant; Captain Ralph Taylor's *Full House* hit the Sumitoma Copper Refining Company; Lieutenant Joseph Westover in *Strange Cargo* attacked a Mitsubishi Heavy Industries installation; Lieutenant Charles McKnight's *Top Secret* bombed Yokkaichi Harbor; and the others went to a variety of similarly specialized targets. After the ten-plane mission, two of the crews reported that their results were "unobserved," but the other eight were all able to report "excellent." It was a reflection of the unusually high degree of training. The usual pilot and bombardier made twenty practice visual bomb runs; the 509th's men made hundreds. The group did not lose a man or an aircraft in training or combat operations, and their bombardiers could put a bomb within a five-hundred-foot circle from thirty thousand feet. The performance of the 509th was exceptional: Out of thirty-eight combat sorties, there was only one abort. The strategic rewards of the lead-up pinpoint strikes

Captain Ralph Taylor and the crew of Full House *after a mission. (Dulin)*

There were four missions staged through Iwo Jima in July, involving both the 58th and 313th wings, and four mining missions in August. **Airborn** *is one of a long line of 444th Group airplanes on the barren island.*

were of little account, but the results did prove that the 509th was a pretty hot outfit.

By the end of July the group was ready to carry out its real mission. The timing was looking good. The atomic bombs had to be dropped visually, so weather became an even more than usually critical factor. Early in the year Arnold had held a high-level meeting in his office to select a probable time for the atomic bombing, and considered a long-range forecast by Air Force Weather Service's Colonel Irving Krick, which predicted favorable conditions over the proposed targets between August 5 and 10. Early in June Tibbets had been informed that one atomic bomb would be available for use on August 6.

*   *   *

Since 1941, Secretary of War Henry Stimson had been directly responsible to the President for the entire atomic-bomb undertaking. According to Stimson, there was never any doubt in Roosevelt's mind that the bomb would be used, and this stance was adopted by Truman when he took over in April 1945 and learned the full facts about the project.

Although there was some dissension in the scientific force working on the bomb, the scientific panel advising the committee (which in turn advised the President) saw " no acceptable alternative to direct military use." The bomb had not yet been tested, but already Arnold, in conference with Groves and others, had selected certain targets in accord with advice given by an "interim committee" of eminent civilians advising the President on atomic matters. The target should be "a military installation or war plant surrounded by or adjacent to houses and other buildings most susceptible to damage." For best psychological results and experimental results it was thought that the target city should be one that was relatively untouched; this immediately ruled out the half dozen largest cities in Japan. Arnold named Kyoto, largest unbombed city, Hiroshima next largest, Niigata, and Kokura. Later he ordered LeMay not to attack these cities by conventional means, but reserve these for the 509th Group and possible atomic bombing. Kyoto, at the insistence of Stimson and against the judgment of Arnold, was removed from the list because of its significance to the Japanese as a national shrine of religion and culture. Nagasaki was then added to the list, apparently by LeMay's staff, although it was not considered an ideal target for atomic attack.

The four designated cities became the subject of intensive study by intelligence officers in Washington and the Marianas.

As the war ended, the B-29s were really paying their way; this is the 498th Group's Miss Lace, *with forty-nine missions without an abort. (T. C. Griffin)*

One of the joint chiefs, Admiral Leahy, was skeptical of the bomb, and there were others in the military, including LeMay, who believed Japan could be conquered by air and sea power alone. Arnold had received a briefing from LeMay on Guam in June that had been so thoroughly convincing that he sent LeMay straight back to Washington to present it to the joint chiefs. The case for finishing the war with the B-29s, without an invasion and without an atomic bomb, was presented by LeMay on June 19, but he was not able to convice General Marshall, or an angry Admiral King. Arnold became the only top military man to counsel President Truman against using the new bomb.

Nevertheless, the strategy adopted and accepted by Truman was that Japan would have to be invaded unless something remarkable occurred. Hospitals were already being built on Tinian to help cater for the expected thousands of casualties; B-29s were being fitted to permit fifty-gallon drums of napalm to be dropped on the beaches; and specially modified Superforts, able to carry eleven-ton "Grand Slam" bombs, were being tested at Eglin Field, and fifty would be ready for action about September 1945.

Some in Washington believed Japan could be brought to surrender if the Emperor's office was kept and if the Japanese way of life was not destroyed. Secretary of War Stimson summed it up as "promising destruction if Japan resisted, and hope if she surrendered."

On July 26 the Potsdam Declaration, signed by Truman, Churchill, and Chiang Kai-shek, was released. It called for Japan's immediate capitulation and made no reference to the Emperor, ending with the warning, "The only alternative for Japan is prompt and utter destruction."

Ten days before, at Alamogordo in New Mexico, the first atomic bomb had been exploded. The experiment was highly successful, the bomb as powerful as any had dared hope. When reports of the test reached Potsdam, Stimson conferred with the President and with Marshall and Arnold concerning the employment of the bomb. The ultimate decision on timing, and target, would rest with the President, but Arnold urged that Spaatz, as the field commander responsible for delivering the weapon, be given as much latitude as possible in the choice of the particular target from the list. This authority was granted.

The decision to drop the bomb was Truman's, and he accepted the heavy responsibility. When Premier Kantaro Suzuki advised the Japanese press on July 28 that the Potsdam ultimatum would be "ignored," he had chosen the wrong word, and it was interpreted as an outright rejection.

Spaatz had actually received his directive for the 509th to "deliver its first special bomb as soon as weather would permit visual bombing after about August 3," on July 25. The President authorized this so that the "military wheels" could be set in motion. His final decision to use the bomb was not made until he was returning from Potsdam.

The fissionable materials were rushed to Tinian as soon after the July 16 test as possible, and Groves had already sent the scientists needed to complete the assembly job.

By August 1 the 509th was ready to go. Spaatz's directive had set August 3 as the earliest day for the attack, and thereafter it was a question of waiting for a break in the weather. With only two bombs available, the drop would have to be made visually. LeMay, as Spaatz's chief of staff, would decide when the weather was suitable.

The 509th's field order indicated that the primary target was Hiroshima. Located on the underside of Honshu, with a harbor opening onto the Inland Sea, it had been an important port of embarkation, although the mining campaign had recently dried up its traffic. But for the restrictions imposed by Washington, Hiroshima would probably have been burned down by LeMay's B-29s long before.

Early on August 1, in a controlled-temperature building on Tinian, the assembly of the first atomic bomb, known as "Little Boy," began. The device was relatively simple and foolproof: Uranium 235 at each end of a long gun barrel, brought together by a proximity fuse.

The day for the attack was selected as August 6, and briefing of the crews began two days before. They were shown films of the Alamogordo test, but no mention was made of an atomic device, simply a bomb with a force equivalent to twenty thousand tons of TNT. The crews were instructed to avoid smoke clouds and warned of the critical distance the plane should be from the bomb when it exploded. They were also issued with protective glasses.

Every crew wanted to fly the mission, and every crew was capable of flying it, but Tibbets quite naturally took it. On August 5 his aircraft was taxied to the pit where the assembled bomb lay, and the five-ton device was jacked up into the bomb bay. Tibbets ordered a painter to apply his mother's name, Enola Gay, to the aircraft. The B-29 was left under guard and at midnight the fliers assembled for a weather briefing. August 6 was looking good, with high visibility and little cloud predicted.

Even this mission had its prosaic aspect: The planes had to be fueled, the kitchen staff had to prepare over ninety lunches for the airmen, armorers had to load a thousand rounds of fifty-caliber ammunition per gun in each plane.

While the crews for the combat strike were still at the mess, the trucks took the crews of the weather planes to their B-29s. Soon after, the three aircraft moved out. As Major Claude Eatherly taxied *Straight Flush* from its hardstand, a B-29 was suddenly bathed in a bright light. It was *Enola Gay*, being set up for crew photographs.

The Hiroshima weather plane: Major Claude Eatherly's Straight Flush. *(John Grahagan)*

Eatherly's B-29 roared down the runway and headed for Hiroshima, sixteen hundred miles away. *Jabbitt III* and *Full House* quickly followed, on their way to check the secondary targets, Kokura and Nagasaki.

*   *   *

Straight Flush reached Hiroshima shortly after seven o'clock in the morning, and crossed the city twice to be sure that the target, particularly the aiming point, was clearly visible. A message confirming good conditions at the primary was flashed to Tinian and the *Enola Gay*. Eatherly headed back to the Marianas, passing the three strike planes somewhere along the way.

Tibbets had taken off in *Enola Gay* at 2:45 A.M. Two minutes later he was followed by Major George Marquardt in the camera plane, then Major Chuck Sweeney's *The Great Artiste*, loaded with blast gauges and other equipment.

As *Enola Gay* leveled out over the ocean, Navy Captain William Parsons and Lieutenant Morris Jeppson armed the bomb. Conventional bombs were always armed on the ground, but with this one the risk was considered too great.

The three B-29s rendezvoused over barren Iwo Jima. Down below Lieutenant Charles McKnight and his crew, who were parked just off Iwo Jima's airstrip, relaxed. If anything had gone wrong they were to take the place of *Enola Gay*, but they were not needed.

The three B-29s began the long climb to bombing altitude, and the crew members settled down to their tasks.

As Japan came nearer, Tibbets made his way through the aircraft, giving final instructions, and near the coast Parsons had a final look at the bomb. Everything was just right.

The bomb run began 25 miles out from Hiroshima, *Enola Gay* roaring along at 328 miles per hour. Twelve miles and just over two minutes from the target the bombardier took over. He could see Hiroshima clearly, 31,600 feet below him, and at 9:15 A.M. he released the bomb. The airmen pulled the goggles over their eyes—a few, including Tibbets, forgot—and less than a minute later the bomb exploded 2,000 feet above Hiroshima. Tibbets had already put *Enola Gay* into a violent 150-degree turn, rehearsed so many times, and was miles from the target.

Down below, Japan's eighth largest city was beginning a new day. The 245,000 residents felt that they had somehow been spared the fire bombings that had destroyed the other large cities, but could not have known

The Hiroshima instrument plane: Major Charles Sweeney's The Great Artiste. *(John Gahagan)*

The Hiroshima camera plane: Necessary Evil. *(Gahagan)*

why. There had been an air-raid alert earlier that morning, but it was only one plane, and the Japanese were used to the single, snooping B-29s.

Suddenly the whole sky was a blinding light, and walls crumbled and glass shrieked through the air. Fires began everywhere, and a terrible fire wind raged through the city. More than 4 1/2 square miles of the city were flattened, and a shroud of dust and smoke darkened Hiroshima.

When the bomb detonated, *Enola Gay* was illuminated by the ball of fire. The two escort planes, their crews watching the explosion through goggles, reported that the flash was "deep purple, then reddish and reached to almost eight thousand feet; the cloud, shaped like a mushroom, was up to twenty thousand feet in one minute, at which time the top part broke from the 'stem,' and eventually reached thirty thousand. . . . The stem of the mushroomlike column of smoke, looking now like a giant grave marker, stood one minute after the explosion upon the whole area of the city, excepting the southern dock area . . . this column was a thick white smoke, darker at the base, and interspersed with deep red."

Although the two escort B-29s were fifteen miles from the target, they, like *Enola Gay*, were buffeted by shock waves that rippled from the base of the massive atomic explosion. Tibbets turned *Enola Gay* to look at the target, instructing his tail gunner to watch the cloud and let him know when it was out of sight. Three hundred sixty-three miles from Hiroshima it was fading from view.

Within five hours after the strike Lieutenant Omer Cox in *Valiant Lady* and Lieutenant Thomas Kendall in a second 3rd Photo Squadron F-13 were over Hiroshima; they reported vast destruction, but fire, smoke, and dust were still so bad that no accurate estimates could be made.

News of the mission was flashed to Truman, then on board ship on the way to the United States. His public announcement of the event, drafted at Potsdam, was released in Washington sixteen hours after the bomb fell. In it the President again warned the Japanese people of "a rain of ruin from the air."

Still there was no offer of surrender. On August 1 there had been only enough fissionable material for two bombs, but production was speeding up. While the world waited for the Japanese to respond, the B-29s kept hitting Japan. On August 7 the Toyokawa naval arsenal was bombed by B-29s from four wings. The next day Yawata, still high on the priority list for conventional attack but bombed only twice from Chengtu in the early days, was attacked. Yawata was not a good radar target and had been slotted for a daylight mission. Eleven groups from three wings were dis-

Colonel Paul Tibbets brings Enola Gay *back from the mission that changed the world.*

patched, their bomb bays filled with a mixed load of incendiaries, but contrary to the weather forecast, they ran into thick clouds over Yawata. Smoke from fires started by the first planes further covered the city, and more than half the force had to bomb by radar. The results were only fair. A strong fight had been expected, so the mission was covered by three groups of Thunderbolts from Ie Shima. The Japanese did come up, and although the fighters got about a dozen, the enemy was able to shoot down one B-29 and five Thunderbolts. Later that afternoon 314th Wing B-29s bombed the Tokyo arsenal, and that night the 313th mined seven fields, while the 58th Wing flew a fire mission to Fukuyama.

The intention had been to use the two atomic bombs at close intervals if the first did not suffice, and apparently there was some thought of running the second mission on August 11. When bad weather was predicted, the strike day was advanced to August 9.

The operational plans were very similar for the second bomb—the fact that a new and more efficient plutonium bomb, dubbed "Fat Man," was to be used made no difference to the B-29s. Again there were three planes in the strike force, but there were only two weather planes, as there were only two possible targets. The first choice was Kokura, a city near the northern tip of Kyushu, with the aiming point a vast Army arsenal. The secondary target was Nagasaki, on the western coast of Kyushu. Its excellent harbor had been losing its importance, but the city's industry had grown. Niigata, on the western coast of Honshu and 160 miles northwest of Tokyo, was considered too distant.

This second atomic mission went off much less smoothly than the first. The weather planes took off in the early hours of August 9, followed by the strike force eighty minutes later. Major Chuck Sweeney was carrying the bomb in *Bockscar*, while Captain Fred Bock was in *The Great Artiste;* there seemed no reason to move the scientific instruments from one plane to another, it was easier to simply swap airplanes. The third aircraft was commanded by Major James Hopkins, with movie cameras and observers. The standby plane on Iwo was Captain Ralph Taylor's *Full House.*

Major Charles Sweeney making his last-minute inspection before Bockscar *takes off on the second atomic mission. (Fred Olivi)*

When *Bockscar* reached seven thousand feet Sweeney turned over the plane to Captain Don Albury and his copilot, Lieutenant Fred Olivi, and went back to catch some sleep in the tunnel. The engineer was anxiously watching his fuel gauges, because just before takeoff he had discovered that a transfer pump was not working and there were six hundred gallons of fuel they would not be able to use. He reported the problem to Sweeney and Tibbets, who decided that they must go, and could get more fuel at Iwo on the way home anyway.

Bockscar, *which dropped the plutonium bomb on Nagasaki. The nose art was added after the mission.* (Dulin)

The rendezvous point was Yakoshima. A few minutes after they reached it, the crew of *Bockscar* received a coded message from Lieutenant Charles McKnight in the weather plane over Nagasaki: Conditions there were "hazy, clearing rapidly, two tenths cloud coverage." Earlier they had had a similar promising report from the plane over Kokura, *Enola Gay,* being flown by Captain George Marquardt.

Shortly after eight o'clock, Japan time, *Bockscar* and *The Great Artiste* linked up, but there was no sign of Hopkins. The two B-29s circled, the crew of *Bockscar* concerned because of their slender fuel reserve. Hopkins was actually nearby, but higher and at another point. Sweeney was beginning to worry, and after forty minutes of meandering around the sky he signaled Bock to close up, and the two B-29s headed for Kokura.

The radar picked up Kokura, and the bomb run began. The bombardier, Captain Kermit Beahan, could see parts of the city, but the aiming point, the arsenal, was hidden by haze. Beahan said, "no drop," and Sweeney went around to begin a second run. *Bockscar* came in from a different angle, and Beahan spotted the river that ran by the aiming point, but still could not see the arsenal. Again no drop, then a third bomb run, which also failed. Flak from the west, around Yawata, was starting to seek the Superfortresses.

Bockscar's fuel situation was critical, and Sweeney decided there was no point in trying any more. The B-29s set a new course for Nagasaki.

Sweeney knew he had barely enough fuel for one run over the secondary target, and he would still need luck to make it as far as Okinawa.

At Nagasaki the weather conditions had changed and the city was under heavy clouds. Sweeney wanted to make a radar drop, but that was strictly against orders; he was faced with a major decision, and he chose to drop the atomic bomb by radar if it could not be done visually.

Over the edge of the city the clouds seemed to thin out, and while *Bockscar* continued her radar approach Beahan was able to find a break in the clouds. He took over. "Fat Man" dropped from the bomb bay, and Sweeney racked *Bockscar* away to the left.

There was a great flash, which stunned the crews of *Bockscar* and *The Great Artiste*. The whole sky was illuminated by a purplish-white light. A mushroom cloud, white and red at the top, gray and black at the base, had soon climbed higher than the B-29s. Ed Buckley, the navigator on *Bockscar*, had watched the bomb on the radarscope and saw half the target "suddenly dimmed out to a flat nothing." Everything that had been there reflecting into his scope had just disappeared.

Bockscar narrowly made it to Okinawa, with Bock following. About an hour later, Hopkins' plane also turned up.

*   *   *

Photographs made it possible to estimate very accurately what the bombs had done to the cities. In Hiroshima four square miles were totally destroyed, with only a few shells of concrete buildings standing. The bridges across the seven forks of the Ota River were destroyed or damaged, and a reddish-brown, ashy dust covered everything. Between seventy thousand and eighty thousand people had died, but the exact figure could never be known.

The stories of the survivors underlined the unbelievable aspects of the bomb. A man standing in the entrance of a building recovered consciousness on the third floor, unaware of how he got there and unhurt except that later his hair fell out. Witnesses said the bomb exploded above the Aioi Bridge, a modern concrete-and-steel structure, and the blast lifted the bridge into the air, twisted it, and it fell back in almost the same place. The heat of the bomb could be felt ten miles away, and survivors of Hiroshima had strange burn patterns over their bodies where light clothing, or another part of the body, or an object, had partly protected them from the bomb's heat radiation: The heat started thousands of fires, and the blast turned all kinds of objects into deadly missiles. Then there was the black rain that came as a result of vaporization and then condensation of moisture in the boiling atomic cloud. A fire wind raged through the ruined city. There were thousands of wounded, many of them doomed to die as the atomic age was born.

At Nagasaki the air-raid shelters were very good by Japanese standards, mainly tunnels in the hills and cliffs. When the weather plane flew over in the morning there was plenty of time for the people to have reached shelter, but the Japanese Government had decided to downplay the Hiroshima bombing and suppressed any mention of "atomic bombs." While many Japanese might have learned about the event from American radio broadcasts and propaganda leaflets, the true effects of the bombs were beyond comprehension. The government did warn the people to wear clothing covering their whole bodies and seek shelter no matter how few B-29s appeared, but these instructions were taken lightly, as they were never explained.

At Nagasaki the area destroyed was an oval, but much less in area than Hiroshima, less than 1½ square miles. It was not possible to make an exact total of lives lost, but official Japanese figures were 23,753. It was obviously far fewer than at Hiroshima, but the Strategic Bombing Survey estimated 35,000.

*   *   *

When the second bomb exploded over Nagasaki on the morning of August 9, the inner council of the Japanese Government was in session discussing surrender terms. The 509th Group's deputy commander, Colonel Tom Classen, and Captain John Wilson had taken off from Tinian in two B-29s a couple of hours before the second mission was airborne. They were on their way back to the States to pick up the third and fourth bombs as soon as they were ready.

So while the war dragged on agonizingly, Emperor Hirohito and Premier Suzuki had in fact already decided to accept the terms of the Potsdam Declaration. The surrender followed the atomic attacks so closely that they are often seen to have been the decisive factor, but that does not seem to be the case. Many Japanese had realized that they were beaten; some when Saipan was invaded, some when the Philippines were lost, some a lot earlier.

Although the ruler to the people, the Emperor's role was actually divine rather than practical. Much of his contact with the government was through his lord privy seal, and both the Emperor and his government were advised by elder statesmen. However, the real power in Japan's ruling structure was the military, and fear of the radical militarists slowed any moves for peace. The bureaucracy and the *Zaibatsu*, the great industrial combines, had power but were divided, and the general public was hardly considered.

The loss of Saipan caused the Tojo cabinet to fall, but although there were clandestine attempts to begin a peace movement, the new government had no mandate to end the war. As failure mounted upon failure, the peace movement had grown, but stealthily, partly because of fear of the Army, partly because public reaction could not be assessed: The people were still being completely misinformed about the actual way the war was going.

By February 1945 the Emperor had received a warning from some of the elder statesmen of how serious the situation was, and in March there was some thought in the Cabinet of negotiating a peace. The invasion of Okinawa was quickly followed by the dismissal of Premier Kuniaki Koiso's government and the formation of a new Cabinet under Admiral Kantaro Suzuki, a former Navy chief of staff.

Apparently Suzuki received a virtual imperial injunction to end the war as soon as possible, although he put on a display of spurring the war effort. The long delay between the Emperor's vague directive and final surrender indicated Suzuki's fear of the militarists.

There was a difference of opinion, even when it was obvious that the war could not be won. Some wanted immediate peace, others clung to the hope that some small victory might give Japan a position to bargain from. In May initial steps were taken to sound out the Soviets on the possibility of interceding with the United States. The approach to the Soviets was met with evasion and disinterest.

At a meeting with the Emperor early in June nobody dared advocate peace, and the proposal of the military to fight to the end was apparently unchallenged. Within a couple of weeks, however, the Emperor directed that a means for terminating the war be found, while the fight for the homeland went on.

In Tokyo reactions to the Potsdam Declaration were mixed. Some were in favor of immediate acceptance, others objected to it. Much of the debate turned on the threat against war criminals, the fate of the Emperor, and the future of the Japanese way of life.

The Cabinet, with the Emperor's consent, decided to make no immediate reply, and it was Suzuki's unfortunate phrasing of this decision in a press release that was accepted by American leaders as a flat rejection.

When the Hiroshima bomb was dropped the Emperor was again advised to accept the Potsdam terms, to which he voiced no objection, but again the military resisted. On August 8 the Soviet Union declared war on Japan.

In an early-morning conference on August 9 Suzuki and the Emperor decided on immediate peace. Later that morning the small council met but ended in deadlock, as did a Cabinet meeting convened that afternoon. Suzuki then asked the Emperor to meet with the inner Cabinet, and after several hours the Premier suggested that the Emperor's view be sought and accepted. Hirohito said he had decided "that this war should be stopped"; by then it was the early morning of August 10. The full Cabinet was reconvened and decided unanimously to accept the Potsdam terms except where they threatened the prerogatives of the Emperor.

Within a few hours the decision had been sent to the United States via the Swiss and to the British and Soviets through Sweden. The American reply came first, in a broadcast from San Francisco on August 12 at four o'clock in the morning, and more formally through the Swiss the next day. The delay was caused by Washington's concern that giving any ground might be seen as weakness. Though there was no intention of destroying the imperial office, the American reply was indirect and to the militarists was unacceptable. Finally, on the morning of August 14, the Emperor called the Cabinet together on his own initiative and reiterated his opinion that the war should be ended. Finding nothing objectionable in the American proposals, he asked his ministers to prepare for his signature an imperial rescript accepting the Potsdam Declaration. This was done in an afternoon session, and the document was sent out that night. The American reply directed an immediate cessation of hostilities and the arrangement of a formal surrender. At noon on August 15 the Japanese first learned of the surrender, and for all but the official class the news came as a complete surprise. In spite of earlier fears there was no general revolt.

For the Twentieth Air Force the interval between the declaration and its acceptance was a time of great activity and frustrating uncertainty. After the Hiroshima attack there had been hope in the Marianas that the surrender would occur within a matter of hours. When this did not happen, Washington ordered Spaatz to continue planned operations until further notice. In regular day and night missions, B-29s were out on the next four days, and the propaganda campaign was intensified. B-29s dropped leaflets informing the Japanese of the Potsdam Declaration, the nature of the atomic bomb, and the Soviet Union's entry into the war.

The 40th Group's B-29s began carrying the Kagu Tsuchi design toward the end of the war. The weather vane symbols denote this airplane's mission. (Vic Seely)

By the end of the war several stylized nose motifs were is use, or being developed, in the 313th Wing. The 6th Group used a red and white streamer with the group's Jean Lafitte emblem. Captain Robert Litchfield's El Pajaro de la Guerra was a group original airplane and carried both unit markings and a highly individual crew decoration. The "Apple a Day" insignia, an eagle rid-ing a bomb with a red apple as the fuse, was first painted on the forward bomb-bay doors; then each of the B-29's missions was re-corded by a hand-painted miniature on the nose. The yellow background paint for the last eight mission insignia has run when applied to the glossy black dope undersur-faces. (Gahagan)

When news of the Japanese note of August 10 was broadcast, Spaatz limited B-29 operations to precision bombing, fearing that area missions might complicate the negotiations. This involved canceling a strike due to bad weather, and the cancellation was unfortunately interpreted by the press as a cease-fire order. Believing that a resumption of B-29 attacks would in turn be played up as an indication that negotiations had failed, Truman on August 11 ordered Spaatz to halt all strategic operations, even to the extent of recalling planes that might be in the air. With negotiations still hanging fire on August 14, Spaatz was directed to resume bombing.

In December 1944 a contest had been held to select a name for the 462nd Group. Kalberer presented a bottle of whiskey to the winner, Corporal Charles Walters, for "Hellbirds." A prolonged series of contests failed to produce a suitable insignia, so one showing a B-29 over the top of the globe was selected "temporarily," and used throughout the war. (Teed)

The 73rd Wing used a barb and ball to identify its aircraft, with any nickname painted within the barb. Gravel Gertie *flew forty-nine missions with the 500th Group.*

Hap Arnold wanted as big a finale as possible, hoping that the Tokyo area could be hit by a thousand planes; the Twentieth had put up 853 on August 1, and Arnold thought the number could be rounded out by calling on Doolittle's Eighth Air Force, but Doolittle did not think it was worth the risk. Spaatz still wanted to drop a third atomic bomb, on Tokyo, but considered the city a poor target for conventional bombing. Instead, he proposed dividing his forces among seven targets. The 58th Bomb Wing drew Hikari naval arsenal, the 73rd Wing hit the Osaka arsenal, the 313th Wing bombed the Marifu railroad yards. That night the 315th bombed the Nippon Oil Company at Tsuchizaki, part of the 313th and 314th wings went to Kumagaya, although thirty-nine 313th planes went mining, and the 73rd and 314th wings sent a force to the Isesaki urban area. The 509th Composite Group dispatched eight B-29s to drop five-ton "pumpkins" on targets in Koromo and Nagoya.

In all, over eight hundred B-29s bombed the various targets, and

Even after two atomic bombs had been dropped, the war dragged on. The 6th Group's White Huntress *roars out from* Tinian. (USMC)

thankfully there were no losses. Before the last Superfortress returned, Truman announced the unconditional surrender of Japan.

One of the first planes back on the morning of August 15 was flown by Colonel Carl Storrie, who had taken command of the 314th Wing late in July. Storrie led his old group, the 29th. "We had a special cargo," he said. "We played alarm clock. All the rest of the aircraft carried fire bombs, but we had four-thousand-pounders and went in to wake up the

population of Kumagaya. They were fixed to salvo and had fuses for
aerial bursts at about one hundred feet above ground to get maximum
blast effect. . . . We were at sixteen thousand and could feel the concus-
sion. It was a dirty trick. We figured the Japs would think it was another
atomic bomb."

The last week had been frustrating for the politicians, frustrating for
the generals, but those who suffered most were the crews of the B-29s.
The idea of dying on the last day of the war was unacceptable; the general impression was that the war was over, but somehow was not ending.
The intricacies of diplomacy meant little to the crews on Saipan, Tinian,
and Guam. One of the 468th Group's squadrons recorded the prevalent
feelings of those days:

"On Saturday, August 11, we heard the radio tell of the civilian reaction through polls on the question of accepting Japan's proposal. This
did not sit well and there was much gnashing of teeth and full-bloom
cursing on this expression of opinion. It was not appreciated and many of
the men will carry it back with them. To bring this to a head we were
alerted and ordered to brief Hikari naval arsenal, which we did at six that
evening. It was a terrible letdown after the mission had been called off the
night before; but perhaps it would be canceled. Everyone hung around
intelligence, pacing the floor, smoking cigarettes, talking, and shoving an
ear right up against the speaker. Then finally we got the news. The Jap
proposal had been accepted with the meaning of the Emperor more
clearly defined. The wire arrived from Twentieth Air Force HQ that the
mission was canceled. The crews were awakened and told they could go
back to sleep. It was a cause for celebration. But all Sunday there was
nothing to do but wait and wait. Peace or war? Peace or war? But the
radio could say nothing but 'The war goes on!' Then we got the word to
unload the ships, to take the bombs out of the bays, and hunt up all of our
cargo platforms.

"Then we received the news that a major U.S. naval unit had just been
hit off Okinawa and the Third Fleet was striking Tokyo. Monday again
we were told to stand by. At noon, told to reload but given no target,
briefing time, or takeoff time. We went to bed not knowing what. It was
no good; by eleven o'clock everybody was up having coffee at the mess
halls. Then the blow struck. Briefing at three for the Hikari arsenal
again. What was the delay in the Jap reply? It was a hard thing to send
out crews thinking that peace would come momentarily. There was a variety of expression of opinion. Some wanted to wait and not endanger another life, others wanted to drop a few more persuaders, while others
said we shouldn't even let the bastards surrender.

"Our planes took off. Tuesday morning we heard the ridiculous cry of the Japanese that they had just received the note. Back at base we paced the floor wondering and waiting for the bombs-away message from Hikari. The message finally came through and indicated perfect visual bombing. Toward late afternoon the word started getting around that Domei had reported the acceptance of the Potsdam Ultimatum. We didn't know whether to believe it or not. After an interminable time our planes started to land late that night. It was the night of Tuesday, the fourteenth of August. About ten o'clock as we were in the heat of interrogation we accounted for all our planes and breathed a sigh of relief. Then we heard Washington acknowledge that a note from the Japanese had been received. The sweat started all over again, but the bright, shiny morning of the 15th revealed it was true. The war was over."

Ed Hering, a 315th Wing armorer on Guam, recalls the last mission as an "off-again, on-again circus—we thought we might have to unload it, but it finally took off." For the first time, the 315th had had to load one-hundred-pound bombs, very hard and tiresome to load. Mechanics and others were recruited to help, but loading the aircraft still took about twenty-eight hours straight.

The historian of a group on Saipan perhaps summed it up best: "The ending of the war was the greatest morale factor that has befell this group since the time of activation."

Mission of Mercy

There was still plenty of work for the B-29s. Weather and photo-reconnaissance missions continued, but about a third of the B-29 effort was devoted to transport, as the bombers supplemented regular cargo planes in the preparations for the formal surrender and the initial occupation of Japan.

Immediately after hostilities ceased, Spaatz directed that the Twentieth provide "a display of air power . . . continuing and increasing between August 19 and V-J Day." Operational plans called for almost daily flights over the Tokyo plain by B-29s drawn in rotation from the five wings, all planes to carry ammunition but no bombs. Those missions, like the surrender ceremony, were postponed due to weather and other complications. The first exhibition, a low-level flight of nearly one hundred B-29s, was staged on August 30, in conjunction with the landing at Atsugi Airfield of MacArthur and the 11th Airborne Division. A similar force was over again the next day, and on September 2, as the surrender ceremo-

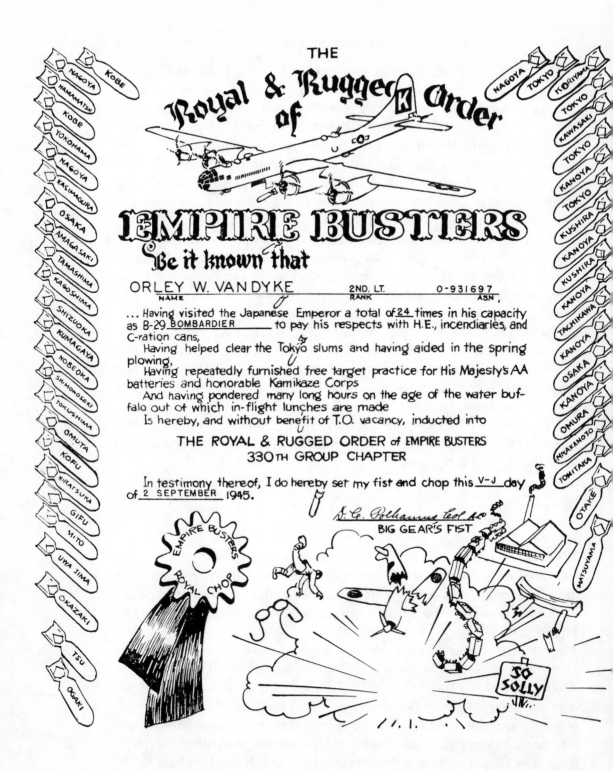

The diploma issued to 330th Group veterans at the end of the war. (Orley Van Dyke)

B-29s from the 58th and 314th wings line Saipan's runways as they prepare for the mercy missions to prison camps. (Reineke)

nies were conducted on board the battleship *Missouri*, a force of over four hundred B-29s circled above. During the rest of the month the B-29s flew thousands of ground personnel on sight-seeing expeditions over the remains of Japan.

Meanwhile, other B-29s had regularly been over Japan, China, Manchuria, and Korea on a more important mission, an errand of mercy that contrasted sharply with the wartime missions. The B-29s were supplying prisoner-of-war and internment camps until the inmates could be evacuated. The range and capacity of the B-29s made them ideal for the job, and three days after the surrender Spaatz laid the whole responsibility on the Twentieth Air Force. The total number of camps was then estimated at about 300, of which about half had been identified by intelligence officers. The list was revised on the basis of more precise information furnished by the Japanese Government, and in all, 154 camps were supplied by the B-29s in August and September.

Engineering officers on Guam developed methods of packaging supplies in "blocks" and of installing cargo platforms in the bombers. The supplies, including food, clothing, and medical kits, were furnished in the Marianas, and twelve thousand parachutes were flown over from Manila by B-29s in the first installment. The first drop was to the Weihsien camp near Peiping on August 27. Finding the place took some time, and the drops were hard to get off correctly, each plane making pass after pass to toggle out the eight gasoline drums crammed with supplies. Some of the parachutes failed to open, and the prisoners flattened against walls or ducked for cover as the rations hit. Some drums seemed to burst open on impact after plunging nearly seven hundred feet; others landed intact. The prisoners dashed to the bundles, pausing only to wave their thanks.

Within five days most of the camps had received their first delivery, and a second delivery was flown, followed by regular supplies to camps as yet not reached by ground parties. Some items were furnished on demand — plasma and other medical supplies, even beer and ice cream.

The effort was not without cost: Eight B-29s were lost on the mercy missions.

The camps did yield some of the survivors of B-29 losses. A 315th Wing aircraft was asked to pass on a message, sent with a walkie-talkie the prisoners had at a camp near Mukden, that "Captain Campbell and nine

The 6th Group's Reamatroid, *stripped of guns, flying "on the step" between Iwo Jima and Tinian after a supply drop to Osaka in August 1945. (Ray Pritchard)*

A 500th Group B-29 swoops low over the Wangpoo River after dropping supplies to the Pootung internment camp, China. This airplane, Z-58, is currently being restored by the Florence Air and Missile Museum, which located her at the Army's Aberdeen Proving Ground and rescued her in 1974. (USA)

members are in a POW camp at Mukden"; these were the survivors of the 462nd's *Wild-Hair,* downed by an aerial bomb before reaching the target on December 21, 1944. On August 31 crews observed the words "Ross 498th" displayed staked out on the ground at a Shikoku camp: This was Lieutenant James Ross, a survivor of the 498th Group's *Antoinette,* which had disappeared on the May 24 Tokyo mission. These incidents led to hopes that many missing fliers might turn up alive; a few did.

In the middle of June 1945 it was decided to paint the undersides of production B-29s black, and similar work began on combat airplanes in the theater. Not a great number had received their paintwork by the end of the war. This 19th Group B-29 had her black paint applied on Guam. (Roy Fagan)

The last B-29 to be shot down during World War II was the 500th Group's *Hog Wild* — she went down on a supply mission on August 29, a victim of Soviet fighters. The incident began when *Hog Wild*, with Lieutenant Joseph Queen and his crew, was delivering supplies to a camp near Hamhung, Korea. In the camp area a couple of Soviet Yaks moved up on the B-29's wings and waved "in a friendly manner." The pilots of the fighters signaled Queen to follow them, which he did, and they led him to a small airfield about ten miles from the prison camp. Apparently the fighters believed Queen was searching for a landing strip, and when the B-29 turned toward the prison camp to complete its mission, the fighters fired a burst across its nose and motioned it to land. Queen decided to head for Iwo Jima, and changed course, and when he was about five miles past the coast the Yaks appeared to have left them. Then a couple of minutes later one of the Soviet fighters made a pursuit curve on them and opened fire. Queen ordered his crew not to return the fire.

Hog Wild was badly shot up. No. 1 engine began to burn, and the fire could not be extinguished. Queen had already turned back toward the small airfield as flames lapped over and under the B-29's wing and streamed back past the tail. He was at about two thousand feet and afraid that the plane might explode. He told his crew to bail out, and six had jumped before the fire eased and Queen decided to make a landing.

He got the B-29 down safely, and the Soviets at the field extinguished the fire by throwing sand on it. Then Queen and his crew were thoroughly searched.

The Soviets became apologetic after Queen convinced them of the reason the B-29 was in the area, but even so, when he was allowed to go to the plane to gather personal equipment that night, he noticed that all papers, the airplane commander's handbook, and other items were missing. And the next day, when Queen and some of his crew began walking toward their plane, a Soviet major motioned them to stop; when they continued he tapped the pistol on his hip to show he meant it.

By the morning of August 31 all of Queen's crew who had jumped had been safely rounded up, and the following day he was allowed to contact Saipan. When he went to *Hog Wild* to use the radio he saw that all the emergency equipment in the plane had been ripped out, and parachutes popped and cut up.

It was decided that spare parts would be flown in by transport to repair the B-29, and Queen kept in daily contact with Saipan until a C-46 transport finally arrived on September 11. Then it was decided to salvage *Hog Wild* rather than repair her, and all the flight instruments, gun sights, bomb-sight radar, and other equipment were removed and loaded in the transport plane. The Soviets returned some of the equipment they had removed.

One of the most interesting figures in the drama was the Soviet "interpreter" who had been brought to the air base, a Major Kruglov. Queen described him as a ground engineering officer who displayed "superior knowledge of the B-29 . . . the first day when we landed he remarked about it being a new B-29 as several switches and things were in different places than in B-29s he had seen."

No lives had been lost in the incident, which the Soviets described as a "mistake," explaining that sometimes American aircraft had been captured and flown by German crews, and that they thought *Hog Wild* may have been a B-29 in enemy hands.

*   *   *

Japan had been defeated without an invasion. Colonel Cecil Combs defined the B-29s' role as "the implied task of bombing the b'Jesus out of Japan," and that task had been thoroughly carried out. Although the B-29 attacks were generally considered as preludes to an invasion of the Japanese home islands, there had always been the underlying hope, and later belief, that Japan would surrender before that became necessary.

With its first role always strategic bombardment, the Twentieth Air Force had faced severe handicaps. Control from Washington proved to be "clumsy," although it did protect the B-29s from wasteful diversion to tactical operations. The logistical problems in using the B-29s from the China bases meant that their potential could never be fully realized, and the weather conditions severely hampered the early operations from the Marianas. Before the fire blitz in March 1945, less than 8,000 tons of bombs had fallen on Japan. Over the next five months, around *139,000 tons of bombs* were rained on Japan; during the fire blitz alone a greater tonnage was dropped in 10 days than had been dropped in the entire 9 months preceding it.

In 14 months of operations the B-29s dropped nearly 170,000 tons of bombs, most of them in the crescendo of the final 6 months of the war. Over 12,000 aerial mines had been laid, and there were the hundreds of miscellaneous sorties—Superdumbo flights, fighter navigation flights, weather missions, leaflet missions, radar countermeasures, and radar-scope and photo-reconnaissance missions. The total amounted to over 34,000 effective sorties. The B-29 gunners claimed over 2,000 enemy planes destroyed, probably destroyed, or damaged. The cost was 414 B-29s, 147 of them combat losses to Japanese flak, fighters, or a combination of the two. There were 3,015 B-29 crewmen listed as dead, wounded, or missing; for each of those men, about 100 Japanese had died. Sixty-five of Japan's most important cities had been put to the torch, and over 150 square miles had been burned out.

The B-29s had come a long way from the "experimental" phase, and they had covered the distance quickly.

To the Japanese, the B-29 was the symbol of their defeat, and there was a strange admiration for the "power and beauty" of the bomber. When an alarm was sounded people would ask each other, "Are the invading planes B-29s?" If it was rampaging fighters there was a sense of overwhelming relief.

After the war, Japanese civilian and military leaders agreed that the Tokyo raids on the nights of March 9 and May 25 were the most disastrous. When asked which raids had the greatest effect these two appear with almost monotonous regularity, with some adding the atomic bombings. Premier Suzuki summed up: "It seemed to me unavoidable that in the long run Japan would be almost destroyed by air attack so that merely on the basis of the B-29s alone I was convinced that Japan should sue for peace. On top of the B-29 raids came the atomic bomb, immediately after the Potsdam Declaration, which was just one additional reason for giving in and was a very good one and gave us the opportune moment to open negotiations for peace. I myself, on the basis of the B-29 raids, felt that the cause was hopeless."

When General Spaatz took over the B-29 force in the Marianas he described it as "the best-organized and most technically and tactically proficient military organization that the world has seen to date."

Although the Japanese situation was declining before the B-29 attacks reached their peak, the attacks further crippled production and dislocated it. The mining campaign had been eminently successful, and Japan was literally starving.

By their all-out, massive attack, using every means at their disposal, the Superfortresses had achieved their purpose: an airpower victory. A truly strategic air force had been born.

Don Reilly Respicio Holmes, January 13, 1981

Appendix

SUPERFORTRESS PRODUCTION

Five factories built the total of 3,960 Superfortresses. The three XB-29s —41-002, 41-003, and 41-18335—were built at Boeing's Seattle plant. The company produced 1,634 more at Wichita, Kansas; Bell built 668 at Marietta, Georgia; Martin produced 536 at Omaha, Nebraska; and Boeing's plant at Renton, Washington, built the other 1,119. The first five aircraft built at Marietta and the five built at Omaha carried serial numbers drawn from the first Wichita production. The stripped B-29Bs were all built by Bell at Marietta, and initially were built in normal "blocks," but then a practice of alternating them with fully armed airplanes began.

BOEING, WICHITA (BW)

Model	Serial Numbers	Model	Serial Numbers
YB-29	41-36954 — 41-36967	B-29-65	44-69805 — 44-69904
B-29-1	42-6205 — 42-6254*	B-29-70	44-69905 — 44-70004
B-29-5	42-6255 — 42-6304	B-29-75	44-70005 — 44-70104
B-29-10	42-6305 — 42-6354	B-29-80	44-70105 — 44-70154
B-29-15	42-6355 — 42-6404		44-87584 — 44-87633
B-29-20	42-6405 — 42-6454	B-29-85	44-87634 — 44-87683
B-29-25	42-24420 — 42-24469	B-29-86	44-87684 — 44-87733
B-29-30	42-24470 — 42-24519	B-29-90	44-87734 — 44-87783
B-29-35	42-24520 — 42-24569		45-21693 — 45-21742
B-29-40	42-24570 — 42-24669	B-29-95	45-21758 — 45-21792
B-29-45	42-24670 — 42-24769		45-21813 — 45-21842
B-29-50	42-24770 — 42-24869	B-29-96	45-21793 — 45-21812
B-29-55	42-24870 — 42-24919	B-29-97	45-21743 — 45-21757
	44-69655 — 44-69704	B-29-100	45-21843 — 45-21872
B-29-60	44-69705 — 44-69804		

* Except for 42-6222, 42-6224, 42-6233, 42-6235, and 42-6243 (first five Bell), and 42-6229, 42-6230, 42-6231, 42-6232, and 42-6237 (first five Martin).

BELL, MARIETTA (BA)

Model	Serial Numbers	Model	Serial Numbers
B-29-1	42-6222, 6224, 6233, 6235, 6243	B-29-5	42-63366 — 42-63381
	42-63352 — 42-63365	B-29-10	42-63382 — 42-63401
		B-29-15	42-63402 — 42-63451

320

Model	Serial Numbers
B-29-20	42-63452 — 42-63501
B-29-25	42-63502 — 42-63551
B-29-30	42-63552 — 42-63580

Model	Serial Numbers
B-29B-30	42-63581 — 42-63621
B-29B-35	42-63622 — 42-63691

B-29B-40 serials were 42-63692 through 42-63751 except for 63737, 63744, and 63750, which were all B-29-40s, and 44-83890 through 44-83895, except for 83894. The B-29B-45 serials were 44-83896 through 44-83943 except for sixteen aircraft—83900, 83904, 83908, 83911, 83914, 83917, 83920, 83923, 83926, 83928, 83930, 83932, 83934, 83936, 83938, and 83940—all of which were B-29-45s. Between 44-83944 and 44-83958, all *odd* numbers were B-29-45, all *even* numbers were B-29B-45. Between 44-83959 and 44-83961 were B-29B-45s, 44-83960 and 44-83962 were B-29-45s. Between serials 44-83963 and 44-84008, the *even* numbers were B-29-50, the *odd* numbers B-29B-50. From 44-84009 to 44-84056, the *even* numbers were B-29-55, the *odd* were B-29B-55. The *even* numbers between 44-84057 and 44-84103 were B-29-60s; the *odd* numbers, B-29B-60s. Finally, the B-29-65s carried the *even* numbers between 44-84104 and 44-84152, and the B-29B-65s the *odd* numbers; 44-84155 was a B-29B-65, and 44-84156 was a B-29-65, the final two Superfortresses from Bell in Georgia.

MARTIN, OMAHA, (MO)

Model	Serial Numbers
B-29-1	42-6229, 6230, 6231, 6232, 6237
	42-65202 — 42-65204
B-29-5	42-65205 — 42-65211
B-29-10	42-65212 — 42-65219
B-29-15	42-65220 — 42-65235
B-29-20	42-65236 — 42-65263
B-29-25	42-65264 — 42-65313
B-29-30	42-65315 — 42-65383

Model	Serial Numbers
B-29-35	42-65384 — 42-65401
	44-27259 — 27325
B-29-40	44-27326 — 4427358
	44-86242 — 86276
B-29-45	44-86277 — 44-86315
B-29-50	44-86316 — 44-86370
B-29-55	44-86371 — 44-86425
B-29-60	44-86426 — 86473

BOEING, RENTON (BN)

Model	Serial Numbers
B-29A-1	42-93824 — 42-93843
B-29A-5	42-93844 — 42-93873
B-29A-10	42-93874 — 42-93923
B-29A-15	42-93924 — 42-93973
B-29A-20	42-93974 — 42-94023
B-29A-25	42-94024 — 42-94073
B-29A-30	42-94074 — 42-94123
B-29A-35	44-61510 — 44-61609

Model	Serial Numbers
B-29A-40	44-61610 — 44-61709
B-29A-45	44-61710 — 44-61809
B-29A-50	44-61810 — 44-61909
B-29A-55	44-61910 — 44-62009
B-29A-60	44-62010 — 44-62109
B-29A-65	44-62110 — 44-62209
B-29A-70	44-62210 — 44-62309
B-29A-75	44-62310 — 44-62328

F-13 CONVERSIONS

Model	Serial Numbers	Model	Serial Numbers
F-13-20-BW	42-6412		44-61533
F-13A-35-BW	42-24566 —		44-61577 —
	42-24567		44-61578
F-13A-40-BW	42-24583		44-61583
	42-24585 —	F-13A-40-BN	44-61659
	42-24586	F-13A-45-BN	44-61727
	42-24588		44-61734
	42-24621	F-13A-50-BN	44-61810
F-13A-50-BW	42-24803		44-61813
	42-24805		44-61815
	42-24810 —		44-61817 —
	42-24811		44-61819
	42-24813		44-61822
	42-24816 —		44-61832
	42-24817		44-61843
	42-24819		44-61847
	42-24821		44-61854 —
	42-24829		44-61855
	42-24833		44-61857
	42-24860		44-61860
F-13A-50/55-BW	42-24869 —		44-61862
	42-24871		44-61866
	42-24877	F-13A-55-BN	44-61924
	42-24881		44-61929 —
F-13A-5-BN	42-93849 —		44-61931
	42-93856		44-61933 —
	42-93863 —		44-61934
	42-93872		44-61939
F-13A-10-BN	42-93874		44-61945 —
	42-93879 —		44-61948
	42-93880		44-61951
	42-93900		44-61960 —
	42-93903		44-61961
	42-93912		44-61981
	42-93914		44-61986
	42-93919		44-61989
F-13A-15-BN	42-93926		44-61991
	42-93933		44-61999 —
	42-93965		44-62000
	42-93967 —	F-13A-95-BW	45-21761
	42-93968		45-21763
F-13A-20-BN	42-93992 —		45-21766
	42-93993		45-21768
F-13A-25-BN	42-94054		45-21775
F-13A-30-BN	42-94074		45-21777
	42-94080	TF-13A-20-BN	42-93987
	42-94113 —		42-94000
	42-94114		42-94022
F-13A-35-BN	44-61528	TF-13A-30-BN	42-94081
	44-61531		

SUPERFORTRESS SPECIFICATIONS

	XB-29	YB-29	B-29	B-29B	B-29A
LENGTH	99'				
WINGSPAN	141' 3"				142' 3"
HEIGHT	27' 9"				
WING AREA	1,736 sq. ft.				1,738 sq. ft.
EMPTY WEIGHT	70,140 lbs.			69,000 lbs.	71,360 lbs.
GROSS WEIGHT	135,000 lbs.			137,000 lbs.	135,000 lbs.
ARMAMENT	10 x .50-cal, 1 x 20-mm		10-12 x .50,20-mm	2 or 3 x .50-cal	10– 12 x .50-cal, 1 x 20-mm
POWER PLANT	R-3350-13	R-3350-21		R-3350-23, -23A, -41, -57, -59	
BOMB LOAD	20,000 lbs.				
MAXIMUM SPEED	357 mph at 25,000 feet			364 mph	357 mph
CRUISING SPEED	200-220 mph			210-225 mph	200-220 mph
SERVICE CEILING	31,850 ft.			32,000 ft.	33,000 ft.
RANGE	3,250 – 4,100 miles			4,200 miles	4,000 miles
NORMAL CREW	7	11		10	11

Note: the above table of specifications should only be applied generally; range, bomb load, ceiling and speed varied considerably in operational use of the B-29.

While all B-29s were essentially the same, there were several notable modifications among the literally hundreds of changes, including the four-gun top turret, which began on the B-29-40-BW, B-29A-15-BN, B-29-10-BA and B-29-10-MO; the deletion of the 20-mm tail cannon from the B-29-55-BW, B-29A-20-BN, B-29-25-BA, B-29-25-MO onwards; pneumatic bomb bay doors first fitted to the B-29-55-BW, B-29A-15-BN, B-29-30-BA and B-29-25-MO; increased fuel capacity due to the installation of four additional tanks in the center wing section, beginning with models B-29-25-BW, B-29-5-BA, B-29A-5-BN and all Omaha B-29s.

THE TWENTIETH AIR FORCE

The Twentieth Air Force was activated on April 4, 1944, with headquarters in Washington until July 16, 1945, when it was transferred to Harmon Field, Guam. Commanded by General Henry H. Arnold from April 1944 until Major General Curtis LeMay took over in July 1945. Lieutenant General Nathan F. Twining commanded after August 2, 1945.

The 20th Bomber Command was activated on November 20, 1943, assigned to the Twentieth Air Force and moved to India early in 1944. Commanded initially by Brigadier General Kenneth B. Wolfe, then by Brigadier General LaVerne G. Saunders from July 6, 1944, Major General Curtis LeMay from August 29, 1944, Brigadier General Roger M. Ramey from January 20, 1945, and finally Brigadier General Joseph Smith between April 25, 1945, and the command's inactivation on July 16, 1945. The 20th Bomber Command was stationed at Kharagpur, India, from March 28, 1944, until June 17, 1945, and at Sakugawa, Okinawa, from July 7 to July 16, 1945.

The 21st Bomber Command was activated on March 1, 1944, and stationed overseas at Harmon Field, Guam, between December 4, 1944, and July 16, 1945. Commanders were Brigadier General Haywood S. Hansell, Jr., from August 28, 1944, until LeMay took over on January 20, 1945.

The 58th Bomb Wing was activated May 1, 1943, and first based overseas at Chakulia, India, from April 2, 1944, then at Kharagpur, India, between April 23 and October 12, 1944; at Hijli Base Area, India, from February 8 to February 24, 1945, and at West Field, Tinian, from March 29 to November 15, 1945. Commanded by Brigadier General LaVerne G. Saunders from March 5, 1944, then Colonel Dwight O. Monteith from February 8, 1945, until Brigadier General Roger M. Ramey took command on April 24, 1945. Voice code was "Loyal" during Marianas operations.

The 40th Bomb Group flew its first mission on June 5, 1944, attacking railroad shops at Bangkok, Thailand. It received a Distinguished Unit Citation for the attack on Yawata on August 20, 1944, and a second award for attacking naval aircraft factories at Kure, oil-storage facilities at Oshima, and the industrial area of Nagoya between May 5 and 14, 1945. A third DUC was awarded for raids on light-metals industries in Osaka on July 24, 1945. The 40th Group squadrons were the 25th, 44th, 45th, and 395th, the latter disbanded in October 1944. Overseas bases were Chakulia, India, from April 2, 1944, until February 25, 1945, then West Field, Tinian, from April 4, 1945, until after the war. The 40th's forward base in China was A-1, Hsinching. The group moved to India under the command of Colonel Leonard F. Harman, who went back to the United States as General Wolfe's assistant and was replaced by Colonel William H. Blanchard on August 4, 1944. Colonel Henry R. Sullivan took command on February 16, 1945, then Colonel William K. Skaer after February 27, 1945. Voice call was "Robust," later "Actor."

The 444th Bomb Group flew its first mission against Bangkok, on June 5, 1944. It received its first Distinguished Unit Citation for the Yawata mission of August 20, 1944, a second for strikes on oil-storage facilities at Oshima, an aircraft factory near Kobe, and an incendiary raid on Nagoya between May 10 and 14, 1945. It won its third DUC for the Osaka mission of July 24, 1945. The squadrons were the 676th, 677th, 678th, and 679th, the latter disbanded October 1944. Based at Charra, India, from April 11, 1944, then at Dudhkundi from July 1, 1944, until March 1, 1945. Moved to West Field from April 7, 1945. The 444th's China base was A-3, Kwanghan. Commanded by Colonel Alva L. Harvey from August 5, 1943, until he moved up to the 58th Wing as deputy commander, his place being taken by Colonel Henry R. Sullivan from April 22, 1945; Colonel James C. Selser took command of the group on June 3, 1945. Voice call was "Mashnote," then "Ogre."

The 462nd Bomb Group flew its first mission on June 5, 1944, to Bangkok. It received a Distinguished Unit Citation for the Yawata mission on August 20, 1944; a second award, for strikes on industrial areas of Tokyo and Yokohama on May 23, 25, and 29, 1945; a third DUC for a daylight attack on an aircraft factory at Takarazuka on July 24, 1945. Squadrons were 768th, 769th, 770th, and 771st, the latter disbanded in October 1944. From April 7, 1944, the group was based at Piardoba, India, until February 26, 1945, then at West Field, Tinian, from April 4. Forward base in China was A-5, Kiunglai. Commanded by Colonel Richard Carmichael from August 26, 1943, until he was shot down and captured during August 20 Yawata mission, when Colonel Alfred F. Kalberer took over. Voice call was "Wicked."

The 468th Bomb Group flew its first mission on June 5, 1944, to Bangkok. It received a Distinguished Unit Citation for a daylight Yawata mission August 20, 1944, and second award for incendiary missions against Tokyo and Yokohama between May 23 and 29, 1945. It received a third DUC for a mission to Takarazuka on July 24, 1945. Squadrons were 792nd, 793rd, 794th, and 795th, the latter disbanded in October 1944. The 468th was based at Kharagpur, India, from April 13, 1944, until February 24, 1945, then at West Field after April 6. Forward base in China was A-7, Pengshan. Commanded by Colonel Howard E. Engler from September 8, 1943, until August 3, 1944, when Colonel Ted S. Faulkner took over. Faulkner was lost on the Singapore mission of November 5, 1944, and Colonel James V. Edmundson became the 468th's final commander. Voice call was "Mingtoy," then "Skookum."

The 73rd Bomb Wing was activated November 20, 1943, and stationed overseas at Isley Field, Saipan, between August 24, 1944, and October 20, 1945. Commanded by Brigadier General Emmett O'Donnell, Jr., from March 15, 1944, to the end of the war. Voice call was "Husky."

The 497th Bomb Group flew its first mission against Japanese home islands on November 24, 1944. It received a Distinguished Unit Citation on January 27, 1945, when weather closed the primary target and the B-29s withstood heavy attacks to strike Hamamatsu. A second DUC was awarded for strategic attacks between July 26 and August 2, 1945. Squadrons were the 869th, 870th, and 871st. Based at Isley Field from October 17, 1944, until November 1945. Commanded by Colonel Stuart P. Wright from April 26, 1944, then Colonel Arnold Johnson from February 26, 1945. Voice call was "Happy," then "Shyster."

The 498th Bomb Group flew shakedown missions prior to the Tokyo mission of November 24, 1944. It received a Distinguished Unit Citation for attack on Mitsubishi engine plant at Nagoya on December 13, 1944, and a second DUC for incendiary attacks on urban industries near Osaka and Kobe during the first week of June 1945. Squadrons were the 873rd, 874th, and 875th. The 498th was based at Isley Field from September 6, 1944, until November 1945. The commanders were Colonel Wiley Ganey from March 14, 1944, and Colonel Donald Saunders from August 10, 1945. Voice call was "Mascot," then "Waxwing."

The 499th Bomb Group flew its first mission against the Japanese homeland on November 24, 1944. It received a Distinguished Unit Citation for the mission to the Mitsubishi plant at Nagoya, January 23, 1945, and a second DUC for a series of missions against airfields on Kyushu, April 22 to 28, 1945. Squadrons were 877th, 878th, and 879th. The group was based at Isley Field from September 18, 1944. Commanded by Colonel Samuel R. Harris from April 14, 1944; Colonel Morris J. Lee from March 17, 1945, until he moved up to 73rd Wing as chief of staff on August 13, 1945; then Lieutenant Colonel Walter E. Chambers. Voice call was "Sandy," later "Nordic."

The 500th Bomb Group took part in the November 24 first Tokyo mission, after shakedown missions. It was awarded a Distinguished Unit Citation for the attack on the Mitsubishi plant at Nagoya on January 23, 1945, and a second DUC for incendiary strikes on Kyushu, Osaka, and Hamamatsu, June 15 to 20, 1945. Squadrons were 881st, 882nd, and 883rd. Based at Isley Field from September 18, 1944, until October 1945. Commanded by Colonel Richard T. King from May 5, 1944, until the B-29 he was flying in was lost on the December 3, 1944, Tokyo mission. Colonel John E. Dougherty commanded the 500th from December 5 until after the war's end. Voice call was "Pluto," then "Wisdom."

The 313th Bomb Wing was activated on April 23, 1944, and stationed overseas at North Field, Tinian, from December 24, 1944. Commanded by Brigadier General John H. Davies. Voice call was "Goldbug."

The 6th Bomb Group flew its first mission against Japan proper on February 19, 1945. It received its first Distinguished Unit Citation on May 25, 1945, for a night low-altitude attack on Tokyo, and a second DUC for a blockade of Japan by mining harbors in Japan and Korea between July 9 and 19, 1945. Squadrons were 24th, 39th, and 40th. Based at North Field from December 28, 1944. Commanded by Colonel Kenneth H. Gibson. Voice call was "Daredevil," later "Cuckoo."

The 9th Bomb Group flew its first mission to Japan on February 19, 1945. It received a Distinguished Unit Citation for bombing the Kawasaki industrial area on the night of April 15, 1945. It received a second award for mining operations in the Inland Sea between May 13 and 28, 1945. Squadrons were the 1st, 5th, and 99th. Based at North Field from December 28, 1944. Colonel Donald W. Eisenhart was commander from May 1, 1944, and was succeeded by Colonel Henry C. Huglin on March 6, 1945, when Eisenhart moved up to be 313th Wing chief of staff. Voice call was "Domino," then "Crosstown."

The 504th Bomb Group flew its first mission against Japan on February 19, 1945. It won a Distinguished Unit Citation for the strike on Yokohama industries on May 29, 1945, and again for mining Korean shipping lanes, the Shimonoseki Strait, and the Inland Sea between July 27 and August 14, 1945. Squadrons were the 398th, 421st, and 680th. Based at North Field from December 23, 1944. Commanded by Colonel James T. Connally from April 6, 1944, and by Colonel Glen W. Martin after February 6, 1945. Voice call was "Albatross," then "Gulfbird."

The 505th Bomb Group received a Distinguished Unit Citation for the attack on the aircraft factory at Ota on February 10, 1945, just four days after its first mission. It received a second DUC for mining of Shimonoseki Strait and the Inland Sea between June 17 and July 1, 1945. Squadrons were 482nd, 483rd, and 484th. Based at North Field from December 19, 1944. Commanded by Colonel Robert A. Ping from May 3, 1944, until Lieutenant Colonel Charles M. Eisenhart took command on July 1, 1945. Voice call was "Skeezik," then "Skyblue."

The 509th Composite Group joined the 313th Wing's B-29s to attack Japan on July 20, 1945. The fifteen specially modified Superfortresses were from the 393rd Squadron. Based at North Field from May 29, 1945, and commanded by Colonel Paul W. Tibbets, Jr. Voice call was "Dimples."

The 314th Bomb Wing was activated on April 23, 1944, and was stationed overseas at North Field, Guam, from January 16, 1945. Commanded by Brigadier General Thomas S. Power from August 29, 1944, and by Colonel Carl R. Storrie from July 23, 1945. Voice call was "Rampage."

The 19th Bomb Group flew its first mission against the Japanese home islands during the Tokyo strike of February 25, 1945. It was awarded its first Distinguished Unit Citation for low-altitude incendiary attacks on Tokyo, Nagoya, Kobe, and Osaka between March 9 and 19, 1945, and its second for the attack on Kobe industries on June 5, 1945. Squadrons were 28th, 30th, and 93rd. Based at North Field from January 16, 1945, and commanded by Colonel John A. Roberts, Jr. Voice call was "Kingbird," then "Curious."

The 29th Bomb Group's first mission against Japan was flown on February 25, 1945. The group received a Distinguished Unit Citation for the attack on Omura Airfield on March 21, 1945, and a second for strikes on industrial targets at Shizuoaka, the Mitsubishi plant at Tamashima, and the Chigusa arsenal at Nagoya between June 19 and 26, 1945. The squadrons were the 6th, 43rd, and 52nd. Based at North Field from January 17, 1945. Commanded by Colonel Carl R. Storrie from May 28, 1944, and Colonel Robert L. Mason after July 23, 1945. Voice call was "Dracula," then "Toby."

The 39th Bomb Group flew its first Japan mission on April 12, 1945, striking the Hodogaya chemical plant at Koriyama. It was awarded a Distinguished Unit Citation for a strike against the Otake oil refinery on May 10, 1945, and a second for bombing industrial and dock areas of Yokohama and manufacturing districts of Tokyo between May 23 and 29, 1945. Squadrons were 60th, 61st, and 62nd. Based at North Field from February 18, 1945. Commanded by Colonel John G. Fowler from February 22, 1945, until he returned to the 314th Wing as deputy commander; Colonel George W. Mundy from March 16, 1945; and Colonel James E. Roberts from August 16, 1945. Voice call was "Blackjack," then "Miser."

The 330th Bomb Group flew its first mission against the Japanese home islands on April 12, 1945, attacking the Hodogaya plant. It won a Distinguished Unit Citation for incendiary raids on industry in Tokushima and Gifu, and Kofu hydroelectric power center between July 3 and 9, 1945. It won a second DUC for the strike on the Nakajima plant near Tokyo on August 8, 1945. Squadrons were 457th, 458th, and 459th. Based at North Field from February 18, 1945. Commanded by Colonel Elbert D. Reynolds until August 12, 1945, when Colonel Douglas C. Polhamus took over. Voice codes were "Baldeagle," later "Mizpah."

The 315th Bomb Wing was activated on July 17, 1944, and stationed at Northwest Field, Guam, from April 5, 1945. Commanded by Brigadier General Frank A. Armstrong, Jr., from November 18, 1944. Voice call was "Hyena."

The 16th Bomb Group flew its first mission against the Japanese home islands on June 26, 1945. It received a Distinguished Unit Citation for unescorted missions against an oil refinery at Shimotsu, the Mitsubishi refinery and oil installations at Kawasaki, and coal liquefaction plants at Ube between July 29 and August 6, 1945. Squadrons were the 15th, 16th, and 17th. Based at Northwest Field from April 14, 1945. Commanded by Colonel Samuel C. Gurney from July 11, 1944, and by Lieutenant André F. Castellotti from July 11, 1945. Voice call was "Blueplate," then "Abie."

The 331st Bomb Group flew its first Japan mission on July 9, 1945. It won a Distinguished Unit Citation for attacks in bad weather, fighters, and heavy flak against Ube, Shimotsu, and Kawasaki from July 22 to 29, 1945. Squadrons were 355th, 356th, and 357th. Based at Northwest Field from May 12, 1945. Commanded by Colonel James N. Peyton. Voice call was "Baywood," later "Slicker."

The 501st Bomb Group flew its first mission against the Japanese home islands on June 27, 1945. It received a Distinguished Unit Citation for attacks on the Maruzen oil refinery at Shimotsu, the Utsobo refinery at Yokkaichi, and the petroleum center at Kawasaki between July 6 and 13, 1945. Squadrons were the 21st, 41st, and 485th. Based at Northwest Field from April 14, 1945. Commanded by Colonel Boyd Hubbard. Voice call was "Pathway," then "Bailiff."

The 502nd Bomb Group flew its first mission to Japan on July 15, 1945. It won a Distinguished Unit Citation for strikes on the coal liquefaction plant at Ube, the tank farm at Amagasaki, and the Nippon oil refinery at Tsuchizaki between August 5 and 15, 1945. Squadrons were 402nd, 411th, and 430th. Based at Northwest Field from May 12, 1945. Commanded by Colonel Kenneth O. Sanborn. Voice call was "Stopwatch," then "Temper."

The 1st Photo Reconnaissance Squadron, Flight C, was originally the Photo Reconnaissance Detachment of the 20th Bomber Command, activated in October 1944. Redesignated Flight C, 1st Photo Reconnaissance Squadron, on February 13, 1945. Based at A-1, Hsinching, China, then Harmon Field, Guam, after May 1945. Commanded by Major Harry B. Allen until May 1945, when Captain George B. Alfke, Jr., took over, and Captain Daniel H. Forbes after July 9, 1945.

The flight was attached to the Eighth Air Force and left Guam for Okinawa on July 19, 1945.

The 3rd Photo Reconnaissance Squadron flew its first mission to Japan on November 1, 1944. Based at Isley Field, Saipan, from September 18, 1944, then moved to Harmon Field, Guam, after January 11, 1945. Commanded by Lieutenant Colonel Patrick McCarthy until June 21, 1945, then by Major Robert Hutton. Voice call was "Hellhog."

THE PLANES

The following alphabetical listing includes every individual B-29 name mentioned or illustrated in the book, along with the airplane serial number and unit.

A
Airborn, 42-65268, 444th Group
American Maid, 42-24593, 497th Group
The Ancient Mariner, 42-65296, 500th Group
Antoinette, 42-24751, 498th Group

B
Bad Brew, 42-24594, 497th Group
Bedroom Eyes, 42-24610, 498th Group
Bella Bortion, 42-63355, 468th Group
Belle Ringer, 42-63464, 468th Group
Bengal Lancer, 42-24487, 468th Group
Big Poison, 42-6353, 444th Group
The Big Stick, 42-24661, 499th Group
Bockscar, 44-27297, 509th Group
Bombin' Buggy, 42-6306, 40th Group
Brooklyn Bessie, 42-93854, 1st Photo
Bugger, 42-63610, 331st Group

C
Calamity Sue, 42-6368, 468th Group
Camel Caravan, 42-6333, 468th Group
The Cannuck, 42-24668, 500th Group
Case Ace, 42-6270, 462nd Group
Celestial Princess, 42-24590, 462nd Group

Chat'nooga Choo Choo, 42-24471, 468th Group
Cherry the Horizontal Cat, 42-63564, 29th Group
City of Arcadia, 42-93925, 29th Group
City of Burlington, 42-65304, 19th Group
City of Fort Gibson, 44-69762, 29th Group
City of Los Angeles, 42-65302, 29th Group
City of Toledo, --------, 39th Group
Coral Queen, 42-24615, 497th Group
Country Gentleman, 42-24793, 505th Group
The Cultured Vulture, 42-24901, 6th Group

D
Dangerous Lady, 42-24823, 505th Group
Danny Mite, 44-69777, 498th Group
Dauntless Dotty, 42-24592, 497th Group
The Deacon's Delight, 42-24818, 505th Group
Deacon's Disciples, 42-24492, 444th Group

Destiny's Tot, 42-65284, 9th Group

Destiny's Tots, 42-65293, 497th Group

Devil's Darlin', 42-24629, 498th Group

Dina Might, 42-65280, 504th Group

Ding How, 42-6358, 468th Group

Dixie Darlin', 42-63413, 497th Group

"Doc" Said All I Needed Was—Affection, 42-65266, 504th Group

Doc's Deadly Dose, 42-24780, 504th Group

Double Exposure, 42-93855, 1st Photo

Double Exposure, 42-24877, 3rd Photo

Draggin Lady, 42-24694, 500th Group

The Dragon Lady, 42-63425, 497th Group

E

Eddie Allen, 42-24579, 40th Group

El Pajaro de la Guerra, 42-24874, 6th Group

Ellie Barbara and Her Orphans, 42-63605, 16th Group

Enola Gay, 44-86292, 509th Group

Esso Express, 42-6242, 468th Group

F

Fay, 42-65210, 498th Group

Fever from the South, 42-63497, 500th Group

Fickle Finger, --------, 497th Group

Flak Alley Sally, 42-24878, 6th Group

Fleet Admiral Nimitz, 42-63650, 501st Group

Fluffy Fuz III, --------, 315th Wing

The Flying Guinea Pig, 41-002, Boeing Flight Test

Flying Stud, 42-6320, 444th Group

Forbidden Fruit, 42-24607, 498th Group

Forever Amber, 44-69839, 6th Group

Full House, 44-27298, 509th Group

G

Gallopin' Goose, 42-6390, 468th Group

Geisha Gertie, 42-24763, 498th Group

General Andrews, 44-69888, 39th Group

Gen. H. H. Arnold Special, 42-6365, 468th Group

Georgia Peach, 42-63356, 468th Group

Gertrude C., 42-6334, 468th Group

Ghastly Goose, 42-63541, 497th Group

Gonna Mak'er, 42-65231, 497th Group

Good Deal, 42-24852, 504th Group

Gravel Gertie, 42-65221, 500th Group

The Great Artiste, 44-27354, 509th Group

The Gusher, 42-6356, 468th Group

H

Haley's Comet, 42-24616, 497th Group

The Heat's On, 42-24605, 498th Group

Heavenly Body, 42-63510, 498th Group

Hobo Queen, 41-36963, 462nd Group

Hog Wild, 42-63436, 500th Group

Honorable TNT Wagon, 42-63484, 505th Group

Hoodlum House II, 42-24475, 462nd Group

Hump Happy Pappy, 42-6254, 40th Group

I

Indian Maid, 42-24806, 504th Group

Irish Lassie, 42-65246, 497th Group

Irish Lullaby, 42-24830, 6th Group

Island Queen, --------, 504th Group

J

Jabbitt III, 44-27303, 509th Group

Jackpot, 42-24797, 505th Group

Jo, 42-65337, 444th Group

Joker's Wild, 42-24626, 497th Group

Joltin' Josie, the Pacific Pioneer, 42-24614, 498th Group

"Jook" Girl, 42-65255, 505th Group
Jumbo, 42-63418, 497th Group
Jumbo II, 42-24855, 497th Group
Jus' One Mo' Time, --------, 501st Group

K
King Size, 42-6347, 462nd Group

L
Lady Eve, 42-65211, 498th Group
Lady Hamilton, 42-6274, 468th Group
Lady Mary Anna, 42-24625, 498th Group
Lassie, 42-63356, 468th Group
Lass'ie Come Home, 42-24609, 498th Group
Last Resort, 42-63394, 40th Group
Lethal Lady, 42-6370, 468th Group
Limber Dugan, 42-6230, 468th Group
Little Gem, 42-24596, 497th Group
Little Jo, 42-24611, 498th Group
Loaded Dice, 42-63688, 16th Group
Long Distance, 42-24544, 498th Group
Look Homeward Angel, --------, 6th Group
Lucky Irish, 42-63492, 497th Group
Lucky 'Leven, 42-24695, 498th Group
Lucky Lynn, 42-24591, 497th Group

M
Male Call, 42-63537, 444th Group
Marianna Ram, 44-69732, 497th Group
Mary Ann, 42-24494, 468th Group
Million Dollar Baby II, 42-63532, 468th Group
Miss Behavin', 42-24655, 497th Group
Miss Judy, 44-61555, 462nd Group
Miss Lace, 42-63554, 498th Group
Missouri Queen, 42-6359, 462nd Group
My Naked——, 44-63725, 501st Group

N
Next Objective, 44-27299, 509th Group
Nightmare, 42-6311, 462nd Group

O
Oily Boid, 42-24912, 29th Group
Old-Bitch-U-Airy Bess, 42-6273, 462nd Group
O'Reilly's Daughter, 42-6264, 468th Group
Our Baby, 42-24597, 497th Group

P
Pacific Queen, 42-63429, 500th Group
Pacific Union, 42-24595, 497th Group
Peace on Earth, 42-63412, 497th Group
Petrol Packin' Mama, 42-6219, 462nd Group
Pioneer, 42-6208, 468th Group
Pocahontas, 42-24601, 498th Group
Ponderous Peg, 42-63431, 497th Group
Postville Express, 42-6279, 468th Group
Pride of the Yankees, 42-24676, 500th Group
Princess Eileen IV, 42-65327, 444th Group

Q
Quaker-City, 44-70016, 330th Group
Quan Yin Cha Ara, 42-93853, 1st Photo

R
Raidin' Maiden, 42-6265, 468th Group
Raidin' Maiden II, 42-65276, 468th Group
Ramblin' Roscoe, 42-24664, 500th Group
Ramp Tramp II, 42-24904, 462nd Group
Rankless Wreck, 42-63420, 40th Group
Ready Teddy, 42-63561, 9th Group
Reamatroid, 44-69672, 6th Group
Reddy Teddy, 42-6408, 468th Group
Roadapple, 42-63600, 501st Group
Rush Order, 42-63393, 462nd Group
Rushin' Rotashun, 42-63417, 468th Group

S

Salt-Censored Resistor, 42-65307, 19th Group
Salvo Sally, 42-24699, 499th Group
Sassy Lassy, 42-24867, 505th Group
Satan's Angel, 42-65202, 444th Group
Satan's Lady, 42-24779, 504th Group
Sentimental Journey, 44-70016, 330th Group
Shady Lady, 42-24619, 497th Group
Shanghai Lil, 42-6277, 444th Group
Shanghai Lil Rides Again, 42-24723, 444th Group
Skyscrapper, 42-24599, 497th Group
Sky-Scrapper II, 42-63463, 497th Group
Slick Chick, 42-24906, 19th Group
Slick Dick, 42-24700, 500th Group
Slick's Chicks, 42-24784, 505th Group
Smilin' Jack, 42-24888, 40th Group
Snatch Blatch, 42-65302, 29th Group
The Spearhead, 44-69975, 9th Group
Star Duster, 42-93858, 497th Group
Starduster, 42-6305, 462nd Group
Straight Flush, 44-27301, 509th Group
Strange Cargo, 44-27300, 509th Group
Su Su Baby, 42-24721, 500th Group
Sweat 'er Out, --------, 497th Group

T

Tanaka Termite, 42-24749, 498th Group
Teaser, 42-63526, 497th Group
Texas Doll, 42-24627, 497th Group
This Is It!, 42-6321, 444th Group
Thumper, 42-24623, 497th Group

Thunderbird, 42-63570, 29th Group
Thunderhead, 42-24641, 497th Group
Thunderin' Loretta, 42-24913, 9th Group
Tokyo-ko, 42-24859, 9th Group
Tokyo Local, 42-24687, 500th Group
Tokyo Rose, 42-93852, 3rd Photo
Tokyo Twister, 42-24682, 499th Group
Top Secret, 44-27302, 509th Group

U

Uncle Tom's Cabin, 42-24642, 498th Group
Under-Exposed, 42-93849, 1st Photo

V

Valiant Lady, 42-93870, 3rd Photo

W

Waddy's Wagon, 42-24598, 497th Group
Werewolf, 42-63423, 497th Group
Wheel 'n' Deal, 42-24604, 497th Group
White Huntress, 42-24776, 6th Group
The Wichita Witch, 42-24654, 498th Group
Wild-Hair, 42-24505, 462nd Group
Windy City, 42-6253, 468th Group
Windy City II, 42-24486, 468th Group
Wugged Wascal, 42-24658, 499th Group

Y

Yokohama Yo-Yo, 42-24621, 3rd Photo

Acknowledgments

Trying to tell the story of the greatest airplane of World War II was a challenging task. There were many facets of the story, and one of my main considerations was to try to regain a perspective that I felt had been lost due to the airplane's involvement with the birth of the nuclear age.

To do this, I needed the help of people who were intimately involved with those facets of the story, and I would like to thank them here.

The Boeing Company gave me support of a kind I have never experienced before. Gordy Williams dug deep into the company's files and his own collection to provide the material I needed. Pete Bowers allowed me to take advantage of his unparalleled knowledge of the company and its products. Al Lloyd searched records and contacted B-29 veterans within the company on my behalf—tech reps, combat crew members, and people involved in the test program. Also from Boeing was John Swihart, who provided invaluable material on the 313th Wing.

While I am neither a trained nor a true historian, I owe a great deal to someone who is: Murray Green. Murray's research into Hap Arnold, for a biography of the general, naturally involved key areas of the B-29 story, and he was gracious enough to share crucial parts of his vast files with me. Not only did he provide interview material with the late Jake Harman and K. B. Wolfe, but also interview material with Paul Tibbets and General Curtis LeMay. In addition, Murray sought specific information from General LeMay on my behalf.

Various offices of the USAF naturally provided the material that is the core of the book. Mrs. Virginia Fincik and Dana Bell of the 1361st Audiovisual Squadron once again helped me to locate elusive photos to illustrate the book, and Captain Rick P. DuCharme of the Magazine and Book Branch fulfilled all my requests for assistance. John Fuller, the Air Weather Service historian, led me to fully understand the part weather played in the B-29 story, while Lieutenant Marc S. Martens of Eglin AFB supplied test reports. Royal Frey and Chuck Worman of the Air Force Museum, where *Bockscar* is displayed, helped, as they always have, and Judy G. Endicott of the Albert F. Simpson Historical Research Center gave valued assistance. Donald R. Lennon provided some unique mate-

334

rial from the Frank A. Armstrong, Jr., papers in the Manuscript and Collection of the East Carolina University.

John Mitchell, over the course of many letters, led me from the early days of the Accelerated Service Test Branch to the operations of the 3rd Photo Squadron on Saipan and Guam, and those letters gave me a feeling for the times.

Denny Pidhayny of the 58th Bomb Wing Association has one of the most extensive collections of B-29 material, and he drew selectively from this to help me tell my story, as well as providing guidance and just about every kind of help on call. Glenn McClure of the 73rd Wing Association and Dick Keenan of the Twentieth Air Force Association were also generous in letting me use their resources. (The following organizations can be contacted at these addresses: 58th Bomb Wing Association: Joseph E. Pokraka, 1730 LaPorte Avenue, Whiting, Ind. 46395; 73rd Bomb Wing Association: 105 Circle Drive, Universal City, Tex. 78148; Twentieth Air Force Association: Box 5534, Washington, D.C. 20016.)

Sam Tagaya provided me with both specific and background material on the Japanese fighter defense organization and operations against the B-29s.

The veterans of the various B-29 groups who provided memories, documents, diaries, and photos are all listed separately, by their unit, but I will thank them here for their willingness to share their recollections with me, and for their faith in this project.

Barry Gilkes, who has helped me with all my books, was again able to provide unique material as was Charles B. Mayer. Others who helped in various ways were Dave Aiken, Dr. Dean C. Allard of the Naval Historical Center, Rhodes Arnold, Jeff Brown, Kay Brunisma, Don Chappell, Richard Ditty. A. O. Evans, Bruce Fraites, Roger A. Freeman, Ed and Eric Furler, Rowland P. Gill, Jim Goodwin, T. C. Griffin, Steve Grivno, Robert Hernandez, Bert Hale, Ed Jablonski, Curtis Johns, Mrs. Minnie F. Jenkins, Tom and June Jones, Fred Johnsen, Howard Levy, Roy Logan, Carl Mahakian, Norm Malayney, Dave Menard, Anton Muraski, Don Norton, Merle Olmsted, Harvey Pyles, T. R. Reid, Robert J. Ruffle, Charles Russo, Kenn Rust, Milt Sheppard, Frank Smith, and Ranny Sprenger.

The select bibliography at the end of the book does not include a lot of the material extracted by Denny Pidhayny from his collection, nor does it include the unofficial histories of the 6th, 9th, 19th, 40th, 330th, 444th, 462nd, 497th, 500th, and 505th bomb groups, and the 73rd Wing, all of which were referred to during the preparation of the book.

The core of the book is the material yielded by forty rolls of microfilmed histories of all the B-29 groups, from the USAF's files at Maxwell

Air Force Base, Alabama. Most of the "floating" quotes in the book come from those official histories or Craven and Cate's fine volume.

Conspicuous by their absence from the select bibliography are the rash of books about the Hiroshima mission, particularly the handful dealing with Claude Eatherly, pilot of the weather plane. While I have read most of these books over the years, I decided for my story to go back to the official files of the 509th Group and a few veterans. When Claude Eatherly died, several newspapers were still calling him the "Hiroshima pilot"; the log of the Hiroshima mission kept by Tibbets' copilot, Bob Lewis, realized eighty-five thousand dollars at auction during 1978. Fact and fiction have run together to produce what might be called quasifact. A 1978 newspaper article called Paul Tibbets a "living symbol of that awesome day"; another called the *Enola Gay*, then gathering dust in a Smithsonian Institution warehouse, "an awesome, monstrous sight," with "the horror of its deed thirty-three years ago clinging to it." If I've told the story of the atomic bombings with a little less drama than their impact deserved, it was probably in an attempt to regain some kind of perspective about them, particularly in a story about an airplane. The continuing vilification of Paul Tibbets and his airplane is tragic and shameful.

This book probably would not have gone ahead had it not been for Larry Reineke, an intelligence officer with the 497th on Saipan, and later on Iwo. Larry first began helping me with a book about the B-24, then with one about the Fifth Air Force. Knowing that he had extensive knowledge of B-29 operations, and a collection of related material, were enough to assure me that I would have a strong foundation to work from. That's how it worked out: Larry's letters, diaries, albums, books, and magazines (including a complete collection of *Brief*, the theater's lively, factual magazine), plus his contacts, insured that the story of the 73rd Wing would be one of the easier parts of the story to put together.

My editor, Harold Kuebler, has faith in these books, and that also makes life a great deal easier for me, in many ways. My association with him through three books has been a pleasure, and his advice has always proved to be right on the mark. His assistant, Nan Grubbs, has fielded my queries and displayed abundant patience and kindness as the book took shape.

The B-29 story did not end at World War II, but the B-29 had played the part planned for it. After the war B-29s served in a variety of roles, and dropped more bombs in Korea than they did in World War II. That's another story, and I hope to tell it soon.

Steve Birdsall, Sydney, Australia

Contributing B-29 Veterans, World War II

Victor N. Agather, Wright Field
L. J. Arents, 462nd Bomb Group
Prentiss Burkett, 499th Bomb Group
Jonas Carpenter, 330th Bomb Group
Leonard W. Carpi, 9th Bomb Group
Thomas J. Classen, 509th Composite Group
Ray C. Clinkscales, 500th Bomb Group
Winton R. Close, 444th Bomb Group
R. M. Cordray, 500th Bomb Group
Edward W. Cutler, 497th Bomb Group
Edward T. Donnelly, 498th Bomb Group
Keith W. Duffield, 497th Bomb Group
James L. Dunavent, 3rd Photo Squadron
John C. Earl, 500th Bomb Group
Ray Ebert, 497th Bomb Group
James V. Edmundson, 468th Bomb Group
Jack R. Ehrenberg, 497th Bomb Group
Elden M. Elliott, 330th Bomb Group
Paul F. Evans, 40th Bomb Group
Roy E. Fagan, 19th Bomb Group
Stanley Fisher, 19th Bomb Group
Tom Friedman, 40th Bomb Group
Harry Frumen, 444th Bomb Group
John Gahagan, 6th Bomb Group
Frank P. Gendusie, 19th Bomb Group
Harry H. George, 6th Bomb Group
Kenneth H. Gibson, 6th Bomb Group
Robert F. Goldsworthy, 500th Bomb Group
Thomas C. Griffin, 498th Bomb Group
Haywood S. Hansell, 21st Bomber Command
Horace E. Hatch, 500th Bomb Group
Charles B. Hawks, 29th Bomb Group
Arthur M. Heith, 6th Bomb Group
LeRoy Henry, 501st Bomb Group
Edward Hering, 501st Bomb Group
Marvin Hooker, Boeing Field Representative, CBI

Ken Hurley, 330th Bomb Group
Francis J. Johnston, 444th Bomb Group
Don Julin, 497th Bomb Group
Richard M. Keenan, 444th Bomb Group
John A. King, 509th Composite Group
Joseph M. Kucera, 330th Bomb Group
Stan Lee, 462nd Bomb Group
James R. Leon, 444th Bomb Group
Wilfred N. Lind, 497th Bomb Group
Glenn E. McClure, 500th Bomb Group
John W. McKenna, 444th Bomb Group
James D. McWethy, 19th Bomb Group
Jim Marich, 39th Bomb Group
Glen W. Martin, 504th Bomb Group
Clyde Matteson, 331st Bomb Group
Don S. Midlam, 504th Bomb Group
John Mitchell, ASTB, 3rd Photo Squadron
J. B. Montgomery, 21st Bomber Command
Richard M. Morgan, Boeing Chief Tech. Rep., Marianas
Jim Morrison, 1st Photo Squadron
Fred J. Olivi, 509th Composite Group
Harold L. Otstot, 505th Bomb Group
Pete Paterson, 3rd Photo Squadron
James L. Pattillo, 468th Bomb Group
Donald H. Phillips, 497th Bomb Group
Denny D. Pidhayny, 468th Bomb Group
Robert A. Ping, 505th Bomb Group
Edward Porada, 500th Bomb Group
J. Ivan Potts, 40th Bomb Group
Ray Pritchard, 6th Bomb Group
Edward G. Prunuske, 498th Bomb Group
Larry Redmond, 444th Bomb Group
Lawrence F. Reineke, 497th Bomb Group
Don Roberts, 6th Bomb Group
H. Evan Roberts, 6th Bomb Group
S. Clay Sandhofer, 462nd Bomb Group
George Savage, 19th Bomb Group
Robert E. Sebring, 500th Bomb Group
Noah D. Showalter, Boeing Flight Test
Ernest A. Sikes, 499th Bomb Group
George A. Simeral, 29th Bomb Group
Dick Snodgrass, Boeing Tech. Rep., Guam
Henry J. Stavinski, 468th Bomb Group

John Swihart, 9th Bomb Group
Cecil E. Tackett, 500th Bomb Group
Paul W. Tibbets, 509th Composite Group
Ray Tolzmann, 468th Bomb Group
Charles O. Trabold, 462nd Bomb Group
Paul A. Trump, 6th Bomb Group
Orley Van Dyke, 330th Bomb Group
James R. Veeder, Boeing Flight Test
Bob Voyles, 501st Bomb Group
Homer E. Walker, 497th Bomb Group
George C. Wallace, 468th Bomb Group
Bob Watson, 497th Bomb Group
Don C. Whitworth, Boeing Flight Test
Al Williams, 499th Bomb Group
Morris Woodward, 9th Bomb Group

Select Bibliography

Army Air Forces. *Pilot's Flight Operating Instructions for Army Models B-29 and B-29A Airplanes.* Washington, 1944.

——. *Erection and Maintenance Instructions for Army Model B-29 Airplane.* Washington, 1944.

Arnold, Henry H. *Global Mission.* New York: Harper & Brothers, 1949.

Berger, Carl. *B-29: The Superfortress.* New York: Ballantine Books, 1970.

Birdsall, Steve. *B-29 Superfortress in Action.* Warren, Mich.: Squadron, 1977.

Bowers, Peter M. *Boeing Aircraft Since 1916.* London: Putnam, 1966.

Collison, Thomas. *The Superfortress Is Born.* New York: Duell, Sloan & Pearce, 1945.

Craig, William. *The Fall of Japan.* New York: Dial Press, 1967.

Craven, W. F., and Cate, J. L. *The Army Air Forces in World War II,* Vol. V. Chicago: University of Chicago Press, 1953.

Freeman, Roger A. *Camouflage & Markings, Boeing B-29 Superfortress.* London: Ducimus, 1975.

Gurney, Gene. *Journey of the Giants.* New York: Coward-McCann, 1961.

Johnsen, Frederick A. *The B-29 Book.* Tacoma, Wash.: Bomber Books, 1978.

Kato, Masuo. *The Lost War.* New York: Alfred A. Knopf, 1946.

LeMay, Curtis E. with Kantor, MacKinlay. *Mission with LeMay.* Garden City, N.Y.: Doubleday & Company, 1965.

Mansfield, Harold. *Vision.* New York: Duell, Sloan & Pearce, 1966.

Maurer, Maurer. *Air Force Combat Units of World War II.* New York: Franklin Watts, 1963.

——. *Combat Squadrons of the Air Forces World War II.* Washington, D.C.: U. S. Government Printing Office, 1969.

Morrison, Wilbur H. *Hellbirds.* New York: Duell, Sloan & Pearce, 1960.

Olmsted, Merle. *Aircraft Armament.* New York: Sports Car Press, 1970.

Stout, Wesley W. *Great Engines and Great Planes.* Detroit: Chrysler Corporation, 1947.

Tuchman, Barbara W. *Stillwell and the American Experience in China.* New York: Macmillan, 1971.

Index

Illustration captions are shown with the page number in italics. Where there is both text and illustrative matter, the page number is roman.